What the critics said about Ngaire N

Female Crime is an impressively unifi
tone and thesis and supported throughout
And it is a powerful one...
Women and Criminal Justice (US)

Ngaire Naffine has opened a door on masculine bias and posed
relevant questions for anyone interested in redressing the balance.
Times Higher Education Supplement

Naffine's book may be quite important if it does finally force feminists
to take a critical look at [these] sociological theories of female crime
and deviance... [it] comes as a timely reminder that this sociological
work does exist and that it should not be automatically validated
simply because it is not biologistic.... Naffine gives a good sense of
the complexity and variety of such explorations and the disputes they
have engendered.
Beverly Brown, Sociology (UK)

[Female Crime] is informed by the tradition of feminist scholarship
which has challenged modes of analysis and categories of thought in
disciplines such as philosophy, psychology, political science and
sociology.
George Zdenkowski, Sydney Morning Herald

Female Crime represents a significant step forward in the quest to
construct accurate and realistic portrayals and explanations of
women's crime.
Tribune

WOMEN'S STUDIES BOOKS OF RELATED INTEREST

LAW AND THE SEXES

Explorations in feminist jurisprudence

Ngaire Naffine

ALLEN & UNWIN
Sydney   Wellington   London   Boston

First published in 1990
Allen & Unwin Australia Pty Ltd
An Unwin Hyman company
8 Napier Street, North Sydney, NSW 2059 Australia

Allen & Unwin New Zealand Limited
75 Ghuznee Street, Wellington, New Zealand

Unwin Hyman Limited
15–17 Broadwick Street, London W1V 1FP England

Unwin Hyman Inc.
8 Winchester Place, Winchester, Mass 01890 USA

National Library of Australia
Cataloguing-in-Publication entry:
  Naffine, Ngaire.
  Law and the sexes.

  Bibliography.
  Includes index.
  ISBN 0 04 442210 5.

  1. Sociological jurisprudence. 2. Women — Legal status,
  laws, etc. 3. Equality before the law. I. Title.

340.115

Library of Congress Catalog Card Number: 89–082451

Set in 10/11.5 pt Bembo by Setrite Typesetters Ltd., Hong Kong
Printed by Chong Moh Offset Printing Pte Ltd, Singapore

Contents

For Carol Bacchi

Acknowledgements

A number of people have helped me to bring this book to fruition. Alison MacKinnon made useful suggestions about Chapter 2. Carol Johnson and Sue Tongue read a large part of the manuscript and offered helpful advice. Sharyn Roach also read some of the manuscript and her suggestions did much to improve my understanding of the legal profession. Stephen Parker went to considerable lengths to help me strengthen and deepen the analysis throughout. The points he raised often added new dimensions to the argument. I thank Delia Rickard for her advice and encouragement. Finally, I wish to thank Carol Bacchi who was unstinting in her time and effort, who read and reread the manuscript with enormous patience, and who was always generous with her ideas and enthusiasm. Though none of them is responsible for the final result, I am grateful to them all.

Introduction

If ever we pick up a book about law, or talk to a lawyer about the nature of legal work, or consider the written pronouncements of members of the Bench, we gain some impression of law's view of the person, the central character of law. This person may well seem to be at some remove from the sort of people we encounter in our daily lives, a slightly alien being we might wish to emulate for his business acumen or we might spurn as too calculating, too programmed, too self-interested, perhaps too ruthless. Though we may be unaware of it, these rough impressions we acquire of the legal person, the individual who represents the classic litigant, challenge law's own idea of itself. This is the notion of the blind maiden, balancing the scales of justice, dispensing her services with perfect impartiality. It is the conventional legal view, supported by many learned treatises, which asserts that law does not operate with a specific individual in mind, that it favours no one type of person. In its purported objectivity and neutrality, law is supposed to adopt a common approach to all.

In this standard view of law, that which professes its impartiality, the legal person is presented as a human norm: a prototypical person whose aims and concerns law must anticipate and respond to if it is to ensure a well-run society. A central claim of this book is that the intimations we gain from our legal encounters that the law is not neutral in its stance on the person—that it presupposes a very particular type of individual—are in fact well grounded. Despite its claims to blind justice, this book will argue, the law contains a quite specific notion of the model person, the paradigm citizen, and the type of social order he is believed to inhabit. (This is a deliberate use of the male pronoun which connects with the argument of this book.) This is true of law across the three countries which form the subject of this work. It applies equally to the systems of justice operating in England, in the United States of America and in Australia.

In its endeavour to reveal bias in law, this book operates at several levels. At the more superficial level, the aim is to show that those who administer the law do not necessarily behave as they say they are obliged to do. That is, they do not invariably treat all people equally, in a detached, dispassionate and therefore supposedly fair and impartial manner. Nor does the law oblige them to, as they say it does. For while we are often told that the clarity and certainty of law ensures the certainty, predictability and fairness of justice, there is in fact considerable room for judicial manoeuvre within the law. In a very practical sense, then, law does not inevitably adhere to its own rhetoric of treating people alike, without fear or favour, in an impartial and objective manner. At this level of analysis, it will also be suggested that the legal ideals of impartiality and objectivity, ideals which are so often invoked by the Bench to establish its essential neutrality, may be neither achievable nor desirable goals, as they are currently conceived by law.

At a deeper level, the endeavour of this book is to show that there is a problem of sex and class bias built into the very forms of law. It is at this stage of analysis that we are introduced to the legal individual who forms the focus of much of this work. The argument is that while law professes to organise around a sort of universal person, abstracted from his social context, a person who could be anyone anywhere, in fact the law endows its legal subject with a very specific set of qualities. And it is these values, priorities and general approach to the world which are reflected in the way law conceives and carries out its task of dispensing justice. A second challenge to law to be advanced at this level is that the very notion of human abstraction—the idea that you can identify an essential human being disconnected from time and place and then endeavour to meet his needs—is fundamentally flawed. Impartial justice, it will be suggested, cannot be secured by ignoring the specific qualities of people and by assuming that we are all interchangeable units which function roughly along the line of law's legal person.

At least two intellectual movements have shaped the arguments of this book. One is the Critical Legal Studies movement. According to Critical Legal Scholars, the central focus of their approach is the exploration of 'the manner in which legal doctrine and legal education and the practices of legal institutions work to buttress and support a pervasive system of oppressive, inegalitarian relations' (Fitzpatrick and Hunt, 1987:1). The branch of legal criticism to which the present work belongs is that which seeks to identify the assumptions under-lying theory. More specifically, this work focuses on the assumptions the law makes about the nature of the legal subject and the way in which human beings associate (Hunt, 1987:14).

This book also has strong lines of connection with feminist criticism of an interdisciplinary nature. There is now a substantial feminist literature which addresses the sexism of scholarship in the social, human and natural sciences. In particular, such work questions the human model which informs thinking in the different fields of learning. Repeatedly, feminists tell us, notions of human nature have been presented as universal, as non-gender-specific. Scholars from a range of disciplines have thus purported to be dealing with abstracted beings who could be anyone—male or female. The contribution of feminists has been to reveal the necessary maleness of these models and to question the validity of the theory which has been developed with such skewed ideas of humanity (Naffine, 1987:Ch. 8).

It is by reading between the lines of the law books, by examining the principles, the concerns and the values espoused by the law and those who interpret it, that we can begin to discover some of the key qualities which define the human being in legal thought. As this book will endeavour to show, in at least three vital respects, the legal person cannot be regarded as a standard person. One of these pertains to sex, another to class, a third to gender. In short, the argument to be developed below is that the legal model of the person implies a man, not a woman; it implies a successful middle-class man, not a working-class male; and it implies a middle-class man who demonstrates what one writer has termed a form of 'emphasised' middle-class masculinity. That is to say, he is a man, he is a middle-class man, and he evinces a middle-class style of masculinity.

A close examination of the aims, priorities and methods of law also tells us a good deal about those individuals who are, in effect, omitted from the legal model of humanity. Indeed this exercise reveals that a large part of the community is either excluded from, or subordinate in, the legal view of the social world. This book is about both the model legal person and about the people who fall short of the ideal. It argues that there is a deep-seated bias in much of our law, a bias in favour of those who best approximate the legal ideal of the person and against those who do not, a bias which shapes, and is reflected in, the form of law and how it goes about its task of providing justice.

Of those individuals who are given a subordinate place in the legal scheme of things, the largest single group is women. A good portion of this book examines the nature of law's construction of women and their role as something other than the legal person. Women, it will be argued, have been specifically excluded from the legal notion of the juridical subject who is expected to inhabit and flourish in the public world of the marketplace. Women have been assigned, instead, a secondary domestic role as care-giver in the private sphere of the home. This book considers why this subservient role has been assigned to women and what it means for women, in terms of their actual dealings with the law, to be omitted from the legal notion of the person.

This work is also about men. It is about the men who are seen to succeed according to middle-class notions of masculinity—and who therefore do well in law—and about the men who are seen to fail. Critics of law's bias against women have been surprisingly silent on the question of legal bias against certain types of men, bias which is informed by issues of gender as well as of class. The concentration of their gaze upon women has tended to obscure the fact that law displays a preference for a particular style of maleness and appears to punish other forms. It displays this preference in its values, its priorities, its doctrines and its methods, indeed in its very orientation. In each of these ways, as we will see, law reflects the world-view of a certain middle-class type of man. Because feminists have often perceived men, uniformly, as the oppressors of women, the problem of legal sexism which has men as its objects has remained largely unaddressed. The contention of this book is that it is essential to understand the legal view of men, as gendered subjects, as well as the legal view of women, if we are to explain and tackle the problem of legal sexism.

Law's preferred person, it will be contended, is a monied, educated, middle-class man who thrives in the competitive marketplace. His masculinity is implicit in his healthy sense of rivalry, his assertiveness or even aggression, his sense of his own rights, of his own place in the world, his essential individualism. This man of law is successful as a man and as a man of the market. He is calculating and restrained. He knows how far to push his own suit to stay within the bounds of acceptable behaviour. He knows how to win on the terms of the market. The law respects his individualism, his sense of his place in the world. It not only values and protects his material interests but it offers a style of justice which mirrors the personal style of the man of law. Law and the man of law are *simpatico*.

The man of law, the classic litigant, represents a dramatic contrast with another sort of man who enters the courts more as a legal object than as a legal subject. Such men are to be found every day, passing through the criminal courts. They represent the disadvantaged men of society who have failed in terms of the market: the impecunious, the unemployed. Such men are also failures according to acceptable standards of middle-class masculinity. Not for them the cut and thrust of the male boardroom, where masculinity is a calculated balance of aggression and restraint. Theirs is a cruder, rougher style which offends middle-class male notions of propriety and leads to trouble.

This book is about all these people. Its purpose is to question a still central tenet of law, that it is perfectly impartial in its dealings with all those who come before it, both in its operation and in its basic form, to challenge law's very construction of its own impartiality (is it appropriate? is it possible? do we want it?) and to spell out some of the ways a law which purports to treat people equally in fact shapes and controls the lives of men and women, preferring some and punishing others.

Though this book is about men as well as women, feminism provides the perspective. The principal object of feminism in the present legal context is to show the large degree to which law has failed to accommodate women in its view of the legal person. But feminism also provides the vantage point from which to criticise law and its relation to men. While it is more usual for feminism to address the situation of women, a feminist approach is also able to show the discordance between the legal model of the person and the attributes and needs of social groups other than women. In other words, feminism provides a site from which to view law's failings with respect to both the sexes. Feminism thus can serve to highlight the inability of law to provide for all who do not fit its conception of humanity.

This interpretation of law and its sexist and class construction is developed in the following manner. Chapter 1 considers what other feminists have had to say about male bias in law and how the present work connects with and contributes to feminist legal thought. The book next considers the official account of law, that it is a fair and unbiased system for the scientific resolution of social disputes, and presents an initial riposte to this standard view. Chapter 3 extends this challenge by maintaining that there are critical problems with law's very conception of its own impartiality. Here it is also argued that, contrary to what law says about itself, legal theory, legal doctrine and legal method all in fact reflect a quite particular and partial approach to the social world and the social person. In Chapter 4 we observe the way in which certain members of the legal community help to sustain this social vision by implicitly endorsing its view of humanity in their legal work and also by failing to offer a dissenting or even critical voice. Chapter 5 then examines in some detail the key attributes of the legal person. It considers who is included in the model and who is expressly or implicitly excluded.

In Chapter 6, we look at the position of the failed men of the legal process, the bread and butter of the criminal courts. Chapter 7 then addresses the place of women in the law. It considers the effects of the traditional role assigned to women by law, as domestics and care-givers. It also questions the success of some recent efforts to have women included in the legal model of the person via sex discrimination laws. Finally, Chapter 8 draws together the various strands of the argument and suggests some possibilities for change.

1

Feminist excavations

The body of writing on law and how it shapes and constrains the lives of women is substantial. Since about the early 1970s, feminists have been challenging the sexism of a wide range of substantive laws—abortion, rape and pornography are some key areas—and there are now several excellent reviews of this literature (deCrow, 1973; Atkins and Hoggett, 1984; O'Donovan, 1985). More recently, feminists have begun to take issue with legal writing within their own particular legal speciality. Thus we are now beginning to see feminist analyses of such standard legal categories as contract, tort and family law (Boyd and Sheehy, 1986).

In the following discussion of feminist legal criticism, the aim is not to canvass the now considerable literature on how discrete laws or categories of law oppress women. The intention is more specific: to trace major developments in feminist thinking and theorising about the law as a whole—as a core of doctrine, as a system and as an approach to the social world—through a close examination of the arguments advanced in certain key works.

This more theoretical form of feminist legal criticism has a short history. Feminist legal theory in fact still seems slight when compared with the efforts of feminists from other disciplines such as political science, philosophy and even the natural sciences (Graycar, 1986a; 1986b). Legal feminism has indeed lagged behind the success clearly achieved in these other areas. It has nevertheless followed closely enough in the same general direction, advancing its understanding of its subject by a similar set of intellectual moves. This therefore suggests that feminist legal theory is importing ideas from these other progressive sectors and developing from there, albeit somewhat less vigorously (Olsen, 1984a; Harding, 1986).

Feminist legal literature addressed to the law as a whole can be divided into three approaches. These are by no means mutually exclusive: they all intersect and overlap and arguments are carried over from one to the other. Indeed it is possible to discern a steady accretion of feminist knowledge on the law, so it is perhaps useful to

conceive of the feminist legal project as a sort of archeological dig
into law, rather than as a series of discrete interpretations in which
each new theorist has abandoned or rejected the insights of her
predecessors. With each new phase, with each new excavation, has
come a more penetrating understanding of the relation between law
and masculinity which has built upon and benefited from the findings
of earlier feminist thinkers. The common project of each of the
feminist critiques of law has been to challenge law's own account of
itself as rational, fair and objective and hence adequate in its treatment
of women.

Following a rough chronology (one can find contemporary writing
from each school), the first phase can be characterised by its concern
with the male monopoly of law. Here the focus is on women's
struggle to achieve equality within the present system in the face of
specific male efforts to preserve male dominance both within the
legal profession and in the general public sphere. In the first phase,
the principal concern is with how the male personnel of the law have
operated upon sexist principles to the detriment of women. The
feminist challenge is directed specifically to the legal claim to fairness
and impartiality in relation to law's dealings with women. The
argument is that the men of law have been blatant in their male bias:
they have specifically endeavoured to preserve their own power and
to keep women in their place.

In the second phase of feminist writing, the argument of male bias
is extended to encompass virtually every aspect of law. Here the
grievance is not confined to the first-phase claim that law is peopled
by men and therefore biased in their favour. Rather the objection is
to what is seen as a deep-seated male orientation in law which infects
all its practices. The law, it is said, embodies a male culture, a male
way of doing things. Law is therefore corrupted for women by its
inherent masculinity. The feminist task is to devise an entirely new
law for women.

The third feminist account of law again extends the challenge and
further complicates the story. Here much of the attack is mounted at
a conceptual level with a view to showing how sexism informs the
analytical categories with which law defends its impartiality. The
effect is to expose the disjuncture between the rhetoric of law and its
sexist practice. Third-phase feminists challenge the very concepts law
invokes to defend itself as a just and fair institution. While law, they
say, professes to be rational, dispassionate, value-neutral, consistent
and objective, it is in fact none of these things. The reason is that law
defines these terms in a very particular and masculine way—one
which omits and devalues the qualities associated with the experience
of women. Indeed the very choice of these ideals as the guiding

principles of law, it is said, indicates a masculine bias.

For third-phase feminists, the actual relation between law and the patriarchal social order is complex and variable. While law, inevitably, is intimately connected to the values and priorities of a sexist, male-dominated society, that relationship is historically contingent, shifting and multifaceted. It is therefore too simple to characterise law as uniformly masculine in its orientation and its priorities. And yet it is true to say that law serves to stifle dissent to the inequitable arrangements it supports and to produce consent to its way of doing things by invoking its rhetoric of fairness and impartiality.

According to the third-phase theorists, the problem of law for women therefore goes beyond the sexism of its representatives or any legal culture of masculinity one might discern. Rather, the problem is that law presents itself in a way which is specifically designed to demonstrate its essential neutrality in relation to the sexes (and other social categories) while in fact the very mode of its self-presentation is deeply gendered. And yet by maintaining the appearance of dispassionate neutrality, law is able quietly to go about its task of assisting in the reproduction of the conditions which subordinate women (as well as other social groups). In other words, the concepts invoked by law to demonstrate its essential justness—concepts such as 'impartiality', 'objectivity' and 'rationality', are gender-biased in their very construction. Nevertheless, they still supply the means by which law maintains the appearance that the social inequality which it oversees is social choice and not oppression.

First-phase feminism: the male monopoly

The largest body of feminist work on law is about the pursuit of formal equality for women: from the acquisition of citizenship to the introduction of anti-discrimination legislation. It describes a male monopoly in the public sphere which a male-controlled law has supported systematically. Its goal has been the removal of legal constraints on women and the acquisition of equal civil rights designed to allow women to compete freely with men in the marketplace (Scales, 1981:427).

This first phase of writing contends that legal men have used their position of dominance to keep the public sphere a male preserve. In the courts and in the parliaments, men have actively sought to exclude women from positions of influence. The aim of feminists is thus to have women placed fully on the legal agenda, to have full legal rights extended to women.

A distinguishing feature of the first phase is its tendency to accept, and approve, law's own account of itself when it is not dealing with women. Law is seen therefore to be essentially a rational and fair institution concerned with the arbitration of conflicting rights between citizens. The problem with law is that it has not yet developed full and effective public rights for women. It was once overtly discriminatory. Today it indirectly denies women rights by constituting a subordinate, domestic role for them in the private sphere (Olsen, 1986).

In the first-phase analysis, the present character and outlook of law are largely left intact. The prevailing idea is accepted that law should be (and can be) impartial and reasoned. The objection is to the failure of law to adhere to its own professed standards when it invokes discriminatory laws and practices. That is, the objection is to bad law.

Two books figure prominently in the writing of first-phase feminism. Both are substantial works which endeavour to treat in a comprehensive fashion the problem of legal sexism. In *Sexism and the Law*, Albie Sachs and Joan Hoff Wilson (1978) examine male bias in legal thinking in Britain and America in the nineteenth and twentieth century. *Women and the Law*, by Susan Atkins and Brenda Hoggett (1984), is principally about the legal treatment and construction of British women today.

To Sachs and Wilson, what is wrong with law, from the point of view of women, is that it constitutes a male monopoly. Far from being the agents of social change, legal men have determinedly fought women in their bid to enter the professions and public life. Sachs and Wilson see this as an effort by men to protect male interests: to preserve jobs for the boys and to keep women in the home performing their domestic labours. In the nineteenth century, male control of the Bench and the Bar was perfect and so the traditional male view of women as dependent homemakers prevailed. In the face of massive resistance from the legal profession (we are told that judges were 'enthusiasts for inequality'), women struggled valiantly to be treated as equals, both as citizens and spouses. We sought even to find a place alongside men at the Bar. Though we have made substantial gains, men still dominate the legal profession and, at best, 'manifest a grudging tolerance rather than a facilitative welcome to women entrants' (Sachs and Wilson, 1978:226).

Sachs and Wilson have been criticised for restricting their analysis to sexism in legal attitudes, as if this were a sufficient explanation of the law's oppression of women (Smart, 1984:17; Graycar, 1986a:108). More particularly, there have been objections to their failure to examine critically the character and ideology of law. Implicit in their writing, it is said, is an uncritical acceptance of law's own view of the social world (as a community of competing and self-interested strangers). Dissatisfaction has been expressed also over the failure of Sachs and Wilson to raise questions about the possible sexism of law's method: how it endeavours to resolve social conflict through a competitive and aggressive adversarial system. Instead, they seem to display a tacit faith in much of the legal system, wishing only 'to see the law functioning as a better instrument for serving the community' (Sachs and Wilson, 1978:x). As we will see in the work of second- and third-phase writers, each of these aspects of law has since been subjected to feminist scrutiny.

Sexism and the Law stands nevertheless as a powerful indictment of the notion of judicial neutrality. It chronicles women's battles for recognition as persons before the law, revealing the wide divide between the judicial view of women and social reality. As the authors observe, 'the myth of femininity was stronger than the evidence of the real females actually before the court' (Sachs and Wilson, 1978:56). It is also a compelling account of women's endeavour to change the legal mind about women.

Prominent in their story of legal sexism are active and political women, engaged in daring and eloquent acts of protest. Not only did the early feminists take issue with the legal view that they should confine themselves to the domestic sphere, but they went to extra-ordinary lengths to make their point. Courageously they pursued their cause, in the face of ridicule, abuse and violence from their male 'protectors'. The courtroom speech delivered in 1873 by American activist Susan B. Anthony provides a fine illustration of such female resistance. Here she defends her 'crime' of voting and advances a case for universal female suffrage:

> For any State to make sex a qualification that must ever result in the disfranchisement of one entire half of the people ... is ... a violation of the law of the land. By it, the blessings of liberty are forever withheld from women and their female posterity ... To them this government is not a democracy ... It is an odious aristocracy: a hateful oligarchy; the most hateful ever established on the face of the globe ... this oligarchy of sex, which makes the men of every household sovereigns, masters; the women subjects, slaves; carrying dissension, rebellion into every home of the Nation, can not be endured. (Sachs and Wilson, 1978:86)

The other example of feminist analysis of the first phase is Atkins and Hoggett's *Women and the Law*. In this volume, the authors operate as conventional lawyers within the given framework and categories of law, the format of their book reflecting the traditional divisions. Hence there are chapters on the law's sexist treatment of women within the 'public' sphere of work and others on the law's approach to women within the 'private' sphere of marriage, sexuality and violence in the home. And yet their volume is more than just an atheoretical compendium of laws affecting women. Atkins and Hoggett attempt to theorise the sexism of law by drawing connections between different discriminatory legal practices and identifying a number of sexist themes running through the law. They show, for example, how the law has consistently viewed women as less responsible than men. They also note the uniform legal construction of women across the different areas of law as primarily wives and mothers. Consistently, the law has imposed on women the roles of child-bearer, child-rearer and domestic servant. The central organising idea, however, is of a male monopoly of law. It is the proposition that men, who dominate the legal system, have used it for their own devices—to preserve a powerful public role for themselves and to cast women in a less desirable, subordinate domestic role.

Notwithstanding subsequent developments in feminist legal thinking which (as we will see) have greatly extended the challenge of the first-phase theorists, it would be wrong to see this early work as fatally flawed by the limitations of its vision, as too short-sighted in its focus on the male personnel of law. The contribution of the first phase to women's struggle for legal change has been considerable. Not only does it represent the first feminist excavation into the male foundations of law, the first archeological dig, but its challenge to male dominance of legal institutions and to discriminatory legislation has been instrumental in reshaping and reforming much of the law for women. Indeed one writer goes so far as to say that it represents 'the single most important feminist legal strategy ... the theoretical underpinning of the entire women's rights movement in law' (Olsen, 1984:12). By demonstrating how laws which constrain only one of the sexes, and seem to work for the benefit of the other, fail to meet law's own self-professed standards (of fairness, rationality and impartiality), it has indicted law on its own terms and supplied the intellectual framework for women's demands for equal treatment. Its sustained attacks on legal sexism have also come close to winning for women formal equality within the substantive law.

Second-phase feminism: the male culture of law

Feminists of the first phase, such as Sachs and Wilson, appear to believe that law could operate fairly and for the common good if only it would recognise the equal rights of women. The second-phase feminists are more swingeing in their critique of law's claim to impartiality and justice for all. These are merely high-minded principles which legal men have employed as protective cover. They obscure law's actual partiality: its preference for men and their view of the world. The truth is that men have fashioned a legal system in their own image. They have developed a harsh, uncaring, combative, adversarial style of justice which essentially reflects their own way of doing things and therefore quite naturally advantages the male litigant. Law treats people as unfeeling automatons, as selfish individuals who care only for their own rights and who feel constantly under threat from other equally self-absorbed holders of rights. This is a male view of society, they say, which ignores and devalues the priorities of women—those of human interdependence, human compassion and human need.

Second-phase feminists also take issue with law's conception of its own objectivity. This is a highly suspect notion, they say, not just because it has been used as a smokescreen to conceal male bias but because it invokes a particular approach to the social world with which many feminists take issue. Law's objectivity, they say, seeks to invoke a detached, dispassionate approach to social conflict. In the rhetoric of law, impartiality is secured by the maintenance of a healthy distance between the 'fact-finder' and the subjects of the dispute. This is the means by which judges maintain their closely guarded neutrality and hence their objectivity. To second-phase feminists, detachment may not be the best approach to resolving disputes: involvement and close proximity to the subject may be better.

The belief that because men have the numbers in the legal system they make sure it represents their interests is merely the starting point of the second-phase feminist criticism of law. At this point it could be described as a variety of male monopoly theory reminiscent of the work of Sachs and Wilson. Thus: 'The judiciary remains overwhelmingly male. Judges have grown up in a patriarchal culture; their attitudes are inevitably shaped by their life experiences and by their position as the beneficiaries of male supremacy' (Polan, 1982:302). But the theory then is taken to its logical extreme. Law is deemed to be essentially an expression of masculinity, not only in its content but also in its *modus operandi*: 'The whole structure of law—its hierarchical organisation; its combative, adversarial format; and its un-deviating bias in favour of rationality over all other values—defines it as a fundamentally patriarchal institution' (Polan 1982:303).

The proposition that law is imbued with the culture of men moves beyond the claim that law is made by men and therefore tends to entrench their position of dominance. The indictment is more far-reaching. Law, it is said, is conceived through the male eye; it represents the male perspective. It starts from the male experience and fails to recognise the female view. To Janet Rifkin (1980:84), for example, law is 'a paradigm of maleness', a 'symbol and a vehicle of male authority'. Law treats as axiomatic the subordination of women to men: it is culturally a male institution which serves to ensure that men remain the dominant sex.

There is little point in seeking to improve women's position within this masculine legal framework: it has no room for women. What is needed is social revolution, not reform. 'Thus, it is not so much that laws must be changed: it is patriarchy that must be changed' (Polan, 1982:303). And from another feminist critic: 'Without a fundamental reordering of societal institutions and values, women cannot begin to achieve true parity' (Rhode, 1986:158).

The most prolific and widely quoted writer of the second phase is the American feminist Catharine MacKinnon. Consistently, her central argument has taken the form of a dispute with other feminist writers on the nature of the 'woman question'. MacKinnon maintains that it has been fundamentally misconceived. For too long, feminists have interpreted the problem of women's oppression in terms of women's differences from men; women's inferior position has been explained in terms of their failure to achieve the standards of men. Consequently some feminists have striven to advance the position of women so that they can be as good as men and therefore justify equal and like treatment. Where women have displayed distinctive 'weaknesses' (such as pregnancy) some feminists have sought to have such female differences recognised as legitimate reasons for the special protection of women.

Feminists have misread the problem, according to MacKinnon (1985:21). Both strategies (that is, 'like' and 'special' treatment) try to fit women to an existing system instead of asking what the system would look like if women, not men, were its starting point. She explains: 'If you see gender as a hierarchy—in which some people have power and some people are powerless—you realise that the oppositions of either being the same as men or being different from men are just two ways of having men as your standard.' To MacKinnon, gender is not a question of difference but a question of dominance. The central issue for feminists is to address the fact that the sexes are not equal. Instead, men have the power to dominate and to oppress women and they do so by controlling our language, our culture, our social and legal institutions, and thus, most importantly, our bodies.

MacKinnon's several analyses of the nature of men's power over women all have as their central theme the 'intimate violation of women by men' (MacKinnon, 1979:1). The core of the problem of women's powerlessness is the 'institutionalised' nature of 'male sexual dominance of women'. In an early work, MacKinnon (1979) examines the impact of male dominance on the workplace where it takes the form of sexual harassment. Sexual intrusions, she claims, are a constant and pervasive feature of working life for women and yet the law has been singularly ineffectual in offering protection or redress.

In her later writing, MacKinnon (1982; 1983; 1985; 1987) extends her criticism to the law and the state, *in toto*, maintaining that both are fully implicated in the sexual oppression of women. MacKinnon pulls no punches. Her work is full of strong statements about the sexism of law and its institutions. Developing the notion that 'sexuality is the linchpin of gender inequality' (1982:533), that men's nearly total power over women resides in their ability to reduce women to 'walking embodiments' of men's sexual needs (1982:534), MacKinnon charges the law with endorsing and entrenching this state of affairs, rather than supplying solutions to women.

MacKinnon's (1983:644) indictment of law is thorough: 'The law sees and treats women the way men see and treat women.' At every level, the law reproduces sexual experience from the perspective of the male, not the female, and thereby ensures male control over the bodies of women. Thus rape, prostitution and obscenity laws have little to do with the physical security of women and everything to do with preserving men's rights over female sexuality. Indeed, they positively help to eroticise the sexual abuse and exploitation of women. Here we see MacKinnon taking a line reminiscent of the first-phase feminists. That is to say, men who dominate the law are in a position to use it to further their own ends and they do so with a vengeance. To illustrate:

> To the extent possession is the point of sex, rape is sex with a woman who is not yours [in most jurisdictions, you may rape your wife] ... If part of the kick of pornography involves eroticizing the putatively prohibited, obscenity law will putatively prohibit pornography enough to maintain its desirability without ever making it unavailable or truly illegitimate. The same with prostitution. (MacKinnon, 1983:644)

The maleness of law, however, goes beyond its practice of pre-serving male sexual interests in women. To MacKinnon (1983:645), law's maleness is not limited to the substance of any individual law but extends to law's very style, its form, and its view of the world. In other words, 'law not only reflects a society in which men rule women [but] it rules in a male way'. When law professes to be neutral and value-free, it calls itself objective. Through a leviathan structure of rules, regulations and ritual language, it endeavours to present itself as 'dispassionate', 'impersonal' and 'disinterested' and to conceal its real interests. The reality is that law is not impartial; it is equated with the male viewpoint, and detachment and disinterest are qualities, valued by men, specifically invoked to obscure the masculinity of law's bias.

To MacKinnon the problem is not just the invocation of the concept of objectivity to obscure the reality of law's male bias. The problem is that objectivity itself as a guiding principle may not be ideal even if it were possible to realise it in the sense that law conceives it—that is, as 'aperspectivity', as absence of a point of view. For what it demands is a degree of distance and detachment from social problems and social disputes which may in fact be better arbitrated and solved by processes which entail participation and involvement: in short, closeness to the subject. The problem of legal objectivity—in particular, the question of whether it is possible to achieve the state of pure detachment and value-neutrality which those who administer the law claim to do—is one which will be specifically addressed later in this book. For the purposes of the present review of feminist theory, it is sufficient to note here some of MacKinnon's observations on the shortcomings of the concept.

Catharine MacKinnon has had a considerable impact on feminist thinking about law, particularly among American theorists. Her protagonists accept that the culture of law is male, that legal institutions and legal methods display an essential masculinity. David Cole, for instance, describes law as operating 'like a man's mind'. Law, he declares, 'is identifiably male, in its implicit substantive norms, its adversarial operation, and its paternalistic remedies. The law reflects male "value judgements" so deeply and pervasively that male values begin to look like neutral normative standards. The feminist perspective exposes the substance and procedure of law as inherently male-biased' (Cole, 1984:50—51). In other words, law embodies a male culture at every level of its operation. It is not just that the content of law reflects male interests but that law goes about its task in an aggressively male way—hence the adversary system (whose style of masculinity will be considered later in the book). And all this is done in the name of objectivity and fairness.

Implicit in this argument is a suggestion that women would do things better. It is assumed that 'women's subjugated position provides the possibility of more complete and less perverse understandings' (Harding 1986:26). Feminism, it is claimed, offers to law the insights of the second sex, 'a new vision of the world from the perspective of women' (Thornton, 1986:22). According to a number of writers of this school, women possess particular qualities which could form the basis of a more desirable legal system.

Ann Scales (1986), another exponent of MacKinnon's thesis, has considered what a legal system might look like if it were moulded in the image of women, not men. Her starting premise is that there is such a thing as a male and a female legal or ethical style: that justice means different things to men and women. Drawing on the work of psychologist Carol Gilligan (1982), Scales contends that boys and girls are brought up to see the social world in different ways and so develop opposing styles of moral reasoning. Boys, who are encouraged to detach themselves from their mothers and flourish as independent beings, develop an 'ethic of rights'. Their priority becomes the preservation of the autonomy of individuals against the claims of others. By contrast, girls are allowed to stay close to their mothers (because they are the same sex and will one day be mothers themselves) and so come to value relationships. Their style of justice is an 'ethic of care'. It gives priority to responsibility for others, to loving and preventing harm. (Though feminists, such as Scales, have absorbed the ideas of both MacKinnon and Gilligan, one must not conflate the two approaches. MacKinnon disputes the idea of a female ethical style which she sees as the convenient artifact of men. And yet we may still observe a good deal of common ground: both women indict the maleness of the prevailing legal ethic.)

Scales deplores the existing male style of law. She objects to its rigid focus on the rights of disconnected individuals. This is an uncaring law whose sole concern is getting right abstract principles without reference to the particular human beings involved. In it, competing claims between individuals are settled bloodlessly, according to standards of supposed fairness and impartiality. People must be treated alike whatever the individual need, whatever the social context and whatever the unfortunate consequences for nearest and dearest. The alternative female mode, she speculates, 'expand[s] the available universe of facts, rules, and relationships to find a unique solution to each unique problem' (Scales, 1986:1381).

To Scales, there is no compromise solution. The male 'rights-based' approach is incompatible with the female 'ethic of care' and therefore must go. The female approach is to be preferred because it is authentic: it reflects the real nature of relations between people—as interdependent and complex (no two cases are alike)—and rejects the inauthentic male mode which sees the social world in terms of the abstract competing claims of identical individuals. As Scales explains:

> The rights-based side of things, for all its grand abstraction, describes a pretty grim view of life on the planet. It treats individuals in society as isolated monads, as natural adversaries

who must each stake out his own territory and protect it with the sword/shield mechanism of 'rights'. This model of aggression is half of what is required for holocaust. (Scales, 1986:1391)

The theories of Carol Gilligan have influenced the thinking of a number of other legal critics who equate law with the culture of men and who advocate a new female style of justice to supplant the present one. To such feminists, women have special virtues: in particular, they share a greater sense of responsibility for others and accord priority to the virtue of caring. A female style of justice, it is claimed, would focus on conciliation as opposed to the more combative male legal style, which stresses, selfishly, the need to preserve the unimpeded rights of individuals to pursue their own ends. Thus one legal writer demands that we 'build on broader feminist values that transcend the legal individualist legacy'—a legacy which conceives us as all as discrete and detached individual units, always potentially in conflict, never benefiting from the good offices of others (Rhode, 1986:158). To another what is needed is an 'ideology of solidarity and collective decision-making characteristic of much ... feminist thinking' (Kingdom, 1985:154). Still other writers talk in terms of a new female language of responsibility in law, one which will supplant law's current concern with the rights of the individual to remain free from the hostile interventions of others (Bottomley, Gibson and Meteyard, 1987:54).

Implicit in all these statements is the second-phase feminist argument that law has a male character: it embodies a male norm and is thus an expression of masculinity. The feminist project is to expose the maleness of law and, for some, it is to devise a new legal approach which is more in harmony with the lives and thus the culture of women. It is on both of these points that the feminists of the second phase can be distinguished from the writers of the third phase.

Third-phase feminism: legal rhetoric and the patriarchal social order

Third-phase feminist theory concedes that law is both male-dominated and full of biases, one of which pertains to the sex of the litigant. However, it resists the notion that law represents male interests in anything like a coordinated or uniform fashion. The reason is that law is not the coherent, logical, internally consistent and rational body of doctrine it professes to be. Part of the feminist challenge here is to the very concepts law has employed to represent itself as a fair and impartial institution. Law, they say, is not to be regarded

—as it has traditionally—as a neutral and dispassionate institution which accordingly resolves disputes and organises social relations justly. The various epithets conventionally used to describe law, such as 'rational', 'autonomous' and 'principled', are in fact male legal ideals. They describe a set of qualities to which men might aspire but they are not, and could not be, the truth of law because nothing in life is ever organised in this way. Vital dimensions of human existence, dimensions conventionally associated with women, are missing from law's depiction of itself. The reality of law is that it is 'as irrational, subjective, concrete and contextualised as it is rational, objective, abstract and principled' (Olsen, 1984:16).

Another concern of the third-phase feminists is to show that while law presents itself as autonomous and value-neutral, the truth is that law reflects the priorities of the dominant patriarchal social order, priorities which are themselves not always coherent or consistent but which generally constitute women as the subordinate sex. Also central to third-phase feminism is an explicit rejection of grand theory and a commitment to the study of particular instances of law's oppression of women.

Two writers dominate the literature of the third phase. Though one addresses the sexism of English law, the other the implications of American justice for women, they have arrived at remarkably similar conclusions. Both agree that law should not be regarded as a unity, as a single set of cultural values. Law, they say, is as complex and contradictory as the dominant social order it reflects. Though it lays claims to rationality, consistency and uniformity in its approach to the social world, in fact it has no one colour, no essence. Though it professes to be independent of the values of the society it serves, in fact it is intimately linked to those values, which are themselves mixed and contradictory.

Law therefore is not simply a vehicle for men's oppression of women, as the first phase suggested. Nor is it simply an embodiment of the values of the male culture, as the second phase thought. Indeed law is unable to muster the degree of rationality, internal coherence and consistency which both approaches necessarily imply. And yet law remains an important site of feminist struggle because of the many ways it constrains and controls the lives of women.

The British author Carol Smart has been writing about the problems of law for women for well over a decade. Her earliest work criticised the processes of criminal justice from a feminist perspective (Smart, 1976; 1981). Since the early 1980s, she has concentrated mainly on family law and its implications for women (Smart, 1982; 1983; 1984a; 1984b; 1986; Smart and Brophy, 1985). In the course of her writing she has advanced and maintained a consistent position on the nature of the law as a whole: both as a system and as a body of doctrine.

The large degree to which family law intrudes on the lives of women is the reason why Smart selects it as the focus of her analysis. This category of law, she tells us, has determined the structure of the family, and it is the family which constitutes the major site of women's oppression. It is therefore legitimate to generate a feminist account of law's relation to women from the study of just one of its many branches (Smart, 1982:144).

In an early paper on historical developments in British family law, Smart develops her thesis. Having documented changes in the complexion of family law since the nineteenth century, Smart (1982:144) observes a substantial improvement in its approach to women to the point where 'it is no longer possible to assert that family law is oppressive of women in a simple and direct fashion'. Women were once denied any rights to their children or to any degree of financial independence. Now the law can be seen positively to champion their cause. Not only does it now respect maternal rights to custody but it also seeks to protect wives and mothers 'against the worst excesses of masculine abuse'. And yet there persists in law a view of women as economic and social subordinates to their husbands. Legal decisions about the family are still based on a highly traditional notion of the family form in which the husband engages in paid work outside the home while the wife performs maternal and domestic labours.

It is this tension in family law which forms the basis of Smart's thesis. On the one hand, the law is an agent of social reform for women. On the other hand, it still helps to keep us in our place. The feminists of the second phase were therefore simplistic in their interpretation of law as 'a tool of patriarchal oppression', for law helps as well as hinders women. Smart (1982:144) specifically rejects the notion of 'a simple, instrumental relationship between law and the structures of patriarchy'. Yet she is also convinced that law is vital in defining a traditional role for women. In short, law is complex and contradictory in its treatment of the female sex.

In a study of English family law of the 1950s, Smart (1983) both narrows the focus of her analysis and extends and elaborates her theory of law. Here she observes the judicial construction of women's family role at the point of divorce over a single decade and finds a mixture of approaches. Some judges adhered to the letter of harsh matrimonial laws which treated property acquired with the husband's earnings, and in his name, as strictly his own, whatever the wife's contribution in the way of domestic services. This left women high and dry after the dissolution of the marriage. Other judges were more merciful and sought to provide a just solution for the 'deserving wife'. This was a mixed blessing for women: it meant that judges were able to employ their own moral evaluations to favour women who adhered more closely to conventional notions of the ideal domestic woman of the 1950s. For Smart, the feminist message of her findings is again that the operation of law is a complex thing: its personnel act in different ways and for different motives. The law is not invariably anti-woman, though it tends to favour a view of woman as dependent wife and mother.

Smart is at pains to distance her view of law from any form of conspiracy theory. Thus she distinguishes her work from that of the first-phase writers Sachs and Wilson who identifed the law as a whole with the interests of the men running the system. The fact that one can find moments in legal history when the law has positively benefited women (she cites the legal requirement that men pay maintenance) is taken by her as evidence of the uneven nature of law: male interests are not inevitably given legal priority. Moreover, it is often far from clear what those male interests might be, were they always to be represented, or just how they might best be served. What is more, the male conspiracy theory tends to leave out the dimension of class. If the law favours men, it often does so selectively, to the disadvantage of working-class males.

In *The Ties that Bind* (1984), Smart extends her analysis of English divorce laws and their consequences for women. Here she uses several types of data. In some detail, she examines developments in both the judicial interpretation of family law and in legislation regulating the conditions of divorce from the 1950s to the early 1980s. The problems for women of matrimonial property, maintenance and the custody of children all come under her gaze. She also reports the outcome of her interviews of Sheffield (England) magistrates and solicitors operating in the area of family law, highlighting their views on gender roles.

Though Smart (1984:xiv) makes a number of far-reaching claims about the oppressive nature of both law and legal practice for women, she denies that her purpose is 'to produce the definitive grand theory on Law and Patriarchy'. She is more interested in explaining 'the specificity of women's oppression' by observing the operation of a single area of law which looms large in the lives of many women. Smart chides those who would seek to develop general feminist theories of law, describing such efforts as 'misguided'. She wishes 'to deconstruct ideas about law as a monolithic, homogeneous power which controls women and is exercised by men' (Smart, 1984:xii). Consistent with this aim, her concluding statement in *The Ties that Bind* stresses the uneven development of law on the family. Thus, 'I do not see the law simply as a conservative force which intransigently resists change ... On the contrary, law itself is seen as a multi-faceted system of regulation, containing its own contradictions, and most importantly, capable of change and positive influence and not just negative restraint' (Smart, 1984:221).

In spite of her many reservations about the value of a feminist interpretation of the law as a whole, Smart's various pronouncements can be seen to cohere as a general, internally consistent theory of law. Basically she maintains that law does not live up to its rhetoric of consistency, rationality and fairness; that law is in fact profoundly sexist but in a fitful and uneven manner—that is, in the manner of the social order which law helps to reproduce. Thus she observes that different judges have different opinions, legal priorities change from one case to another, the laws in any one area do not fit neatly together so that they could be said to represent a single set of interests. And yet, in spite of its complexity and muddle, law can still be seen to assist in the reproduction of the dominant patriarchal social order. It does this by slotting people into household units, constituted through marriage, with a breadwinning husband–father at the head, and a subordinate woman performing the unpaid offices of wife and mother, sustaining the traditional 'family values'. Indeed the woman's place is vital to the peace, good order and stability of the patriarchal order: 'She can prevent delinquency by staying at home to look after the children, she can reduce unemployment by staying at home and freeing jobs for the men, she can recreate a stable family unit by becoming totally dependent on her husband so that she cannot leave him. *She* is the answer' (Smart, 1984:136).

It is this patriarchal arrangement, which is supported by law, which ensures the social and economic insecurity of wives and mothers and therefore oppresses women as a sex. Both within legally sanctified marriages and after their dissolution, women are still expected to give priority to the unpaid work of child-rearing and are placed in a position of considerable financial vulnerability in carrying out this assigned task.

In a recent statement on legal sexism, Smart (1986) presents a synthesis of her various arguments, calling it 'the idea of the uneven development of law'. Here she reiterates her proposition that law is not a unity, not 'a simple tool of patriarchy', but has many dimensions. Significantly, for women, law both encourages and hampers change. To illustrate her point, Smart draws our attention to changes in the English laws governing abortion. The legal avail-ability of abortion represents an improvement in women's position in that it increases our control over our bodies. But what the law giveth it taketh. Abortion laws have invested considerable authority over women's reproduction to a male-dominated medical profession.

A further demonstration of Smart's theory of the uneven nature of law is provided by domestic violence legislation. In the 1970s, the British government introduced laws designed to provide remedies for battered wives. Though these reforms might have been more extensive, they represented nevertheless a real gain for women, at least in theory. In practice, however, there was little change in the position of battered women for the simple reason that law-enforcers did not like the law. Non-compliant police made it difficult for women to proceed against violent husbands; a conservative judiciary imposed restrictive interpretations on the legislation, further limiting its value. Domestic violence laws therefore fell prey to the problem of uneven development. 'Law-as-legislation [was] undermined by law-in-practice' (Smart, 1986:119; see also Parker, 1985).

In a similar vein, the American legal critic Frances Olsen (1983; 1984a; 1984b) believes that it is wrong to attribute to law a male essence or an 'immutable nature'. Feminists have found too much consistency of style and character in law, says Olsen, when in fact law has no clear line, no identifiable persona. It is neither all male nor consistently anti-female. Also in tune with the thinking of Smart is Olsen's claim that there is much that is good for women in law. It does not simply represent the interests of men, as the second-phase writers suggest. Feminist struggles have won for women real reforms which should not be discounted in the rush to condemn law as sexist.

What Olsen does object to in law, however, is its function as a powerful tool of male propaganda. A male-dominated legal system presents law to the world in terms of a set of characteristics and priorities which are valued by men. Thus law is said to be just, fair, principled and objective and to have a public, rather than private, orientation: it is concerned with the weighty matters of public life, not with the running of the home. Law's lofty claims for itself include an ability to arbitrate impartially the competing rights of individuals (when they enter the public sphere) and to ensure the equality of treatment of all citizens.

In reality, says Olsen, law possesses no such rationality or unity of purpose. Moreover, the ideals of objectivity and impartiality to which law aspires are, to Olsen, in themselves inherently suspect. All human decision-making, she maintains, is inevitably a complex mixture of abstract and concrete thinking, of objectivity and subjectivity. Indeed, 'objectivity is necessarily subjective'. The implications of this last statement will be considered in some detail later in the book, where the problem of legal objectivity will be subjected to scrutiny.

The false portrayal and exaltation of law by men as a rational synthesis of rules designed to settle the disputes of public individuals presents several problems for women, according to Olsen (1984a). For one thing, law's positive identification with values men think are important (such as rationality and objectivity) both overlooks and implicitly downgrades the opposing set of characteristics convention-ally associated with women (such as emotionality and sensitivity). This has had the effect of defining law as a male profession, of justifying the exclusion of women from legal practice. Men are seen as rational and objective, fair and principled, and so should control a legal system which embodies these values. Women are the antithesis: they are emotional, personal, irrational. Hence law is an unsuitable job for a woman.

According to Olsen, our male-oriented law presents a view of social organisation which is positively damaging to all women. Law splits the world into public and private, and into male and female, and then identifies itself with the male and public world, and purports to confine its activities to this sphere. Meanwhile, the private sphere is in certain respects left unregulated and the women who are con-signed to the domestic realm are deprived of legal redress. Women are left in the home tending children, without a wage, and without the protections that law offers to public individuals—such as the right to sue for payment for services provided or (until recently) the right to seek remedies for physical or sexual abuse. By deeming the home to be beyond its sphere of influence, the law ratifies the unequal private roles of men and women (Olsen 1983:1505).

Notwithstanding its rhetoric of non-intervention in the home, (a myth which will later be challenged) in other ways law has gone to considerable efforts to define and construct a role for women in the private sphere (Olsen, 1985). Along the same lines as Smart, Olsen maintains that law has played an active role in the reproduction of the dominant patriarchal social order and usually in the name of the sanctity of the home. She draws our attention to a series of laws operating last century (mainly now repealed, though, as we will see, their legacy remains) which assumed that the natural place of women was in the home as economic and social dependants of their husbands. For example, the husband possessed the legal right to choose the family domicile and the wife was obliged to live there. He was also 'the juridical head of the family' in that he was entitled to control and admonish his wife and children and to act on their behalf as the financial head. Thus law reinforced the power of husbands over wives within the home, a form of domination which was taken to be part of the natural sexual order, though it clearly needed the law's intervention to secure the 'natural' sexual hierarchy.

With Smart, Olsen also views the law as both oppressive to women and as uneven in its treatment of the sexes. There is insufficient method and system in law for it to be invariably unfair to women. Like Smart, Olsen claims to see through the law's rhetoric of rights and principles to its essential disunity. To both writers, women are not as victimised by the forces of the law as the second phase would have it. Smart and Olsen therefore seek to restore the first-wave notion (generally abandoned in the second phase) of women's power to fight back, to resist. Though they concede that there is much in law that is bad for women, they do not underestimate the achievements of early feminism (Olsen 1984a:16). They acknowledge that women have engaged in 'concrete struggles', that 'some feminist gains have been and will continue to be achieved in the legal arena' (Olsen, 1984b:401). Thus 'much of the legislation that has been enacted over the last century in the area of family law has had an appreciable effect on the economic status of women, particularly on wives faced with divorce' (Smart, 1981:43).

Still feminists are right to perceive law as a central arena of debate because law remains an important part of the construction of, and constraints on, women's social role. Law helps to perpetuate a view of the family which keeps women in their place as subordinates to male authority figures who still largely control the purse.

The contribution of Marxist theory

There is by now a considerable tradition of analysing law and the legal process from a Marxist perspective. Without attempting an exhaustive taxonomy of legal theories informed by Marxism, one can still note the diversity of Marxist approaches to law. For example, some writers have conceived the relation between law and class in a fairly simple and straightforward fashion. Thus law has been seen to serve directly the interests of the capitalist class by giving priority to, and protecting, rights to property. It has also been observed that litigation is such an expensive undertaking that it is out of reach of all but the most privileged. To others, the law is thought to be directly repressive in the sense that it manipulates and controls the activities of powerless groups, by criminalising behaviour which is seen to threaten or challenge the rights of the propertied to a quiet life (Chambliss and Seidman, 1971).

Still others have tried to construe the class character of law as a more subtle and invidious but no less powerful thing. In these interpretations, law is seen less as a direct servant of 'the possessing classes', to borrow a term from Carol Pateman (1988), less as their specific instrument than as a valuable prop to the stability of the dominant capitalist mode of production. One way that it achieves this stability is by fostering the impression that we are all free and equal legal subjects. Law thereby stifles dissent and mutes dissatisfaction with what are in fact inherently inequitable social arrangements. In other words, the class function of law, in these accounts, is seen less as instrumental and repressive than as economic and ideological (Cotterrell, 1984:116).

In view of the strength and richness of the Marxist tradition of legal criticism, it is surprising that it has exerted such a limited impact on feminist analyses of law. The preceding discussion of feminist legal theory did not include a Marxist-feminist strain simply because one has yet to be developed. Although certain feminist writers have emphasised the ideological functions of law, in the manner of the Marxist theorists (Smart in particular), none have in fact sustained a specific focus on the problem of law's relation both to class and to sex.

The one feminist writer who has explicitly brought Marxist theory into her analysis is Catharine MacKinnon. Her use of Marxist legal criticism, however, has been confined to a study of its parallels with feminist theory, and ultimately MacKinnon rejects the Marxist view as unhelpful to women. Specifically, it fails to expose the maleness of law and the state. MacKinnon thus proceeds to examine the law as an instrument for the male oppression of women, making little of the different impact of the legal system on men and women of different classes. Men are grouped together as a single category, an undifferentiated class: the oppressors. Together they are seen to benefit from the sexist institutions of law. Women, the oppressed, form the other category. What is missing from this analysis is an account of the different value of law to men of different classes. Women are also viewed as an undifferentiated group which inevitably falls victim to an essentially masculine law.

Carol Smart, by contrast, has alluded to the unevenness of law in relation to both men and women and is sensitive to the problem of class. Both men and women, she says, can benefit from and be oppressed by law. Social status, she affirms, is one of many determinants of law's approach to both sexes. Perhaps because of her resistance to any unified general theory of law, however (she insists that law is marked more by its unevenness than by its consistency), she is unwilling to develop an overarching theory of the effects of class and sex on the law's treatment of the individual. Instead she opts for a study of specific instances in which law has oppressed women, but also notes, in the course of her writing, the vulnerability of working-class men to legal prosecution.

The dominant tendency in feminist legal criticism is to regard men as the source of women's problems, rarely as victims themselves. In

an effort to depict the benefits which accrue to men of what is seen
to be an inherently sexist institution, many feminists have overlooked
the point that not all men benefit equally from legal sexism. The
equation of law with an all-pervasive male culture has often served to
obscure the fact that it is a very particular class of man who derives
the main advantage from law. If law embodies a male norm, it is a
norm which fits a privileged minority of mankind, not the mass of
men.

Men, women and the law

The interpretation of law to be adopted in this book is a contribution
to the shared feminist enterprise of challenging law's claim to objectivity, impartiality and fairness. It has a kinship with all three feminisms discussed above. The ensuing analysis will therefore often
borrow from their propositions, employ their observations and develop
their trains of thought. Indeed the argument of this work is conducted
on several levels which can be seen to reflect the different layers of
concern of feminist legal writing.

At one level, the project involves a direct challenge to law's rhetoric
of impartiality and consistency in the manner of first-phase feminism.
The various efforts made by law's representatives to present their
endeavour as essentially free from bias are therefore subjected to
critical analysis. It will be claimed that, despite their protestations of
value-neutrality, those who interpret and administer the law do not
always treat those who come before them in an equal and dispassionate
manner. In reality, opinion and belief have shaped the responses of
law's representatives, and often those beliefs have been profoundly
sexist. Also to be questioned is the idea that there can ever be a
perfect place from which to view social disputes impartially, free
from value and bias, as law purports to do.

At a deeper level, the feminist challenge of this book owes a debt
to the thinking of both second- and third-phase feminists but is
perhaps more closely connected to the writing of the third phase.
Specifically, the intention is to examine critically one of the most
important organising conceptual categories of law which has been
used to establish law's impartiality. This is the notion of the abstract
individual. As we will see in later chapters, this entails the idea that
law invokes and serves a sort of universal 'man', rather than particular
individuals or social categories, and that it therefore provides equally
for anyone, anywhere, abstracted from their specific place in the
social world. The argument to be developed, in reply, is not only
that the legal idea of human abstraction is fundamentally misconceived

but that, contrary to what we are told, law in fact anticipates and assumes a very particular type of social order in which a particular type of individual is thought to flourish. And it is this individual, not anyone, whom law in fact endeavours to serve.

The ensuing analysis of law's conception of 'man' and society brings together two fundamental social categories, class and gender, which have largely been kept apart in legal criticism. They have belonged to different traditions between which there has been little cross-fertilisation. Marxist writers have argued the class bias in law, but have usually kept silent on the question of gender. They have said, for example, that law advantages the rich (man) and oppresses the poor (man), either directly, by advancing the interests of one over the other, or indirectly, by securing the material and/or ideo-logical conditions which maintain the capitalist social order (O'Malley, 1983). Feminists have denounced the male bias of law, but have tended to depict men as a homogeneous social category. Some feminists have said that law protects the interests of men; others have gone further and said that law has an inherently male style. Still other feminists have shown unease at a uniform depiction of such a complex institution, but have still advanced the view that law helps to reproduce the dominant patriarchal social order. This book borrows from each of these strands of thinking to explain law's construction of, and relation to, both men and women.

Specifically, the argument to be developed below is that while law purports to deal in abstract individuals, in truth it has a preferred person: the man of law, the individual who flourishes in, and domi-nates, the type of society conceived by law. This person is preferred in the sense that the law reflects his priorities and concerns and conducts itself in a manner which is considered, by him, to be both desirable and natural. This being is both a creature of class and a gendered subject. He is one of the possessing classes. His gender takes the form of a certain exaggerated style of middle-class mascu-linity: he is assertive, articulate, independent, calculating, competitive and competent. And these are precisely the qualities valued in the sort of society which law has in mind: a society which is fiercely competitive and composed of similarly self-interested and able in-dividuals; a society which looks very much like the modern free market.

In later chapters we will see that the man of law is a complex construction. He embodies the range of attributes deemed to be both appropriate and successful in the social order anticipated by law. These are in essence the qualities of the successful middle-class man of business. In this account, then, men do not constitute a single, undifferentiated category, which derives a common benefit from law. Instead, it will be argued that different men have different relations to law. There are certain men—the men of law—upon whom law seems to confer an obvious advantage. Other men are more clearly the objects of law, not its users. Though it may be argued that all men benefit from law's endorsement of the patriarchal form of the family, those men who fail the tests of middle-class masculinity, the unsuccessful men, nevertheless do less well before the law and derive fewer benefits from its services than our man of law.

In relation to women, it will be claimed, there has been greater uniformity of approach. Consistently, women have been constructed in a fashion thought to reflect their natural place in the social order. Their traditional role is not as legal subject but as helpmate to the man of law. Their place is not the competitive public terrain of law but the private sphere of the home. Here their duties are to serve the domestic and emotional needs of their husbands, to assume responsibility for children, to provide love and stability, to leave the man of law nourished and free to pursue his own interests in the marketplace. As we will see, women are the linchpin of what Olsen (1983: 1563) has called the 'altruistic, hierarchical, private family', the site where the man of law may recover his humanity in order to return replenished to the alienating, competitive and therefore legally regulated public sphere.

As we will also discover, recent legal endeavours to improve women's place in law by prohibiting sex discrimination have in many ways served only to entrench the dominant legal model of the person. For what is now expected of women, if they insist on equality with the man of law, is that they mimic him in as many ways as possible—that they become pseudo-men of law. In the following chapters, we shall explore the various ways in which modern English, American and Australian law reflects and reinforces this sex- and class-divided image of society. We will also consider the practical implications of such an inequitable system of justice for men of the non-possessing classes and for women who come before the law.

2

Blind justice

The official version of law— what the legal world would have us believe about itself—is that it is an impartial, neutral and objective system for resolving social conflict. This is the dominant notion of law as an intellectually rigorous system. It is the view of law which tends to prevail among lawyers and judges. Consider the following statements on the nature of contemporary law and justice:

> Legal reasoning, whatever it comprises, is supposed to exclude personal bias. If a judge were to announce: 'The evidence about the defendant's negligence is inconclusive, but I shall find against him because I don't like his type', his decision could be described as procedurally unjust ... the reasons he gives must at least be 'universalisable' so that his reasoning is circumscribed by the requirements of formal justice.' (Harris, 1980:259—60)

> in the official vision of adversary procedure the magistrates and judges are neutral umpires in guilt-finding. (O'Malley, 1983:141)

> legal reasoning ... is intellectual and rational ... The judge can come to know enough about the whole complex of law and fact to discover enough of the truth to settle wisely the disputes before the court ... It requires an open and cultivated mind. (Derham, Maher and Waller, 1986:189)

> Justice is the intellectual consideration and resolution of conflict by an impartial and disinterested third party ... [It is] the careful, impartial, disinterested examination of claims and of the nature of the matter ... (Kamenka and Tay, 1986:308)

Divorced from politics, morals and systems of belief, law's task is to discern 'the facts' (as they are referred to in court) and find the truth of any given matter placed before it.

The idea that law and its processes are rational, fair and disinterested is integral to traditional legal thinking. Members of the Bench, in this view, do not invoke their own personal beliefs of the rights or wrongs of an individual or a case. Nor do they operate with any particular set of social or cultural values. Instead, they are obliged to

24

treat all who come before them in an unbiased fashion, fairly and dispassionately. To quote from the English judicial oath, the obligation on the judicial officer is to 'do right to all manner of people ... without fear or favour, affection or illwill' (Pannick, 1988:5). The essence of legal thinking is this notion of the equality of treatment of all before the law—regardless of class, race, sex or creed. This is achieved by what is often said to be the essential impartiality of the judiciary.

According to this official view, law is an internally-consistent process. It is predictable, precise and logical and therefore just. The law and its representatives must therefore be seen to be autonomous. They must appear to be above politics and personal conviction. In the words of the British legal analyst Roger Cotterrell,

> the judiciary guards vital and carefully nurtured characteristics of its own ... authority—the image of impartiality and objectivity in decision-making, a stance of neutrality and aloofness based on judicial wisdom divorced from all political partisanship, and the highest levels of technical expertise and adjudicatory skill. (1984:242)

Those who interpret and apply the law are said to operate at a respectful distance from the individuals to whom justice is dispensed. Judicial decisions are said to employ 'a distinctly legal mode of reasoning' which ensures that they are not tainted by personal opinion (Kairys, 1982:11). Rather, they invoke what is considered to be an objective viewpoint. To quote the eminent jurist Sir Owen Dixon:

> It is taken for granted that the decision of the Court will be 'correct' or 'incorrect', 'right' or 'wrong' as it conforms with ascertained legal principles and applies them according to a stand-ard of reasoning which is not personal to the judges themselves. But it is basal. The Court would feel that the function it per-formed had lost its meaning and purpose if there were no external (that is 'legal') standard of correctness. (Stubbs, 1986:73)

In their self-proclaimed capacity to arrive at just solutions to social disputes, those who interpret and apply the law profess to act with total impartiality. They claim to be able to set aside their own personal convictions, to proceed in a formally legal fashion, and thereby to arrive at the right answer. Such aspirations to the status of objectivity, to what is thought to be scientific rigour, invest the legal process with considerable prestige and power and secure it, to a large degree, immunity from external criticism. For the truly objective decision is not open to question.

The intellectual roots of this belief in the essential certainty and objectivity of law may be found in liberal philosophy which, in its turn, may be traced to English political theory and practice of the seventeenth century. According to the political scientist, C.B. MacPherson (1962:1), 'It was then, in the course of a protracted struggle in parliament, a civil war, a series of republican experiments, a restoration of the monarchy, and a final constitutional revolution, that the principles which were to become basic to liberal democracy were all developed, though not with equal success at the time'. The key ingredient of this struggle, MacPherson tells us, was 'a new belief in the value and the rights of the individual'.

The manner in which liberal 'individualism' has informed the values and orientation of law in the Anglo-American tradition is a matter for the next chapter. Our present concern, however, is with the modern western style of legal reasoning and the debt it owes to liberal thought. Though it is true that this particular style of reasoning has been subjected to repeated challenges, to the point that some argue that there has been a 'turning away from these [liberal] ideals' (Unger, 1976:192–203), it may still be seen to represent the public face of modern western law and to supply its main defence of itself— as the quotations which opened this chapter ably demonstrate.

To explain the relationship between legal reasoning and liberal thought in the briefest of terms, it is from the dichotomous view of the world advanced by liberal philosophy, (but going back even further: Olsen (1984a) suggests perhaps to the time of Plato), that law derives much of its sense of its own certainty. In this divided view of existence, that which is rational can be separated from that which is irrational; thought can be separated from feeling; objectivity can be distinguished from subjectivity; and abstract thinking can be separated from contextual reasoning. And in each of these cases, for each of these 'dualisms', the former is better than the latter. The rational, the intellectual, the objective and the abstract decision is the preferred and superior style of decision-making (Johnson and Scales, 1986:447).

Alison Jaggar (1983:28) calls this liberal intellectual tendency thus to divide the world into a series of polar opposites 'normative dualism' and observes its association with 'the belief that what is especially valuable about human beings is a particular "mental" ca- pacity, the capacity for rationality'. Liberal theorists, according to Jaggar, 'ascribe political rights on the basis of what they take to be the specifically human capacity for rationality, and disregard what they conceive as "merely physical" capacities and incapacities'. That is to say, what identifies a person as a suitable political actor, in the liberal view, is his ability to think abstractly and objectively. And as we saw in the last chapter, this preferred style of reasoning is one which has tended to be associated with the masculine intellect, the antithetical qualities (the emotions, the passions and the affairs of the body) being associated with the feminine persona (Olsen, 1984a:1).

'Liberal legalism' reflects this divided view of the world by its commitment to an intellectual mode which strives to be all of these things: to be intelligent, abstract and rational. By its adherence to particular legal forms, law seeks to secure for itself the intellectual high ground of abstract rationality, of objective thought—that which is uncontaminated by the passions and by personal opinions. By scrupulous adherence to specifically legal modes of reasoning (which will be outlined below), law endeavours to effect a 'radical separation of morals, politics, and personality from judicial action' (Klare, 1978:276). If the correct forms are obeyed, if legal reasoning is followed closely, then judges are able to stand apart from the matters they have to decide upon in a fully neutral fashion and dispense objective justice. The careful pursuit of legal logic 'banishes equivocation by erecting a norm of legitimacy and branding the infinity of other possibilities as illegitimate' (Johnson and Scales, 1986:447).

It is this idea that law can and should be value-free, certain, indeed, accurate, which provides the very foundation of the notion of the Rule of Law itself. This is the theory of law enunciated by the eminent English jurist A.V. Dicey (1959:184−203): that those who make and administer English law are themselves governed by law and that that law is certain and predictable, not variable or optional. 'In this sense', Dicey says, 'the rule of law is contrasted with every system of government based on the exercise by persons in authority of wide, arbitrary, or discretionary powers of constraint.' The virtue of English law is its certainty and predictability, for 'wherever there is discretion there is room for arbitrariness' which in turn 'must mean insecurity for legal freedom on the part of its subjects'. In this traditional liberal view, law is conceived essentially as 'a neutral guardian of the social order' (Unger, 1976:192).

This chapter attempts to do several things. Its first purpose is to pinpoint some of the ways the law sustains its reputation as an essentially impartial institution: as fair, consistent, rational and un-sullied by personal preferences and beliefs. To this end, it considers the type of education which is said to produce such an even-handed and dispassionate profession. It goes on to examine the way law's official explanation of itself helps to maintain the prevailing notion of law's impartiality. This is the theory of legal positivism: law's own definition of its provenance and purpose. The chapter then considers how the common-law doctrine of precedent further entrenches the idea of legal neutrality. This is the theory that law is a rational and predictable process because judges are bound by the decisions of their predecessors.

A second purpose of this chapter is to mount a challenge to law's rhetoric of neutrality, by maintaining that there is in fact considerable room for judicial manoeuvre within the formal constraints of the system. The argument here is that, despite the official version of law as a near perfectly impartial process, opinion and belief are in fact integral to much of its operation. In other words, the intention of what follows is to challenge law on its own terms, in a manner reminiscent of the first-phase feminists. The question posed is: Does law live up to its own rhetoric? Is it consistent and impartial in the sense that the values of those who are critical to its processes do not intrude? Does the law adhere to its own logic? Is it predictable, intelligent and dispassionate?

The project of exposing the disparity between the theory and practice of law is not a new one. In the 1920s and 1930s, the American Legal Realists questioned the idea of formalistic legal reasoning or 'legal formalism'—the idea that by adhering to specific, technical and formal modes of reasoning, law could be freed from any element of subjectivity (Klare, 1978:278; Parker and Drahoss, 1989). 'The realists' approach', according to the legal sociologist Edwin Schur (1968:43), 'was grounded in a radical conception of the legal process.' The Realists took the view that judges did not discover the law, as they professed to do, but rather they made it. Always the judge had to decide which principle to adopt and then a formal legal principle was invoked as justification. 'Judicial precedent and legal doctrine', said the Realists, could 'be found or developed to support almost any outcome. The real decision is made first ... and then it is "rationalised" in the written opinion' (Schur, 1968:43). From this it followed that legal formalism was unable to ensure the objectivity and autonomy of law, as it was said to do. Instead, law was inevitably 'animated by social purposes' (Gordon, 1984).

More recently, Critical Legal Theorists have extended the critique of formalism. Accepting the Realist point that policies and politics necessarily inform legal decision-making (which, for honesty's sake, should be brought out into the open), they have gone on to argue that those policies demonstrate a quite particular political bias—towards the status quo. According to Critical Theorists, law helps to shore up and entrench the existing, inequitable social order by re-presenting it as inevitable and natural, not contingent and variable. It thereby excludes and represses other competing visions of the social world which might challenge the dominant legal view of social life (Peller, 1985; Handler, J.F., 1988). The value of adherence to legal forms is that it continues to generate the appearance of a neutral and even-handed law which offers formal equality to all.

The present chapter is part of this project of challenging the claims of legal formalism and demonstrating the place of value in law. Its task is to rebut the proposition advanced by formalists that legal reasoning guarantees law's certainty and value-freedom. And it does this as a necessary prior step to the critique of legal values to be conducted in the next chapter.

A further purpose of the chapter is to cast doubt on the concept of objectivity itself as a legal ideal—also in the manner of the Critical Legal Scholars. Not only will it be suggested that the notion of law's essential neutrality is an effective strategy for concealing the role of values in law (MacKinnon's important point), but questions will also be raised about the possibility and the desirability of legal impartiality as presently conceived.

In the next chapter, the challenge to law's claims to impartiality and fairness will be conducted at a deeper level. There it will be argued that the problem with law is not just that it is not as good as it says it is, that all would be well if only lawyers and judges could clean up their act. Rather, the problem with law, why it does not dispense equal justice for all, is more deep-seated, indeed is elemental. The suggestion will be that it resides in law's very conceptions of the human being and the social order which are presented as universal but are in fact highly contested.

Legal education

At law schools in Australia, England and the United States, aspiring lawyers are encouraged to perceive and practise the law in a very particular way. Law is often delivered to students as a vast accumulation of cases and legislation which must be comprehended and applied by the budding practitioner. Law is presented as a technical exercise in sorting legal material rather than as a social practice which may reshape the lives of those who enter the lawyer's office or who are brought before the courts. To many law teachers, a critical appreciation of the social, economic or political implications of law seems to be considered inessential. Indeed a good law student may pass through the university encountering little more than thousands of cases with little thought for the human beings to whom they must be applied (Sexton and Maher, 1982:13; Frug, 1988).

The important effect of this style of training is that prospective lawyers may well come to view their task as one which is divorced from politics and personal convictions. Instead, the young lawyer is encouraged to get on with the task of learning and applying a pre-given body of law in an intelligent, rational and objective fashion.

The lawyer's position is one of dispassionate, impartial adviser. Lawyers portray themselves as objective because they are often not required to consider the social ramifications of the legal material with which they work. Their main duty is to consider what law 'is', rather than what law 'ought' to be, to invoke the distinction of the British jurist John Austin (Sugarman, 1986:35). Indeed any agonising about the human consequences of the law may be viewed as positively dysfunctional.

A recent edition of an introductory legal textbook aimed at the trainee lawyer serves to illustrate this traditional view of the lawyer's role. According to Derham, Maher and Waller (1986:43), Dr Johnson's assessment of the role of the profession is still essentially correct: 'A lawyer has no business with the justice or injustice of the cause which he undertakes.' And it is precisely this detachment which is thought to make the lawyer such a reliable advisor. It enables members of the profession to 'act free of the passions and emotions which may be controlling their clients' desires, beliefs and judgements. They can form their own judgement objectively in the light of their own understanding of the law'.

It is true that law schools are changing. Increasingly, legal curricula are reaching beyond the 'black letter' of the law and embracing such non-traditional topics as 'Women and the Law' and 'Aborigines and the Law'. Though this has done much to introduce a social and critical dimension to legal teaching, to show that law has a real-life setting, it may also be argued that such courses shore up the dominant approach. That is to say, the core idea of law as an autonomous discipline, as impervious to outside influences, is preserved. 'Women' or 'Aborigines' are simply added to the traditional curriculum, often as optional extras. They give some spice to the law degree. More importantly, such subjects show that 'The Law' does in fact operate within a social context and has important social ramifications. But they do not change 'The Law' in any important way. Thus, for example, feminist legal analysis is appropriately dealt with in 'the Gender Course' but it does not reshape the basic pedagogy of the traditional, bread-and-butter subjects such as Contract, Tort or Commercial Law.

The sense we have of the lawyer as an uncritical and therefore dispassionate and impartial interpreter of legal material owes much to the strong historical links between legal education and legal practice and the fact that, as a result of this association, in England law came late to the halls of Academe and so came to be regarded as the poor relation within the universities. The effect, as we shall see, was to define the purpose of legal training as the production of expert lawyers who were technically proficient at analysing a given body of law and providing legal advice. It was not primarily to foster in the student a critical and intellectual appreciation of the nature of law in society.

In England there is a longstanding tradition of the legal profession training its own recruits. Before the middle of the eighteenth century, legal training was conducted entirely by lawyers within the Inns of Court. Gradually and fitfully there was a shift of legal education to the universities, which then assumed the task of producing 'recruits to the law'. But even then, law was not accorded high priority as an intellectual discipline. 'Compared with the higher education facilities provided for the younger professions, however, and compared with the provision of facilities for other university disciplines, the professional efforts and the financial commitments were slight' (Derham, Maher and Waller, 1986:51–52).

The dominant style of legal teaching which was to evolve—a style which was self-consciously narrow, prescribed and expository—has been interpreted as a response both to the tenuous place of law within the universities and a desire not to alienate the practising profession which the new law departments were to service. What the new law teachers were trying to achieve through this style of pedagogy, according to David Sugarman (1986), was a distinctive role for themselves as legal educators both in relation to the Bar and the Academy. The territory they carved out for themselves, however, was but 'a narrow ledge', to use Sugarman's term.

Sensitive to the opinions of the profession, to the point of reverence (many dedicated their legal texts to members of the Bench), the law teachers sought not to trespass upon the territory of the Bar and the Bench whose task it was to deal with the content of law and 'the linkages between law and daily life' (Sugarman, 1986:34). At the same time, the law teachers sought to distinguish themselves as a new intellectual discipline within the university by offering a unique body of expertise. And to this end, they attempted to fashion themselves as a distinct legal science. They endeavoured to show that the law 'was ultimately governed by principles akin to the laws of natural sciences and was, thus, a subject worthy of a place in the university firmament' (Sugarman, 1986:30).

More specifically, the new legal educators asserted that their concern was only with the forms and principles of law, not its substance— which was better dealt with by the practising profession. Their interest was in developing a science of law which would help the budding practitioner acquire the necessary technical skills to discern law's inherently rational and logical nature. This in turn required 'that "facts" and "reality" [be] kept at a safe distance'. An appreciation of how the law functioned in action might otherwise destroy the central proposition of the law teachers upon which they founded their science: 'namely, that law was essentially a simple, unified, coherent whole' (Sugarman, 1986:34).

Out of this approach to legal education emerged a particular style of teaching which aimed 'not at breadth but at highly specialised excellence'. The task which the legal educators took upon themselves was the distillation and organisation of law into its most fundamental principles which could be learned and applied to specific legal problems. These principles were in turn set out in the new legal textbooks which were to provide the foundation of university knowledge on the law. In a sense, the new textbooks which laid out the formal science of law became the law as experienced by the law student and so the learning of law became the learning of its formal principles as perceived by the legal educators. The result, according to Sugarman (1986:51), is what we now experience as legal education: 'the teaching of law as a simple set of rules; that examinations test the ability to resolve legal problems by reference to certain "pat" answers; and that law texts and teaching are "vocational" (albeit in a peculiarly narrow and artificial sense) and examination–oriented'.

It is probably still true to say of many university law departments that what they are mainly concerned to inculcate is the profession of lawyering rather than how to think critically about the law. The desired result, at the end of legal training, is a competent lawyer who can analyse and apply legal doctrine in an intelligent and disinterested fashion. As one writer has observed about the American system of legal training, 'the young men [*sic*] who emerge from this process [of legal education] are usually tough-minded, skeptical, pragmatic and resourceful' (Cavers, 1972:300). For the profession wants skilled practitioners, not philosophers.

Australian legal education has largely been patterned on the English university model. The first law faculties drew their staff from the practising profession, whose members taught mainly part-time. There has persisted a close relationship between legal practitioners and the university which is generally sanctioned by the Academy. The idea that the business of the law school is the production of competent lawyers, not legal intellectuals who might challenge the system, continues to be advanced, without apology, in legal texts. Thus: 'If university legal education is to be recognised as having value for professional purposes, such education must be concerned with the lawyer's skills as well as with the lawyer's knowledge. It must do something to prepare the student to master the skills of the lawyer's art quickly and with understanding' (Derham, Maher and Waller, 1986:53).

In a similar fashion, the American law schools have maintained close ties with the profession. They recruit their teaching staff 'from the ranks of successful young lawyers' who then ensure that teaching programmes address the problems which arise in legal practice (Cavers, 1972:302). An important focus is the understanding and application of legal doctrine (Frug, 1988).

A number of academic lawyers have taken the Academy to task for its particular brand of education. The main cost of the narrow intellectual focus of many law schools is said to be a failure to appreciate the social, political and historical framework of law. What is missing also is the human factor. Thus in Australia, Thornton has objected to the 'narrow, doctrinal, atheoretical' style of legal teaching which is to be found around the country. The law, she complains, is taught as if it were a complete and autonomous entity. 'There is little understanding of the study of law as an interdisciplinary, contextual and critical exercise' (Thornton, 1986:22). Of American legal education, it has been suggested that 'any theoretical dimension' of law is often given short shrift (Frug, 1988:1). English analysts of legal teaching have been no less critical of their law schools. According to Bankowski and Mungham (1976:82), the English style of education can be characterised as 'ahistorical, pedestrian and encouraging only a narrow cognitive sense of law'.

In Australian law schools, the curriculum is, in the main, traditional. Following the English model, its principal concern is the standard categories of law, such as torts, contract and property, subjects which are seen to be of immediate use to the legal practicioner. Emphasis is placed upon the study of the workings of specific, discrete laws. Critical discussion of legal theory and social policy is considered, in many law schools, to be peripheral to the central task of the lawyer.

Wherever this traditional style of legal training is offered, social problems tend to be reduced to a series of disconnected disputes between anonymous and interchangeable individuals. Hypothetical cases are manufactured for students who are expected to isolate the 'facts' and then apply the relevant law. The student's task is to arrive at the legally 'correct' solution by reasoning in an intelligent and objective manner. Social conflict and social inequalities are therefore reduced to an impersonal sort of algebra. Injured and injuring parties become A and B; Cs and Ds enter the story to complicate the legal problem. Its resolution is in terms of the degree of fit between the situation of the parties and the given law. Legal technicalities, not the moral rights or wrongs of the case, determine the availability of a remedy. Whether the problem has a larger social cause or solution is simply not the point.

To invoke another metaphor, law is often delivered to the student as a jigsaw puzzle. For much of the time, the required task is skilfully to piece together small sections of the puzzle, without ever having to appreciate the entire composite legal picture and its implications for society. Thus is maintained the impression of a fair, dispassionate and objective treatment of all parties who come before the law. All As will be treated like other As, and Bs like Bs, generally without regard to the social implications of their class, colour, creed or sex, unless of course these factors are deemed to be legally relevant. Indeed, as we will see below, law's much-prized neutrality resides in its refusal to look beyond the immediate facts in its resolution of each new dispute (Thornton, 1986:16—17).

Sexton and Maher (1982) have raised similar objections to the pedagogical methods adopted in Australian law schools. They observe the tendency of many law teachers not to give due weight to the social and economic consequences of legal decisions. They are also concerned that students who undergo a traditional legal education seem not to be required to think deeply about the effect of their legal practice on the rest of the community. 'The net result, despite exceptional courses and exceptional teachers, is to foster the myth of law as an immutable set of principles and lawyers as platonic guardians of those principles for the rest of society' (Sexton and Maher, 1982:12).

Legal positivism

Legal positivism represents the official version of law, law's explanation of itself. It is the dominant model of the legal process in the Anglo-American and Australian legal world, 'the typical outlook of the legal profession [which] informs most legal scholarship and teaching' (Cotterrell, 1984:10).

Legal positivism is fundamental to the constitution of legal thought. It is a key reason why lawyers come to accept the official version of law as legal reality, why lawyers tend not to question the nature and purpose of law but take it as a given. It also helps to explain why the law comes to assume the status of objectivity and why judges become the seekers of truth.

Positivism is a philosophical position. According to Flew's *A Dictionary of Philosophy* (1979:283), its exponents use the term 'positive' in a very particular sense, to indicate 'that which is laid down, that which has to be accepted as we find it and is not further explicable'. Positivists are committed to the scientific method. They believe that 'all genuine human knowledge is contained within the boundaries of science ... [and that] whatever questions cannot be answered by scientific methods we must be content to leave permanently unanswered'.

To the positivist, what matters, scientifically, is what we are able to observe. It follows that moral issues, questions of judgment and belief, are rendered extraneous. The positivist is concerned with the determination of concrete matters of fact, not value, which are beyond the ken of science. Thus the positivist invokes a rigid separation of facts and beliefs and exalts the value-free nature of the scientific method. Science, it is thought, should refrain from making value-judgments about the matters it observes and it should not inquire into the values held by those placed under the microscope (Cotterrell, 1984:10).

Transposed to the legal context, a positivist outlook interprets law as a collection of rules which can be authenticated as valid law by the application of certain formulaic tests. These tests are intended to indicate whether any given rule has issued from a recognised law-maker. If it has, that rule becomes part of 'the data' of law 'which it is the lawyer's task to analyse and order' (Cotterrell, 1984:10). Put differently, law is that, and only that, which has been laid down or 'posited', as John Austin put it, by an appropriate source. Thus to Cross, a rule derived from precedent (to be explained below) was a proper rule 'because it was made by the judges, and not because it originated in common usage, or the judges' idea of justice and public convenience'. And to Kelsen, 'law is always positive law, and its positivity lies in the fact that it is created and annulled by acts of human beings, thus being independent of morality and other norm systems' (all quoted in Simpson (1986:11).

In the view of legal positivists, it is not the lawyer's job to look behind the laws for the values which might inform them. The justness or fairness of any particular law is simply not essential to its understanding and certainly beyond the interest of the lawyer. What matters is that it has gone through the necessary processes to function as official, usable legal material.

In his analysis of law and modern society, the British jurist P.S. Atiyah (1983:103) offers a useful summary of the key propositions which comprise the positivist approach to law:

> first, laws are commands of human beings addressed to other human beings; second, there is no necessary connexion between law and morals; thirdly, the analysis of law and legal concepts is a true 'scientific' inquiry which is concerned with the formal requirements of valid law, and not with its content; and fourth, judges, when deciding new points of law, must confine them-selves to 'legal' arguments and not to moral or policy issues.

Atiyah (1983:104) blames the positivist tradition in law for what he sees as the impoverishment of legal theory and English law. He believes that positivism has contributed to an unwillingness on the part of lawyers to address the moral and political components of law. Positivism may also be seen to legitimate the refusal of most judges to consider the extent to which their particular approach to the world informs their decisions. That is, it lends support to the formalist position that what is being dispensed is always a politically neutral type of justice.

According to the Australian legal critic Margot Stubbs (1986), legal positivism is a highly convenient approach to the law from the point of view of the legal profession. Its doctrine that law is 'an autonomous, self-contained system' renders the perceptions and the methods of lawyers as neutral, value-free and independent of politics. Lawyers are untainted by passions; they rise above commitments to any particular ideology in their disinterested pursuit of their client's interests.

The common-law tradition

Anglo-American and Australian legal thinking is still largely informed by the traditions of the English common law. Within this intellectual framework, the law is interpreted as a rational accumulation of judicial wisdom which has developed 'pragmatically case by case through judicial decisions rather than being elaborated from *a priori* general concepts or legislated in the form of codes or statutes'. Though the legislature is in fact a more important source of new law in the three countries in question, the legal community still tends to think of law in terms of the decisions which emanate from the courts (Cotterrell, 1984:18).

Fundamental to the common-law system is the doctrine of precedent. At its simplest, this means that like cases are treated alike; judicial decisions are made by reference to previous judicial decisions in analogous cases; the present is bound by the past. The idea is that judges look only to the wording of legislation or to the decisions of earlier cases when pronouncing on the law. 'This process is seen as largely deductive', observe Sachs and Wilson (1978:45), 'involving the extension by analogy of principles gathered from previous decisions to the circumstances of new cases.'

The significance of the doctrine for present purposes lies in its claim to lift the legal decision out of the realm of politics and personal opinion. 'It expressly excludes examination of the social or political importance of the issue at hand' (Sachs and Wilson, 1978:45). According to the doctrine, judges do not offer their own views when they hand down a decision. Instead they apply 'a distinctly legal mode of reasoning' which is said to ensure the predictability and essential correctness of their decision (Kairys, 1982:11). Members of the Bench have no authority to invoke their personal politics. They are subservient to the decisions of their judicial predecessors. Their task is to establish, intelligently and systematically, the connection between the case before them and former decisions. The outcome is, then, in a sense, predetermined and thus the values of the individual judge can play no part. Indeed judges may often be obliged to apply a principle which is directly at odds with their personal philosophy, such is the strength of the doctrine.

The doctrine of precedent may seem a relatively straightforward way of deciding cases. In fact, it comprises a complex set of rules indicating which courts bind which courts and which parts of judicial decisions have the force of law. Derham, Maher and Waller (1986) have usefully distilled these rules into five basic principles. The first is that courts are bound by the decisions of higher courts within the same hierarchy. The second is that legal arguments presented to the court may be based on the decision of any superior court. Third, the vintage of an authority or precedent does not diminish its effect. Fourth, the court may hear arguments based on precedents from any reliable source, though they must be, in the court's reckoning, the best available. Finally, courts are not bound by their own decisions and so may overrule themselves if convinced that the previous decision was wrong. The rules of precedent can be seen to give lawyers a good deal of scope to range through both long-past and recent cases to find precedents which support their arguments. Indeed, it is possible to refer to an authority from just about any source.

Further rules govern the determination of just what part of a case is binding. Not everything that the judge says in the course of a judgment is authoritative. Strictly speaking, it is only the actual reason for the decision or *ratio decidendi* which binds future courts. This definition, however, is not as restrictive as one might think. Indeed the accepted test has the potential to encompass much of the judgment. The critical question is whether 'the statement [is] a proposition of law relied upon by the judge as justifying, even as only one course of justification, the decision of an issue presented to him for decision in the course of disposing of the case he was hearing'. In fact it has been suggested that even a point made by the court 'in the course of a line of reasoning' which led to the final decision might be treated as part of the *ratio decidendi*. Moreover, it seems that the general principle implicit in a judicial decision, as well as the nature of the resolution of the specific issue at hand, may be regarded as authoritative (Derham, Maher and Waller, 1986:109, 112). In short, the *ratio* may be interpreted in any one of a number of ways, depending on what legal counsel and the court deem to be appropriate to the case at hand.

The willingness of a court to follow a decision of a superior court may depend largely on the court's evaluation of that previous decision: whether it is thought to embody a sound principle or is considered out of step with current legal thinking. If the case is generally approved, then the decision is likely to be interpreted widely. Effect will be given to what was considered to be the full intention of the Bench. If the case is regarded as unsound, there is a greater chance that the *ratio decidendi* will be interpreted narrowly. The court will endeavour to confine the binding effect of the precedent by arguing that it applies only to identical fact situations.

The doctrine of precedent is clearly a flexible legal tool. And yet it is generally considered by legal professionals to strengthen law's claim to consistency, predictability and impartiality. It is conceived to be an integral part of the body of 'binding, fixed and determinate rules, that pre-exist the dispute and serve to determine the relationship between the parties to it before the matter even comes before the court' (Stubbs, 1986:78). The notion that courts are bound to follow the dictates of their superiors is said to separate legal reasoning from personal, moral or political issues. Judges may not act according to their own caprices. As one American writer observes, 'compulsion to follow precedent is essentially a means of limiting power. It means that a court cannot decide the new case before it according to the impulse it may have at the moment, but must act according to prior decisions' (Dawson, 1972:26).

The doctrine of precedent has been the focus of critical discussion for much of the century, as we saw at the beginning of this chapter. In the 1930s and 1940s, the American Legal Realists were challenging the idea that precedent imparts certainty (Schur, 1968). In the 1960s, the Australian jurist Julius Stone subjected the doctrine to close scrutiny. He remarked on the fact that 'leeways for choice constantly arise'; that while judges might appear to be obliged to follow a 'compelling logic', they were in truth 'free to choose between different results' (Stone, 1964:333). And of course the Critical Legal Theorists are still engaged in their challenge to the idea of legal objectivity (Peller, 1985).

The notion that judges do make policy, that they do not just interpret a received body of law in a formulaic manner, is now even being advanced by the judiciary. Thus in a recent lecture, the Australian Chief Justice, Sir Anthony Mason (1987), referred to the demise of formalism, while the President of the New Zealand Court of Appeal, Sir Robin Cooke (1987), has also commented of late on 'the pretence of legal formalism', acknowledging that rules do not in fact constrain the outcome of a case, that policy intervenes. And yet with all these developments in legal thinking, the official version of precedent— that it imparts a basic neutrality to judicial decisions—may be seen to endure. 'Despite the purported acceptance of the realist claim that law is political', observes Peller (1985:1153), 'something called legal reasoning continues to be used at judicial proceedings and taught in law schools. Legal thinking is still perceived as a distinct way of thinking about (and being within) the social world. Boundaries [still] segregate legal discourse from political rhetoric.' Thus each new generation of law students is instructed at length in its principles.

In the traditional view of the doctrine, the one to be found in many legal textbooks and delivered at many a law school lectern (notwithstanding the growing influence of Critical Legal Studies on legal pedagogy), what judges think personally about any matter placed before them, how they view the problem from their social place in the world, is said to be largely irrelevant. The job at hand is to determine how an issue should be decided by reference to a formal set of principles which guide the judicial decision. 'On the whole, the rules ... are clear and certain. They simply have to be learned as items of positive knowledge which must be acquired by anyone who proposes to work with the common law' (Derham, Maher and Waller, 1986:125). The result, we are told, is consistency, predictability and certainty.

The myth of judicial neutrality

In view of the resilience of the formal doctrine of precedent to criticism from both without and within, it may come as a surprise to learn that few legal analysts seem to accept it at face value. According to Atiyah (1983:135), 'every lawyer knows that fine distinctions are sometimes seized upon to justify departing from a prior decision without an apparent breach in the rules of binding precedent'. This was a fact not lost on the early interpreters of the doctrine. 'Coke, Hale, and Blackstone', McBarnet (1983:163) tells us, 'were all firm exponents of the view that decisions and precedents were not law but merely "evidence of what the law is".' In the 1930s, Holdsworth said on the question of judicial manoeuvrability within the doctrine: 'The manner in which they [the courts] have decided this question has left them many means of escape from the necessity of literal obedience to the general rule that decided cases must always be followed' (quoted in McBarnet, 1983:163—64). More recently, the eminent English legal philosopher H.L.A. Hart (1958:607) referred to 'a penumbra of debatable cases' which inevitably introduces some uncertainty into the law. Such cases, however, he believed to be rare.

Those who are sympathetic to the aims of the doctrine maintain that judicial decision-making is inevitably a combination of common-sense and community opinion. Judicial wisdom, they say, combines a sense of current social values and healthy pragmatism. Although there is a good deal of room for choice within the doctrine, judges usually get their decisions right because they are wise old men with enormous experience. In the words of a current legal text:

> Since judges usually have had 20 or 30 years' experience of legal language and thinking, they have been entrusted with the task of drawing the correct inferences from deduction, induction, analogy and so on ... That means we accept their opinions as good authority ... In all such cases there is the element of risk and the possibility of error—but that is life as we know it ... On the whole the judges do [their job] extraordinarily well. (Derham, Maher and Waller, 1986:190−91)

Others take a less sanguine view (Griffiths, 1977; Kairys, 1982). They dispute the idea of a system of judicial checks and balances implicit in the doctrine. Precedent, they claim, ensures neither impartiality nor predictability. The legal community might think that judges follow what is largely a predetermined course of action, with a healthy dose of common sense thrown in. But in fact the evolution of the common law, through the doctrine of precedent, reflects the values and priorities of the judicial decision-makers. More worryingly, it is said that the doctrine has been used, self-servingly, to obscure this fact and to secure the appearance that judges are always coolly dispassionate.

One critic of the idea of judicial certainty, the English legal writer Maureen Cain (1976), explains the persistence of the notion that judges are able to, and generally do, produce a 'correct' and predictable rendering of law in terms of the social density of the Bench and the Bar and the consequent unity of thought it induces in its members. The legal community, at this level, Cain tells us, is small and socially homogeneous (a point which will be taken up in a later chapter). Only like-minded types are admitted, and dissenting, critical voices are discouraged. The result is a common intellectual outlook, a 'unity of legal thought' in which barristers and judges are actually likely to make similar decisions using similar reasoning: to have an 'identity of legal comprehension'. This in turn gives rise to the necessary 'predictability' and 'impartiality' of the Bench required by the Rule of Law.

To Cain, law is predictable, however, not because of its inherent correctness, not because it is the essential distillation of truth or because it gives an accurate account of reality, but because a common intellectual outlook leads to similar and therefore predictable decisions (rather than a multitude of interpretations informed by different viewpoints). And it is impartial not because it invokes some sort of Olympian or universal intellectual stance but because it is not obliged to accommodate the thinking of those outside the legal community (it is the creation of a single outlook). In other words, the existence of an insulated and homogeneous body of rule-users helps to impose certainty on an uncertain law. It generates a common response to legal problems which in turn creates the impression that there is something inherently right about the judicial process—that this, in-evitably, is the way things are done.

Gary Peller (1985:1155) puts the same point another way. He talks about the 'codes of "common sense" ' shared by members of the legal world which 'freeze the argumentative play of analogy by providing categories that form boundaries' for legal reasoning. In other words, the legal community shares a way of thinking, a way of organising thoughts and ideas, which in fact is a particular cultural product; it is one way of organising and arranging thoughts. It is experienced and represented as objective, formal legal reasoning, however, because other ways of operating are not allowed to intrude. Indeed, 'the contingency and exclusivity of the conventions would be apparent to anyone from a different social group' (Peller, 1985:1157). But these voices are not heard and so how the judges and the lawyers reason is conceived of as the objective and the correct way, not one of many intellectual practices.

Perfect uniformity of outlook, however, is not always achievable, even among the members of the Bench. Cracks do appear in the legal firmament in the form of disagreements between judges. And it is these moments of judicial discord that other critics of precedent have employed to challenge its claims to certainty and to show how social values inform judicial decision-making. Simply, what these critics have done is to compare cases with similar facts in which judges have arrived at opposing decisions. They have then examined the values and interests implicit in such decisions and the reasons why judges might move from one position to another. Sachs and Wilson (1978), for example, use these methods in their analysis of the 'persons' case to demonstrate what they call the 'myth of judicial neutrality'. Indeed, much of their volume *Sexism and the Law* is essentially an indictment of the English common-law tradition and its claims to fairness and impartiality.

According to Sachs and Wilson, the English judiciary blatantly exploited the doctrine of precedent to justify the exclusion of women from the legal category of 'person', with its attendant public rights, such as the right to vote. For over half a century the English Bench maintained this view. Case law, they held, was clear about the principle that, in law, the word 'person' was meant to denote the male sex. Against the claims of the suffragettes, judicial officers repeatedly stated that they had no right to pronounce on the justice of the situation. They were bound by the decisions of their predecessors which established the law in this area. Their personal feelings had nothing to do with the matter. Then, in 1929, the Judicial Council of the Privy Council changed its collective mind. It decided, against the weight of past authority, that women were, after all, 'persons' in the eyes of the law.

What had changed in the 60 years over which the 'persons' cases were fought was not the legal meaning of the word 'person' nor the chain of cases by which it was interpreted. Opinion, Sachs and Wilson maintain, not judicial authority, decided the issue. By the late 1920s, the highest court in the land was committed to a different view of women and their place in public life: 'Lord Sankey and a majority, if not all of his colleagues, thought it absurd that women should be debarred from public office solely on grounds of sex, and even more absurd that the word "person" should be the instrument for achieving this result' (Sachs and Wilson, 1978:42). Notwithstanding this complete turnaround, the Privy Council was still able to refer back to previous cases to justify their decision. As Sachs and Wilson (1978:42) remark, 'it was not difficult for them to write a judgement that paid conventional respect to all the earlier decisions while totally ignoring their effect'.

In her commentary on the Persons Case of 1929, Mary Jane Mossman (1986) explains just how the doctrine of precedent was used to give judicial weight to what was essentially a view of women's proper place. The method adopted by Lord Sankey to justify the court's decision was simply to distinguish the facts at hand. Earlier cases on the subject, he declared, were not precisely the same as those before him. By interpreting these cases narrowly, he was able to show his regard for the views of his predecessors while in fact departing fully from their clear intention, imposing his own judgment of the matter. To Mossman (1986:42), Lord Sankey's decision indicates clearly 'the availability of choice in the selection of facts, in the categorisation of principles and in the determination of relevance'.

Similar observations have been made about the United States' Supreme Court and its imaginative use of the doctrine of precedent. By tracing the chain of logic employed in a more recent set of decisions on the right of free speech in private places, David Kairys

(1982) has shown the subtle interplay between fact and value which comprises judicial thinking. Kairys begins with an account of a 1968 decision (Case A), in which the court upheld the right of union members, engaged in a labour dispute, to picket a store located in a privately owned shopping centre. The court conceded that this was the best way to air their grievance to other local citizens and cited in support of their verdict a 1946 case which upheld similar constitutional freedoms in a 'company town'.

Four years later, however, the Supreme Court (in Case B) declared that an anti-war campaigner could not distribute leaflets in a shopping centre even though political candidates used it as a political forum, because of the large number of people it attracted. The finding in Case A was distinguished on the grounds that a labour dispute was more closely related to the functions of a shopping centre. Then in 1976, the court decided (in Case C) that it would be unconstitutional to treat a labour speech differently from an anti-war speech and so declared that this could not possibly have been intended by the Bench in Case B. The obvious intent of that court must have been to overrule Case A which found in favour of the labour picket. The 1976 Bench then proceeded to use the reinterpreted anti-war case (B) to support its own judgment against the right to picket in a shopping centre.

Despite the convoluted logic required to achieve its verdict, the court in Case C announced that it had no choice in the matter, it was bound to follow precedent. 'Our institutional duty is to follow until changed the law as it now is, not as some members of the Court might wish it to be.' As Kairys (1982:13) points out, 'Unstated and lost in the mire of contradictory precedents and justifications was the central point that none of these cases was or could be decided without ultimate reference to values and choices of a political nature'. Each of the shopping-centre cases depended on the values of the presiding judges: whether they gave priority to freedom of speech or to the right to quiet enjoyment of private property. The doctrine of precedent was then invoked to lend legitimacy to the judicial process.

In Australia, Sexton and Maher (1982) have also challenged the idea of law as a systematic accretion of principles. The focus of their criticism is the large amount of dissension among the judges who sit on the High Court of Australia—a finding which suggests that the unity of legal outlook described by Cain is perhaps beginning to break down, at least in the Australian context. They examine the recent constitutional decisions of this court and discover that few have been unanimous. Indeed many have involved 'a three-to-two or a four-to-three split'. They conclude that there is nothing inexorable or predictable about the process of judicial decision-making. For even at the highest level, the one Bench is unable to agree about the meaning of the law.

The message of this chapter is that law presents itself as one thing when in fact it is another. Law is still often taught, justified and interpreted as if it were a form of science, and therefore a systematic and rigorous exercise. Students are presented with a mass of cases and legislation which they are told are the raw data of law. Positivism reinforces the conventional view of lawyers and judges as technicians whose task it is to organise and analyse the law in a skilful and dispassionate manner. The common-law notion of precedent further entrenches the view that law is a neutral and technical process, whose aim is logic and consistency. Just a brief analysis of the development of case law reveals the spuriousness of law's claim to neutrality. Inevitably there is a vital connection between law and social values which is obscured by the official version of law. Lawyers and judges may well practise their craft in good faith, convinced of their essential objectivity. But, as we shall see shortly, in fact the wheels of law are oiled by deeply held assumptions about the nature of people and about the purpose of society.

The problem of legal objectivity

What emerges from this analysis of law's own assessment of itself as value-neutral is the discovery that the legal ideal of objectivity functions as a smokescreen to conceal the actual social content of law and the place of value in legal processes. Law students do not have to worry about the purposes of law if theirs is purely a technical exercise, devoid of political or social content. And judges can apply the rules laid down by their predecessors, which are perceived as fixed and binding, without being seen to invoke any particular set of values. Law's claim to the status of objective truth means that those who operate within it assume the mantle of truth. Their decisions are therefore seen to be correct in some absolute sense. As a consequence, they do not have the fallibility of a point of view.

Feminists have become increasingly concerned about the use of the notion of objectivity as just such a political tool—as a way of presenting an opinion as truth. Catharine MacKinnon (1982:537), for one, has argued that law's objectivity—what it regards as its point-of-viewlessness—is in fact the male viewpoint (a proposition which will be examined and modified in the next chapter). MacKinnon believes that law's 'purported generality, disinterestedness, and universality', what she calls law's 'aperspectivity', is in fact 'a strategy

of male hegemony'. It is the way that men represent their particular
view of the world as the correct and only one.

Indeed feminists (MacKinnon included) have gone further than
this and have questioned the very endeavour to discover a universal,
objective perspective. That is to say, they have begun to take issue
with the very idea of objectivity: the claim to neutrality, disinterest
and impartiality—to the detached perspective. Sandra Harding
(1986:26), for one, suggests there is no such thing as the correct,
objective, universal, stance which derives its Olympian status from
its detachment or disengagement from the realm of human experience
and values. Rather, there are many inevitably partial understandings
of the world all of which owe their existence to the particular,
concrete experiences of the apprehender. The extent to which there
appears to be a single, objective place from which to arrive at truth
dispassionately (law's apparent claim for itself) therefore is only the
extent to which one particular view point is able to dominate interpretations of reality.

In the light of what we have learned about the nature of legal
reasoning by analogy, Harding's insights seem particularly pertinent
to law. As we have seen, a major way in which law seeks to establish
its sense of certainty and essential correctness is through the notion
that it invokes pre-existing legal principles in an essentially neutral
fashion. Like cases are treated alike and the job of the 'fact-finder' is
simply to find the correct analogy. And yet this process is a complex
one and is further complicated by the fact that one party to the
dispute is trying to establish the appropriateness of one set of analogies
while the other side is trying to establish another.

In this adversarial form of justice (see Chapter 4 for a fuller
account) the goal is not to inquire into the facts of any matter with
access to as much evidence as is available at the time. It is not a
search for the total 'truth', in this sense. Instead it is a carefully
controlled and contrived contest between two parties who each
present a version of events which is most favourable to their own
position. The parties themselves (and hence their lawyers) are 'atti-
tudinally and ethically committed to winning the contest', not to
finding the most honest or the most humane solution. That is, 'the
parties are generally committed to prevailing rather than to discovering
truth' (Goodpaster, 1987:120, 122). Moreover, the rules of evidence
and procedure ensure that each case is presented in a highly stylised
manner and that only parts of each story are deemed to be legally
admissible. Thus the road to legal truth runs through a highly
artificial form of conflict.

Impartial justice is thought to reside in a judicial decision arrived at
after exposure to two opposing versions of an event, which have

been filtered through this legal process. The task of the judge is to consider which is the truer one. (This is not to say that the adversary system endorses dissent or challenge to the legal process. Though the prosecution and defence present different and opposing accounts of a contested story, they are both committed to, and bound by, the legal forms of reasoning. They may be divided by the differences between their allocated roles—as formal adversaries—but they are united in their commitment to the legal way of doing things.) From this it follows that the filtered 'reality' which eventually comes to serve as law's truth, the one that is considered to have been always the correct, the objective, account of events, is the one which is able to impress its truth on the fact-finder. It is the judge's reading of the matter.

The formal processes of justice thus provide a vivid illustration of Harding's point that 'objectivity' is an inherently problematic concept. Though the traditional conception of legal decision-making is that there is a legal truth 'out there' waiting to be discovered by a judge skilled in legal reasoning, the reality is that each case before the court is susceptible of many readings. The task of the lawyer on one side of the courtroom is to render 'reality' in a way which favours the client and to prove this reality by reference to other similar cases. The task of the lawyer on the other side is to find a version of the facts which is most sympathetic to the client and to support this version with suitable precedents. As one legal critic observes, 'An unmentioned premise of our adversary system is that the truth takes sides. Because we do not know which side the truth has taken, we let the sides fight on. The eventual winner is allowed to lay claim to the truth' (A.B. Handler, 1988:4). Ultimately, law's truth is that reading of the case which the fact-finder comes to believe in.

What the judge decides is the truth of the matter is not only a function of the persuasive skills of the advocate but is also a product of the judge's own experience of 'reality'. As Harding explains, we each have a particular understanding of the world informed by our particular experiences of life. Thomas Kuhn (1970) called this a 'paradigm'. It is comprised of our set of assumptions and perspectives on the world which are in turn affected by a host of factors such as our sex, our class, our race and our age. Kuhn maintained that even that last bastion of truth and objectivity, science, is tainted by the paradigm of those who engage in scientific research. It is inevitable, says Kuhn, that the particular perspective of the individual engaged in the processes of discovering scientific 'truth' is necessarily brought to bear on the problem at hand.

So too, and more obviously so, with the judiciary. Inevitably the social make-up of those who people the Bench shapes the reasoning applied in legal decisions. It colours their reading of the problem before them and helps them to decide which version of events amounts to the truth of the matter. The impact of the social composition of the Bar and the Bench on legal perceptions of reality will be considered separately and in some detail later in the book. For present purposes it is sufficient to note that serious objections have been raised to the idea of the perfectly unbiased and value-free perspective, which is so central to traditional legal thinking, and which forms the basis of law's claim to impartiality.

What is worrying about the legal claim to objectivity, however, is not just that it is self-deluding—that there is probably no value-free place from which to view the world— but that it tends to subvert any critical assessment of the values which inform legal decision-making. As Cain (1976) has argued, the closed social nature of the Bar and the Bench even stifles dissent from within (a critical point we will explore later), further strengthening the impression that there is a seamless legal web of knowledge and understanding. Consistency and certainty are attainable only if different points of view (which challenge the sense in the legal forms of reasoning) are not given voice. 'Interpretation must be intellectually bounded to be mutually comprehensible' (Cain, 1976:247). Law's objectivity is therefore, as MacKinnon has noted, a powerful political tool which has served to disguise what feminists have shown to be the often sexist assumptions implicit in the workings of the law. Law's claim to objectivity elevates it to the status of truth. From this exalted position, its fairness and even-handedness is not open to question.

3

The community of strangers

Perhaps the most fundamental claim of Anglo-American law is to to treat people equally. To this end, the agents of the law endeavour to be impartial in their dealings with all who come before them. They seek to dispense justice in a consistent, neutral, objective, dispassionate and systematic manner. The blindfold over the eyes of the legal maiden who holds the scales of justice is meant to signify her freedom from improper influences such as discrimination or favouritism (Gibson, 1987:434). The legal maiden professes to prefer no one type of person who comes before her in her application of the law; nor is she prejudiced against another. She guarantees equal and consistent treatment of all before the law. Her way is to be fair; to be detached and disinterested; in short, to be impartial.

Each of these ideas is to be found in the traditional liberal concept of the Rule of Law, as elucidated by the English jurist A.V. Dicey (1959). We encountered the idea of the Rule of Law in the last chapter within the discussion of legal formalism. There the focus was primarily on that part of the concept which emphasises the need for certainty and predictability in law. Under the Rule of Law, said Dicey, 'persons in authority' are constrained from exercising 'wide, arbitrary, or discretionary powers'. We discovered, however, that the elaborate legal rules which are intended to ensure predictability, certainty, accuracy and therefore fairness in legal decisions are really quite malleable. Opinion and value do shape the law's response to those who come before it, a fact which is most apparent when it generates inconsistencies of approach.

Another ingredient of the Rule of Law, according to Dicey, and that which mainly concerns us here, is the proposition 'not only that with us no man is above the law ... but that here every man, whatever his rank or condition, is subject to the ordinary law of the realm'. In other words, an important characteristic of law in the English tradition is said to be its commitment to an ideal of equality of all before the law (Dicey, 1959:184–203). As we also saw in the last chapter, individual judges and individual Benches have been shown by feminists to impose sexist views, while invoking traditional legal principles to demonstrate their essential objectivity. This discovery, in itself, brings into question the idea that we are all treated by the law in a like and equal manner. The present purpose, however, is to extend and deepen this challenge.

The intention of this chapter is not simply to see whether the law adheres to its own rhetoric of consistency, predictability and detachment; it is not just to ascertain whether the law does indeed offer equality to all who come before it, in the limited sense that the individual or shared values and prejudices of those who dispense the law do not lead to obvious differences in its application, so that some social groups are preferred to others. Feminists such as Sachs and Wilson have already done this job perfectly satisfactorily. The present aim is to go further than this and examine critically law's most fundamental assumptions about how we relate and function as social beings.

It is inevitable that values should inform the law and legal decision-making, as the previous chapter made plain. There is no single place from which to view the world in a detached fashion, as the law professes to do. This is why it is important to resist the claims of the legal formalists (that law speaks with a neutral, value-free and dispassionate voice) and examine the social vision implicit in the very form of law to see whether it provides a sound basis for the equal and fair treatment of all. This requires us to consider just what sort of person and society are presupposed when the law dispenses its supposedly neutral services. In this way we can determine whether the law is inclined towards certain social groups to the detriment of others.

With the granting of most formal legal rights to women and the removal of references to gender from most laws, a process well documented by the first-phase feminists, there has been a tendency in some feminist legal writing to move away from questions of bias within the law itself—though MacKinnon and her followers continue to indict the law as a whole, as well as its various branches, as a fundamentally masculine institution. In some of the new writing, the focus is now principally on questions of substantive inequality for women, that is, with inequality of legal result, rather than with gender inequality within the actual structures and organisation of law. The cogent point being made is that in a gendered world, where the sexes are not equal, the application to women of seemingly gender-neutral laws, laws which purport to treat the sexes as formally equal by invoking a common standard, does not have gender-neutral results (O'Donovan, 1988).

As MacKinnon has noted, the problem for women of getting fair results out of supposedly neutral laws is further compounded by the fact that women repeatedly find themselves judged by a male standard of behaviour when they try to invoke their formal 'equal' rights. That is, women find their actions assessed (for example, when they are trying to get a job) according to male rather than female life-patterns. Equal treatment therefore becomes treatment like a man, and if a woman's situation does not allow her to reach parity with her male counterpart (say, in her work skills or working experience) then it is bad luck for her. She is not a like case and therefore should not be treated like him.

Law's basic method of reasoning by analogy, of treating like cases alike, can therefore work to the positive detriment of women who are likely to differ from the male standard of comparison because of structural social disadvantages (such as responsibility for children) and possibly because of different priorities (they may prefer at some stage of their lives to engage in the full-time care of children and therefore break their career path). Not surprisingly, then, what purports to be equal treatment of the sexes in the actual operation of the law does not amount to equality of result.

It is vital that feminists expose the deficiencies of the legal ideal of equal treatment in an unequal society and endeavour to arrive at practical solutions to this problem for women. It is also vital that they challenge legal reasoning by analogy with its accompanying sexist tendency to use male experiences as the standard of measurement: so that a woman is able to get equal treatment only when she is deemed to be in a similar situation to a man. (Indeed both of these important points will be put to use in this chapter.) But this is not our most immediate concern. Rather the principal interest of this chapter remains with the question of formal rather than substantive inequality. Though it also addresses the problem of bias in the methods of law and in its net effects, the main concern of this chapter is the problem of continuing bias built into the law itself, at its most fundamental level. The argument to be advanced is that there is still a critical problem of bias running through the heart of law, which is to be located in its partial and one-dimensional view of people and the social world they inhabit.

This problem of legal bias, to be recounted below, is far more intractable than anything identified by the first phase of feminists, for it is not confined to the substance of any particular laws. Rather it is intrinsic to the general orientation and form of law as a whole as well as its overall conception of its task. It is as pervasive and problematic as the perceived masculinity of law identified in MacKinnon's writing, though, as we will see, the present analysis of law departs in critical ways from MacKinnon's thesis. The import of this bias is that we have yet to achieve formal equality of all before the law, let alone equality in the administration or methods of law or equality in its real effects.

Outlining the argument

The question posed in this chapter is whether the legal view of humanity and of the social order set appropriate conditions for the law to operate, as it professes to do, without fear or favour. The reply is firmly in the negative. The general argument to be developed is that problems of sex and class bias within the central organising concept of law—its view of the individual—undermine the legal intention to offer an impartial form of justice in the sense that it does not discriminate and does not confer privilege.

The challenge to legal impartiality presented in this chapter occurs at two levels. The first entails a rebuttal of law's claim that its legal subject is a universal, abstract person and that, accordingly, law is not disposed towards any one class of individual or any one set of interests. The second part of the argument extends the challenge to legal impartiality by maintaining that law's very construction of this precept is flawed. The proposition is that in an unequal and complex society, where people are not only differently advantaged but have different concerns and priorities, it is neither fair nor impartial, indeed makes no sense to treat them uniformly as abstract individuals, as if their place in the world did not matter.

The first challenge engages directly with law's claim to be impartial in the sense that it prefers no one type of person. As we will see, law derives its sense of its own impartiality from the fact that it is thought to organise around and to serve an abstract, universal person, not a social type or category. Indeed the existence of an abstract, prototypical individual is vital to law's claims not to discriminate: it is the very justification of that strand of the Rule of Law which defines justice as a common approach to all, or, in the words of Dicey, 'the universal subjection of all classes, to one law' (Dicey, 1959:1), and which therefore assumes that human differences (such as race, creed, sex and wealth) are largely irrelevant for legal purposes. If our legal system has been devised with a human being in mind, then that person is supposed to be a universal being, a human norm, someone who could be anyone functioning anywhere. The legal subject, according to the official view, is a standard individual, abstracted from any particular set of social circumstances: a paradigm person whose needs and priorities law must anticipate and respond to if it is to ensure a well-run society. From this it is thought to follow that law is for everyone, not just for a privileged elite.

The first proposition to be advanced here is that, contrary to the traditional view, legal principles, legal priorities and legal methods in fact all presuppose a quite specific individual whom the law is intended to serve. Law's supposedly abstract person—its human prototype—is not in fact a universal being. Instead, the legal person is endowed with a specific set of characteristics which are presented as universal. As this chapter will try to show, law's preferred person is one who fits in remarkably well with the needs and priorities of modern, industrial, competitive market societies and who therefore flourishes within this context. In other words, he is deemed to be able-bodied, autonomous, rational, educated, monied, competitive and essentially self-interested. (The male pronoun is deliberate as it will be argued that the legal person is conceived of as a man.)

The important consequence of this legal construction of the individual, as we will see later, is that law does not in fact treat all classes of people equally, that it is not impartial. Instead, it performs best for those persons who approximate its model of humanity while providing a less satisfactory form of justice for those who depart in important ways from the model or who are excluded from it altogether. In short, this first set of arguments addresses the problem of the human (and social) model in law.

The second challenge to legal impartiality addresses the very precept of impartiality itself, in particular, its 'individuating, abstract form' (Sugarman and Rubin, 1984:49). Law's professed undertaking is not to deal with social categories but with abstract individuals, human prototypes (people who could be anyone). To reiterate, law derives its sense of its own fairness and justice from its commitment to this view that it does not discriminate between, and is not interested in, different types of people. Instead, it professes to act 'without affection or illwill' to all individuals, whatever their place in the social order, and the way it does this is to abstract people from their particular contexts and examine the merits of their individual cases. It then demands that like cases should be treated alike and should generally only be differentiated on their factual circumstances (Rhode, 1986:152). So if A behaves in a certain manner and so does B, then A and B should largely be treated the same, whatever their place in the world at large (without fear or favour).

Implicit in this process of abstraction is the legal fiction that all As and Bs are equally situated because they are all deemed to possess the characteristics of the abstract individual—that is, they are presumed to be able-bodied, monied, rational, self-interested and autonomous. In civil law, we see this imputation of character in the necessary legal fiction that when we enter into a contract, we are usually assumed to be free, rational and equal and so our bargains can generally be presumed to be fair. In criminal law, we see it in the legal fiction that we are all free, independent, rational and self-determining and therefore should be held personally accountable for our actions. It is therefore fair that if A and B behave the same, they should get similar treatment.

The abstract, individuating form of law, with which this chapter takes issue, is just this. It is law's commitment to a form of justice by analogy, in which people who come before the law, the As and the Bs, are abstracted from their different social locations (the locations which make them different) and then deemed to be similarly situated. To make them equal before the law, they have the character of the abstract individual imposed upon them and so they are generally assumed, for legal purposes, to be free, capable and competitive. Their decontextualised, individual behaviour is then scrutinised to see whether it is sufficiently similar to warrant a similar form of legal response. This process of justice by abstraction is the linchpin of law's guiding precept of, and claim to, impartiality.

The case to be made here is that it is neither meaningful nor fair, that it is not impartial in the way law conceives that word, to adopt a common approach to all by treating people as interchangeable, individual atoms abstracted from their social context. Nor is it fair or appropriate to assume that the mass of humanity is endowed with the qualities of the abstract individual when in fact, mostly, people are not. The argument to be advanced is that it is a nonsense to abstract people from their social contexts, because we are all so much a part of them. In a world in which people do not come before the law as identical and equally placed individuals, it is inappropriate to treat them as if they were. Law's very construction of impartiality as uniform treatment of interchangeable, abstract individuals is therefore flawed. In short, this second set of arguments about legal impartiality addresses the legal practice of abstraction.

In sum, this chapter raises two questions which go to the core of law's sense of its own impartiality. First, it asks whether law's abstract individual is really an abstract and universal person and concludes that 'he' is not. Second, it asks whether it is either meaningful or appropriate for law to depend so heavily for its sense of impartial justice on the concept of abstraction and concludes that it is neither. People are inextricably a part of their social worlds and therefore any legal idea of a standard, abstract person, designed to impose a spurious equality between people, is necessarily a legal fiction and a human impossibility. And yet it does serve a function in that it irons out inconvenient social differences between people, deeming them to be generally irrelevant for legal purposes.

Law and the sexes

This complex interpretation of legal bias represents a departure from the sort of male interest-group or male conspiracy theory of law implicit in both first- and second-phase feminisms. For its intellectual starting point is the notion that, as a rule, those who work with the law generally seek to be fair, to dispense blind justice (though, as we have seen, they are able to impose their particular values when it is thought to suit). At this level, the nub of the argument is that law's principal failing is not so much the inappropriate intrusion into legal decisions of the values shared by those particular persons who dispense justice, that is, the men of the Bench. Rather, the problem is of a more impersonal, more indirect but nevertheless deep-seated kind in that it resides in the fundamental priorities and orientation of law and the legal system.

This is not to say that those who administer and interpret the law do not positively benefit from the prevailing legal construction of the person, in a manner not unlike that described by the early feminists. As it will be argued in the next chapter, there is a nice congruence between the men of law—the judges and the lawyers and the preferred clients of the profession—and the paradigm legal person. Such a close association brings with it certain benefits. Those who approximate the legal model are placed in a most desirable position before the law: as full legal subjects possessed of all the necessary attributes to function effectively within the law.

The *Gesellschaft* conception of law and justice

Law in the Anglo-American tradition finds its roots in liberal political theory, as we observed in the last chapter. There we considered how the liberal commitment to a dichotomous style of thought has served to strengthen the claims of law to be certain, how it has given credence to the view that law could and should be abstract, rational and objective. Now, the concern is with the set of values (rather than intellectual methods) which inspired the classical liberal thinkers such as Thomas Hobbes and John Locke to promulgate their view of the world—values which were to provide the philosophical foundation of what has been called 'liberal legalist jurisprudence' (Klare, 1978:276).

The political scientist C.B. McPherson (1962:1) has summarised the values of liberal philosophy in the term 'possessive individualism', by which he means the belief that political rights and obligations can be deduced 'from the interest and will of dissociated individuals'. The 'possessive' quality of liberal individualism, we are told, resides in its view of the human being 'as essentially the proprietor of his own person or capacities, owing nothing to society for them'. In this view, the individual is free from dependence on others; he is 'neither ... a moral whole, nor ... part of a larger social whole'.

The liberal individualist account of people and their relation to society has played a critical role in shaping Anglo-American law. To Roger Cotterrell (1984:125), 'the individualism of Western law and society' may be described as 'its hallmark'. It is 'a vital current of ideology which has been developed in and through Western legal doctrine'. Indeed, as this chapter will endeavour to show, the liberal concept of the individual permeates legal theory, legal doctrine and legal practice.

Much of the considerable success enjoyed by liberal philosophy, exemplified by its influence on legal thought, lies in its ability to interpret and justify the set of social and economic processes which gave rise to modern market society. The celebrated jurist Henry Maine (1959:168), has described this social transformation as the shift from 'status' to 'contract'. It is a movement 'distinguished by the gradual dissolution of family dependency and the growth of individual obligation in its place. The individual is steadily substituted for the Family, as the unit of which civil laws take account.' The major social theorists have also depicted this change. Max Weber (1968:673), for example, saw it as the shift from a society characterised by fraternal bonds to relations defined by purposive contracts. These he defined as 'contracts neither affecting the status of the parties nor giving rise to new qualities of comradeship but aimed solely, as, for instance, barter, at some specific (especially economic) performance or result'. Ferdinand Tonnies (1955), as we will see below, interpreted the move as one from social relations of *Gemeinschaft* (community) to relations of *Gesellschaft* (association). (A more recent shift in law, away from *Gesellschaft* and towards what has been called a more 'bureaucratic-administrative' form of justice—concerned with public regulation and policy rather than with the rights of individuals—has also been theorised (Kamenka and Tay, 1975; 1986; Unger, 1976; Bankowski, 1979; O'Malley, 1983; Pratt, 1989). While it is not the purpose of this volume to explore the ramifications of this third type of law, it is still useful to note the impurity of the *Gesellschaft* model which, as we will see, not only coexists, uneasily, with its predecessor, the *Gemeinschaft* strain, but may itself be undergoing a transformation as it accedes to the demands of what some have termed the post-liberal, 'corporate' state.)

In short, the liberal notion of 'possessive individualism' both defines and vindicates relations which have emerged in modern market society. These are relations which can be characterised by their limited, instrumental and contractual nature, rather than by their intimacy, kinship or personal obligation. And it is these modern market relations which have shaped law in the Anglo–American tradition, which in its turn, with the imprimatur of liberal individualism, may be seen to justify, organise and regulate those market relations. Or as Cotterrell (1984:126) expresses it, 'law has had a major part to play in developing [the] ideological conditions [of individualism] and is a major form of their expression'.

For the purposes of the following analysis of liberal law and its view of the person, we will borrow extensively from Tonnies and his concept of *Gesellschaft*. The value of this concept is that it serves to summarise the essential liberal tendencies of modern western law. The *Gesellschaft* paradigm of law thus allows us to focus on only those key ingredients of Anglo–American law which have helped to shape much of its basic liberal character and which mark its commitment to liberalism.

The vital ingredients of *Gesellschaft* law, of law in the liberal tradition, have recently been summarised in the following manner:

> It assumes a society based on external as opposed to internal links, made up of atomic individuals and private interests, each in principle equivalent to the other ... It emphasises formal procedure, impartiality, adjudicative justice, precise legal provisions and definitions, and the rationality and predictability of legal administration. It is oriented to the exact definition of the rights and duties of individuals through a sharpening of the point at issue, and not to the day-to-day ad hoc maintenance of social harmony, community traditions and organic solidarity ... Its ideal model for all law is contract and the quid pro quo associated with commercial exchange, which also demands rationality and predictability ... It is at home with the social contract theory of society, with individualism and abstract rights. (Kamenka and Tay, 1986:292)

This is by no means an exact or complete description of any specific form of modern western law, as Tonnies (1955:xix) himself makes clear. Instead, it is to be regarded as a paradigm, an 'ideal type' (in the Weberian sense), or a conceptual model of law which is not intended to negate the various countervailing trends which inevitably exist in any legal system. It is a 'shorthand' for the law we know; it does not seek to set down that law in all its details. Its value in the present context is that it isolates the dominant tendencies in law of the Anglo–American tradition. It therefore provides us with a working model or hypothesis of law, one which frees us from the need to demonstrate all the complexities and contradictions of modern liberal law, allowing us to focus more clearly and expeditiously on law's conception of the person.

Tonnies' theoretical model of *Gesellschaft* (association or society) will also allow us to explore the contrast between these individualistic values implicit in our modern, western tradition of law and what the second-phase feminists have begun to identify (though, clearly, they have not coined the model) as an alternative approach to justice— what Tonnies has described as the opposing values of *Gemeinschaft* (community). In this other tradition, to be found *inter alia* in traditional Chinese legal procedure, in pre-industrial European society and in aspects of communist justice, priority is given to the needs of the community rather than the individual, and the emphasis is on social harmony and moral reciprocity, not competing rights. 'Where Gemeinschaft elevates community ... human relationships and common bonds ... Gesellschaft elevates the abstract individual and his abstract rights and duties in a social contract and a system of abstract and impersonal law' (Kamenka and Tay, 1986:289, 295).

In what follows, the intention is to explain the key elements of *Gesellschaft* law—the dominant strain in our common-law tradition— and to consider what those elements necessarily imply about the attributes and qualities of the supposedly universal legal subject.

Law and the social contract

It has been said that the *Gesellschaft* model of law is 'at home with the social contract theory of society' (Kamenka and Tay, 1986:292). The theory of the social contract is particularly associated with the work of the seventeenth-century British political philosophers Thomas Hobbes and John Locke, and so it is with an assessment of their interpretation of the individual and the social order that we begin our analysis of the legal person.

Hobbes derived his model of social organisation from what he took to be the facts of the human condition. To Hobbes, there was such a thing as a universal human nature which transcended the particular circumstances in which the individual might find himself at any one time or place (again the male pronoun is used because as we shall shortly discover, Hobbes was thinking of men and not of women). Put differently, Hobbes believed in a human essence which preceded and was ultimately more important than any efforts society might make to change and condition its members. The individual came first in Hobbes' scheme of things; the effects on the human being of living in a society came second, as accretions on the essential person. Society did not form men; men formed society (Campbell, 1981:10).

The logical corollary of the Hobbesian idea of the pre-social being is that we are all first and foremost discrete individuals, not interdependent social beings. We come together as separate relatively self-sufficient individuals to form a society of our choosing. Society does not choose us. Our motives for forming a society necessarily pre-exist the society we form and in turn are determined by our universal natures. The universal driving force of the individual, thought Hobbes, was the desire for personal gain, and the sole reason for controlling that desire was fear of its consequences to oneself.

The reason why we formed a society, according to Hobbes, was that our essential egoism, our wish for material self-advancement, threatened our very existence. It was rational for people (and Hobbes believed that we are rational in this sense) therefore to devise a form of social organisation which would secure our ability to pursue our own interests, but only to the extent that they did not threaten the interests of the next person. Thus potentially warring, self-interested individuals came together only to ensure that rational self-interest did not lead to mutual self-destruction (Campbell, 1981:70). In this view of humanity, 'a calculus of prudence rather than a love of goodness is the ideal guiding public behaviour' (Coltheart, 1986:114). To Hobbes, we chose to associate not because of a humane concern or love for others or any sense of shared humanity. We associated because this was the only rational way of ensuring our own protection.

The particular social means by which a balance was ultimately achieved between the competing rights of individuals, according to Hobbes, was the social contract. This was an implied agreement by all citizens to surrender to the state the minimal freedom necessary to allow it to arbitrate the conflicts between individuals and to sanction those who threatened to infringe the freedoms of others (Wacks, 1987:80). The social contract empowered the institutions of law and government which in turn ensured a well-ordered society.

In the political theory espoused by Hobbes, and endorsed by Locke, the most vital function of the state was thought to be the preservation of the right of individuals to negotiate freely in the marketplace in order to advance their individual interests. (This is not to impute to Hobbes and Locke a unanimity of thought. Indeed there were significant differences between the two thinkers on the question of the individual's political rights to the sovereign, in that Hobbes considered the social contract to be binding while Locke thought that people could change governments if they were un-democratic.) A healthy society, to Hobbes, was one in which there was free competition between its members. The institutions of the state were to ensure this individual freedom: their task was to guarantee the rights of individuals to pursue their own cause, as long as this self-promotion did not interfere with the similar freedoms of the next person. John Stuart Mill has provided the 'classic formulation' of this doctrine in his statement that 'the only freedom which deserves the name, is that of pursuing our own good in our own way, so long as we do not attempt to deprive others of theirs, or impede their efforts to obtain it' (quoted in Dietz, 1987:3).

The Hobbesian contractual view of society has been said to advance a 'logic of acquisition'. It gives primacy to the private possession of property and grants permission to the state to interfere with individual freedoms only when security of property (and the person) is under threat. For this reason, the social contract has been described as 'a contract of the propertied' (Coltheart, 1986:114). It has also been said to be about 'the quid pro quo associated with commercial exchange' (Kamenka and Tay, 1986:292).

Blackstone and *The Commentaries*

To observe the influence of the Hobbesian vision of 'man', society and the social contract on the thinking of legal theorists in the *Gesellschaft* tradition, it is useful to turn to one of the most authoritative sources of English law: William Blackstone's *Commentaries*. Published in 1765, *The Commentaries* 'ordered and summed up the preceding centuries of legal development' and so provided a 'jumping off point for new development, both in England and America' (Stone, 1946:247). They went on to assume a central place in legal teaching for almost a century and still feature importantly in legal analysis.

To Blackstone (1978:124), the principal aim of society 'was to protect individuals in the enjoyment of those absolute rights' over their person and their property: the priorities that Hobbes identified and defended. The prerogative of all human beings was to be free to act 'as one thinks fit, without any restraint or control', to exercise 'the faculty of free-will' (Blackstone, 1978:125). The human claim to be free was absolute in the sense that it would belong to persons even in a state of nature. It was absolute in the 'primary and strictest sense' (Blackstone, 1978:123).

In Blackstone's analysis, the laws of England were intimately connected with this essentially liberal view of society's purpose in that their object was to secure human freedom. More specifically, their purpose was to guarantee 'the right of personal security, the right of personal liberty, and the right of private property' (Blackstone, 1978:129). These were the three absolute human rights.

In Blackstone's utopian vision, we see an individual standing alone in a potentially hostile society, ideally unfettered and unrestrained by fellow citizens. That person is an autonomous, independent, human agent. Blackstone (1978:139) is quite clear on the point that the individual is both prior to, and inevitably more important than, the collective of which he is a part. Thus: 'In vain it may be urged that the good of the individual should yield to that of the community; for it would be dangerous to allow any private man, or even any public tribunal, to be the judge of this common good, and to decide whether it be expedient or no.' Indeed the public interest is seen to be synonymous with the protection of the autonomy of the person. The group benefits from the maximum liberty of each of its members.

Blackstone's account of society focuses on the separateness of individuals rather than their interdependence. The human being, he suggests, flourishes when left alone to do his own thing. Blackstone's person is stripped of human need and weakness: birth, death, child-hood and old age are all missing from this vision. The person is abstracted from the emotional and physical realities of the human condition and presented as a healthy adult able to function without the nurture of other caring persons. The ideal human condition, according to Blackstone, is one of freedom from interference from other individuals and from the state. If anything, other individuals represent a positive threat to freedom, not a source of support, and thus the role of law is to limit such interference in the name of individual liberty. The emphasis here is not on social solidarity, on the benefits which derive from our associations with others—the values of the *Gemeinschaft*. Rather, the focus is the 'natural' competition, if not positive hostility, which is thought to characterise social relationships in the *Gesellschaft*.

In his elaboration of the sanctity of the right to property, Blackstone provides us with further insights into the type of person who forms the legal subject in his *Gesellschaft* conception of law. Self-evidently, the legal subject is a property-owner whose sense of a free place in the world depends, in large part, on the continuity and preservation of that ownership. Blackstone (1978:138) conceives an almost sym-biotic relationship between 'man' and his property; one can barely imagine one without the other. So deep-seated is the human need for secure private possession of property that it is 'probably founded in nature'.

The legal person, in Blackstone's estimate, is also a property-owning man and not a woman. As we will see later, Blackstone believed that when a woman married, her personhood disappeared into that of her husband's, and the law in fact reflected this view of things by refusing to recognise the public rights of married women. This exclusion of women from the legal model in fact makes sense of Blackstone's commitment to the *Gesellschaft* idea of human separate-ness and independence. If women were eliminated from public life, they could take care of that side of humanity which was also excised from the *Gesellschaft* model of society. In their role of non-persons, they could nurture the young and the sick and the dying and provide emotional succour for their husbands. In other words, they could preserve the *Gemeinschaft* values within the home, leaving the man free to live out the *Gesellschaft* notion of the individual as the free-standing human atom. Thus the exclusion of women from the legal model was positively functional. Women could not be the free autonomous individuals that Blackstone wanted men to be because someone had to look after the human needs of the family and help the free-standing legal man stand freely.

John Rawls and the original position

The *Gesellschaft* conception of justice is not a historical curiosity confined to the thinking of the eighteenth century when Blackstone was compiling his *Commentaries*. Despite strong countervailing influences (some of which will be outlined below), it still represents the dominant strain in the common law tradition which forms the focus of this book. For a clear contemporary illustration of this type of legal theorising we can turn to a legal treatise recognised as 'one of the most widely read and carefully contructed extant in modern Anglo-American jurisprudence' (Matsuda, 1986:614). In John Rawls' *A Theory of Justice* (1971) we find a modern rendition of the Hobbesian story of the social contract which sheds further light on the qualities of the person in the *Gesellschaft*.

Rawls develops his model of the relation between law and society thus. First he requires us to imagine ourselves in a position where we are stripped of all knowledge of our particular place in the world. Rawls calls this 'the original position'. Here we have no awareness of our personal talents or our social or economic status. Nor, it seems, do we have any knowledge of our sex (though he does not make this plain) or our race. All these aspects of our selves are viewed by Rawls as accretions upon our fundamental humanity. They are simply fetters to our moral thinking, not vital elements of ourselves. In this state of ignorance, what Rawls calls the 'veil of ignorance', we must proceed to decide, as free and equal people, what it is we want in a just society.

To Rawls there are some basic human characteristics which will help us to make this decision. He sees us as heads or representatives of families who are concerned about the well-being of family members and of future generations, but who are in all other respects essentially self-interested and 'mutually disinterested' in the sense that we 'take no interest in one another's interest' (Jaggar, 1983a:31). He is also convinced that we are mainly after our share of 'the primary social goods (wealth, income, power, authority, self-respect and liberty)'. Quite naturally, Rawls believes, we are all striving for individual material success and social status, and the best of all possible worlds is one in which we are all able to achieve these things.

In the original position, Rawls believes that we will make two choices. We will opt for freedom first and equality second. We will do this because as humans (as Rawls conceives of us) we will realise that what matters is that we be allowed to realise our own individual aims, to realise our essential autonomy, to the extent that it is compatible with the autonomy of the next person. The 'mainspring of the sense of justice', to Rawls, is this basic human desire to make society for all its members as voluntary as possible. In the Rawlsian view, the ideal life is one in which the individual can pursue his own path, unobstructed by others, so long as those pursuits do not in themselves interfere with the freedoms of others. Rights, in the Rawlsian scheme, are perceived as zones of non-interference with our fundamental independence.

A number of writers have analysed critically the Rawlsian view of the person. Michael Sandel (1982), for one, has examined the implications of the theory that the individual must be placed in a pre-social 'original position' to discover his most basic values. He takes this to mean that the person is 'an antecedently individuated subject, standing always at a certain distance from the interests it has'. That is, our selves and our experiences are seen by Rawls to be two quite distinct things. Our identity and what we see is right are fixed 'once and for all' and are not shaped and conditioned by our encounters with others in a social context (Sandel, 1982:62). With Hobbes, Rawls is committed to the view of the pre-social being who decides to associate with others only for limited and basically self-serving purposes.

Rawls' account of the person, argues Sandel (1982:62), 'rules out the possibility of any attachments ... the possibility of a public life in which ... the interests of the participants could be at stake'. For to imagine that one's true moral self is that which is stripped of all the layers of our social existence is to relegate our social relations to the inessential. In Rawls' scheme of things, my social connections do not shape my view of what is right; they only cloud it. I am 'always, irreducibly, an active, willing agent, distinguishable from my surroundings and capable of choice' (Sandel, 1982:19).

The identification of freedom as the first human choice follows logically from the Rawlsian construction of the person 'as a sovereign agent of choice, a creature whose ends are chosen rather than given'.

The moral person thus becomes one who prefers, before all else, conditions which enable a full and free expression of the individual will. The moral person is one who chooses a life in which all human beings can pursue their own ends (Sandel, 1982:22).

Mari Matsuda (1986) offers a similar assessment of Rawls' person and the choices he makes. *A Theory of Justice*, she observes, contains a number of tacit assumptions about the nature of the world and the people who inhabit it. In this world, resources are scarce and people will inevitably want as much of them as they can get. Conflict is therefore 'inherent in social life and ... cooperation is preferable only to the extent that cooperation is mutually rewarding'. Though Rawls explicitly denies his commitment to a view of human beings as essentially egoistic, Matsuda feels that this does not accord with his social vision. For his is a world 'where everyone looks after themselves, and where mutual concern is merely an extension of self-interest'. In such a society, where individuals are concerned fundamentally with their own good, not that of others, 'people are wise to place primary value on liberty' (Matsuda, 1986:625).

The feminist philosopher Susan Moller Okin (1987) throws further light on the Rawlsian construction of the person by noting his sexual characteristics. Though Rawls seems to suggest that the person in the original position does not have a sex, his theory proceeds nevertheless on the assumption that his subject is a man and not a woman. Okin draws this conclusion from a close reading of Rawls, focusing on the assumptions he makes about the sort of roles that the person in the original position will go on to assume in the real world.

Okin (1987:50) begins her analysis by noting that Rawls conceives his person in the original position as of no specific sex but nevertheless as a head of a family. He then goes on to assume that this individual will participate in the paid labour market once he enters the real world. This ignores the important point that 'in societies characterised by a gender system (all current societies) a much larger proportion of women's than men's labor is unpaid, and is often not even acknowledged to be labor'. In other respects also, Rawls makes gendered assumptions which reveal that his hypothetical person is male. For example, at one stage he talks about the infringement of human freedom involved in military conscription, suggesting that it may be justifiable in defence of liberty, as long as there is 'no avoidable class bias in selecting those who are called for duty' (quoted in Okin, 1987:50). He makes no mention, however, of the fact that women as a sex are exempt from this form of state interference.

The Australian political scientist Deborah Kearns (1984) strengthens further the feminist critique of Rawls. Her objection is to Rawls' implicit assumption about the structure of the family which he takes to be one of 'the general facts about society'. From a careful perusal of *A Theory of Justice* it becomes apparent that Rawls (1972:467) can imagine no more desirable or natural an arrangement than the nuclear family 'characterised by a definite hierarchy, in which each member has certain rights and duties'. And by his references to the 'various conceptions of a good wife and husband' (1972:468) it would seem that Rawls is importing conventional notions of the respective roles of husbands and wives into his theory. At the same time, however, he fails to acknowledge that those ascribed roles are in fact the products of a sexist social convention—that they do not have an intrinsic or natural quality. 'Rawls just takes it for granted that it means something different to be a wife than a husband, to be a daughter than a son' (Kearns, 1984:199).

Together, the various critiques of *A Theory of Justice* suggest that, in the same manner as Blackstone's *Commentaries*, Rawls takes that human being to be a man and not a woman. Rawls conceives of his subject as a free-standing and independent male who is able to represent the interests of the family in an essentially hostile world. While the husband-father negotiates with the public world, a wife and mother is necessarily assumed to be performing her traditional functions of nurturing the more vulnerable family members who are unable to engage in the cut and thrust of public life (the young, the sick and the old). For the only way the family representative is able to perform his tasks of guarding the interests of the family is by having someone (a wife) take care of the other (family) side of life in the hierarchical family. Interesting questions are therefore raised about the sort of justice decisions which might be made by the care-givers from the original position. In the face of human dependence and human suffering, would they opt for autonomy or interdependence in a just world?

The abstract, individuating form of law

The *Gesellschaft* paradigm of law is not just the intellectual creature of legal theorists such as John Rawls but may also be seen to inhere in various specific doctrines and forms of the Anglo-American system of justice. Most significantly, it is reflected in what has been described as the 'individuating, abstract form' of our law (Sugarman and Rubin, 1984:49). What this means is that law of the common-law tradition tends to operate at a general and abstract level, applying universal rules and principles to everyone.

To achieve this universality of application of legal rules, human beings are not regarded as being comprised of different categories of persons with diverse and differing needs—for whom uniform laws may have different effects. Rather, human beings are generally taken to be separate, individually differentiated and therefore interchangeable legal units who can therefore, meaningfully, be abstracted from their social contexts and brought before the law.

The reference to the 'abstract individuating form' of law is also a comment on the fact that the basic unit of law in the *Gesellschaft* legal paradigm is the individual. That is, the law is essentially concerned with the protection and the advancement of the rights of individual citizens, not with the interests of social groups or collectivities. The law professes not to be interested in the relative position or social power of the individual. Nor is it concerned with regulating and forging social connections between individuals. Instead it takes the individual in glorious isolation and endeavours to ensure what it perceives to be his essential rights as a fully autonomous subject. The 'abstract individuating form' of law treats human beings as 'individual atoms' who can logically be extracted from their social context for legal purposes (Jaggar, 1983:29).

Thus in the forms of law which comprise the *Gesellschaft* legal model, the focus is the independence and separation of human beings whose potentially damaging interactions law seeks to regulate and control. Absent from the vision is a sense of the sort of loving, interdependent community living which is assumed to occur within the family—the values of the *Gemeinschaft*. In other words, the legal subject is conceived of as a potentially threatening (and potentially threatened) individual operating in a society of similar types. The sort of image invoked is that of a person fostering his own concerns in an open, competitive and hostile market. It does not include a view of the person operating for altruistic motives to assist and foster the positions of others—the sort of thing women are expected to do in families.

The most important rights of the individual with which the law is concerned are the protection of one's physical person and also one's possessions from the threat of others. The Anglo-American legal notion of an absolute right of the individual to private property was developed in the seventeenth century (Sugarman and Rubin, 1984:41) and, as we have seen, was accorded a central place in Blackstone's analysis of human rights in the late eighteenth century. It continues to assume a central role in legal thinking.

The twin concepts of individual rights and private ownership have been described as 'fundamental to our legal system' (Braybrooke, Sinclair and Sonneman, 1976:14). This is in direct contrast to legal systems in communist states where individual rights are subordinate to those of the state and property is owned collectively, by the state. The British philosopher Jeremy Bentham expressed the relation between English law and our rights to property in the strongest of terms. 'Property and law are born and must die together', he said. 'Before the laws there was no property: take away the laws, all property ceases' (quoted in Sugarman and Rubin, 1984:23).

In the Anglo-American legal tradition, the individual is not only the basic unit of legal rights, and, in particular, of rights to property. He is also the basic unit of responsibility. Individuals are makers of their own destinies and must therefore suffer the consequences of their actions. Thus 'the legal person standing alone bears responsibility for the acts or omissions attributed to him' (Cotterrell, 1984:126).

This *Gesellschaft* concept of individual responsibility presupposes a number of things about human beings and the world in which they are thought to live. Most importantly, it assumes that we are all fully in control of our actions; that we are not constrained by personal, social or economic circumstances. The focus is on the healthy, the wealthy and perhaps the wise in that the legal subject is thought to be generally free from any encumbrances or responsibilities. Missing from the theory is a recognition of the plight of the young, the old, the weak and the disadvantaged. Nor is the role of those who engage in the direct care of others acknowledged by the concept. Instead, 'people do what they do because they decide they want to' (Parsloe, 1978:9). In the words of the famous American jurist Roscoe Pound, the doctrine constructs 'a picture in which relation is ignored and each man is made to stand out by himself as an economically, politically, morally and hence self-sufficient unit' (quoted in Parsloe, 1978:9).

A logical consequence of the doctrine of individual responsibility is that our particular place in the world is generally deemed irrelevant when we are brought before a court for wrongdoing. The position of the accused person is reminiscent of 'man' in the original position — a highly artificial state of affairs. 'What is at issue is whether or not a rule has been broken, and the individual attributes of the accused, such as wealth, education, race, religion and intelligence and to some extent past criminal history are irrelevant' (Parsloe, 1978:11). Though it is true that criminal law has in many ways tried to ameliorate the harshness of this doctrine of individual responsibility (Garland, 1985), in particular at the point of sentencing when the social characteristics of the accused are considered pertinent, the individual is still largely expected to assume responsibility for his actions, which are considered to be those of a free agent. (Significant exceptions to this rule are the criminal defences of insanity, diminished responsibility, provocation and duress (Freiberg, Fox and Hogan, 1988:66).)

This fundamental principle of our legal system — that we must 'carry the can' for our transgressions — contrasts directly with a legal principle which has gained some recognition in the juvenile sphere of justice but which is still subordinate within the justice system as a whole and is at present under strong attack (Hudson, 1987). This is commonly referred to as 'the welfare approach' and may be seen to have close affinities with the *Gemeinschaft* conception of justice. It is one of the countervailing influences in our *Gesellschaft* law which illustrates the fact that it is not a pure strain, but shot through with contradictions. What is interesting about this other approach to justice is that it provides a model for quite a different view of humanity and in so doing, throws into stark relief the harsh individualism of the dominant model.

The welfare and community view of law, according to Parsloe (1978:181), 'sees children as part of an interacting family group, and sees families in a similar position within the community'. In the welfare model, human behaviour is interpreted as the consequence of 'the interaction between two or more people'. It follows that the individual child's actions must be assessed within the child's network of relationships. Logically, it should follow that the responsibility for youthful offending might sometimes fall on the parents and not on the actual offender. This in turn leads to the legal possibility of actually fining parents for the delinquencies of their children. In England, this idea recently received clear legislative endorsement in the Criminal Justice Act, 1982. Similarly, in Australia, several jurisdictions now allow for the punishment of parents for the crimes of their children (Freiberg, Fox and Hogan, 1988:69). This notwithstanding, the notion still holds within the juvenile sphere that punishment should usually be directed at the child. Thus the most that the welfare model generally achieves is some amelioration of the traditional justice principle that the penalty should fit the crime. Account therefore is taken of the child's family and social experiences in the determination of sentence.

Indeed, the first exposure of law students to the very limited legal notion of our responsibility for others is usually an occasion for the expression of moral indignation. The usual response by the uninitiated is 'why does the law not require us to do more for people (in the manner of the *Gemeinschaft* conception of justice)? How can it be so callous? This reaction of moral outrage is no doubt nurtured by the type of legal problems relished by law teachers when they expound the law in this area.

To demonstrate the law on our responsibility for others, a law teacher is likely to construct a hypothetical legal problem which goes something like this. Our potential defendant is a brutish individual, possibly a sadist, who enjoys witnessing the torment of others. He comes across the victim who is drowning in quicksand. He in no

way assists the process of drowning but he does nothing to help.
Indeed he derives positive pleasure from the spectacle and settles
down to watch. Is he guilty of murder or manslaughter or just a civil
wrong? The unequivocal answer is that he is guilty of none of these
charges. He is under no legal duty whatsoever because he has no
specific legal relationship with the victim. For example, he is not *in
loco parentis* and therefore is not obliged to care for the child in the
manner of a parent. Nor has he sold to the victim a faulty product
which has led to his destruction. In short, our law does not require
us to come to the aid of those with whom we have no formal
relationship. It assumes what might be called, to borrow the Rawlsian
term, 'mutual disinterest'.

The law of criminal responsibility here described is governed by a
critical distinction which our law observes between the notion of
'commission' and the notion of 'omission'. In short, the law on
criminal responsibility says that you can be punished for your com-
missions, if they cause harm to others, but you cannot be punished
for your omissions. This dichotomy may be traced to liberal theory
and the idea that the freedom of the individual from the dictates of
others is paramount. A famous statement on the liberal view which
guides the law in this area is that of John Stuart Mill (1910:72–73).
He said that:

> The only purpose for which power can be rightfully exercised
> over any member of a civilized community against his will, is to
> prevent harm to others. His own good, either physical or moral,
> is not a sufficient warrant. He cannot rightfully be compelled to
> do or forbear because it would be better for him to do so,
> because it will make him happier, because, in the opinion of
> others, to do so would be wise or even right.

In other words, the liberal philosophical position is that we must all
be allowed to pursue our own moral course and that we therefore do
not have to do anything that we do not want to do, whether or not
our omissions permit the occasion of harm to ourselves or to others.

Again the legal vision of society and its members is found to be
one of autonomy and individuality. I am not responsible for you. I
am only responsible for myself. I may not cause harm .to you,
because that would interfere with your individual freedom. But I am
not obliged to intervene on your behalf to further your interests (for
would that not limit my freedom?) no matter the smallness of the
cost to myself nor the largeness of the benefit to you. That is, the
law on the individual's responsibility to another assumes a society of
detached individuals whose autonomy is paramount rather than a
group which gives priority to community and to the welfare of
others.

Law should not interfere in the private sphere

Consistent with the primacy it accords the freedom of the individual, the *Gesellschaft* conception of law advances a principle of minimum interference in what it deems to be the private lives of citizens. Its professed concern is with the interactions between individuals, functioning as individuals, within the public realm. It is the public activities and rights of people which are thought to require legal regulation and protection. What people do in their own homes is basically up to them.

'The idea that private and public can be distinguished is imbued in legal philosophy and informs legal policy', observes Katherine O'Donovan (1985:8). This dichotomy or division between the private and public spheres has its provenance in liberal philosophy. In the public arena, the individual of liberal theory is expected to be calculating and self-interested, to confront a world in which, quite naturally, dog eats dog. Thus it is in this sphere of competition and combat between individual citizens that the law is needed to secure the rights and freedoms of each person thus threatened.

Liberal theory describes quite another world operating in the private sphere. To this place, the liberal citizen can retreat and feel secure from the interventions of other persons and from the state. Indeed the vital liberty of the person is thought to depend on the security of the private realm where the individual can relax, express emotions, love and be loved. For the public person to be free, the private sphere must remain free from the depredations of others and free from legal regulation. The central assumption of liberal theory is thus the central assumption of law: that 'the house of everyone is his castle' (O'Donovan, 1985:12).

Implicit in the standard theory that law confines its activities to the public sphere is the notion that law is for and about the lives and activities of people who dominate this realm—that is, working men. It is quite specifically said not to be for or about those whose lives are conducted primarily within the family and whose principal concerns are family concerns. And yet these other people (the mothers and the wives) are central to the legal notion of the private retreat of the family where *Gemeinschaft* values are supposed to assume prominence. Their specific function is to provide the humanising and tempering influence on the harsh individualism which law presupposes in the public sphere. In other words, the wives and mothers hold the *Gesellschaft* model of society together, though they are not considered to be a part of legal life.

The conventional view that law stays out of the family is one that has been directly challenged by a number of feminists. Writers such as Carol Smart (1984) and Frances Olsen (1985b) have observed the way in which law positively constructs the family and the place of women within it. While law professes to confine its regulations to the public sphere, and thus to leave people free to pursue their own lives in the private realm, in fact it makes a number of assumptions about the social organisation within the family and proceeds to enforce them. As Katherine O'Donovan (1985:14) remarks, 'although the state is reluctant to intervene directly, policies in areas which impinge on the family and which are expressed in legislative, judicial and administrative provisions construct a particular family form. The nuclear family, in which there is a division of labour between wife and husband, is an expression of these policies.'

To take an English example of legal control of family life, taxation laws cast wives in a secondary role by treating men as the main breadwinners. Indeed there are several welfare and social security laws which construct women as the legal dependants of men. Laws which limit or prohibit a woman's right to abortion effectively control the right of women to procreate at times of their own choosing. In many states of America, a husband has the legal right to force his wife to have sexual intercourse, again placing the wife in a vulnerable and dependent position.

Law can also be seen negatively to construct relations within the family. Until only recently the law chose not to intrude on violent relations within a marriage (now violent husbands may even be excluded from the family home). And of course law's refusal to acknowledge the marriage contract as an enforceable financial agreement leaves women who are full-time child-carers dependent on the caprices of a benevolent spouse for their subsistence.

In other ways, law's approach to marriage can be viewed as a positive construction of family relations, and in particular, of the subordinate place of the wife. For one thing, the law positively prevents a man and a woman from drawing up a marriage contract of their own terms and choosing. The 'essentials of the marriage contract' remain 'the husband's duty to support his wife, and the wife's duty to serve her husband' (Weitzman, 1981:338). In other words, when a man and a woman marry, they have imposed on them a contract not of their own making but one which is defined by the state. Their marital status is externally defined by the laws governing the nature of marriage and the respective roles of the parties. To illustrate, the state both expects the wife to perform domestic services for the husband (later we will discuss the law of consortium—the husband's right to sue for loss of domestic services), and prevents the parties from making a lawful agreement in which the husband is bound to pay for these services. The law dictates that they must be performed as a gift. The law also dictates that a marriage is an agreement between a man and a woman. It lays down that a 'husband ' is a man and a 'wife' is a woman (Pateman, 1988:167). People of the same sex are therefore not allowed to enter into a contract of marriage.

In short, there are many ways that law constrains and manipulates relations within the family, belying the *Gesellschaft* proposition that law regards the family as sacrosanct. The implications of the way in which law conceives of the role of women within the family—as subordinate and service-provider— will be taken up later when we consider more closely the sex of the legal person.

The contractual form of law

In the *Gesellschaft* conception of justice, the 'ideal model for all law is contract' (Kamenka and Tay, 1986:292). That is to say, liberal law tends to characterise social relationships in contractual terms. It sees people as current or potential parties to agreements in which they will derive some form of profit. In a legal contract, something is promised (such as goods or services or property) in exchange for consideration (usually money). The role of law is to make such transactions possible, to secure the rights of persons to form contracts of their own choosing from which they will derive a benefit.

This contractual right of individuals guaranteed by law is seen as vital and necessary to human liberty in the *Gesellschaft*. Indeed it is seen to secure two types of freedom. One is quite simply the right to form contracts with others. The other is the right to use and dispose of our property, including property in our labour, as we see fit (O'Malley, 1983:35).

The contractual view of social life assumes that contracts are the beginning and end of social relations. As one political theorist has observed, it assumes that social life 'is nothing more than contracts between individuals'. (Pateman, 1988:59). From the original social contract envisaged by Hobbes, there is thought to be contract 'all the way down'. To the Australian legal writer Pat O'Malley, the contractual form of law 'expresses an individualistic conception of social order based on contractual relations'. In this social vision 'anonymous and abstract individuals negotiate binding agreements based on unfettered choices and according to conditions upon which they agree'. The basic contractual structure of law has also been described, by one American lawyer, as reflecting 'the ethics of free enterprise capitalism and the ideals of justice of small enterprisers, individual merchants and independent craftsmen' (quoted in Cotterrell, 1984:128).

In other words, the contractual emphasis of our law suits the needs and priorities of those who function best in the free marketplace.

The contractual notion of the *Gesellschaft* embodies a major assumption about people and their relations with each other. It assumes that we are basically each the same as the next person and that we are therefore legally interchangeable. It takes for granted the voluntary and equal bargaining power of individuals who enter contracts. It is based on a view of social life 'as composed of independent, freedom-seeking individuals, each of whom avidly pursue[s] his own self-interest' (Feinman, 1983:832). It presupposes separate, autonomous and equal parties who come together on equal terms, haggle and compete, thrash out their differences, and arrive at a fair and mutually beneficial agreement. In this model, we are all thought to function well in 'the quid pro quo associated with commercial exchange, which also demands rationality and predictability'. (Kamenka and Tay, 1986:293).

Again, it is important to remember that we are talking here about a model of law, not law in all its details. The contractual idea of 'the voluntary bargain of free individuals' has been substantially modified since the classical period of the late nineteenth century by an expanding range of laws designed to recognise the unequal bargaining power of people in certain relationships (Cotterrell, 1984:127). It is possible to point to a number of examples of this trend. One is the legal recognition of the vulnerability of tenants when entering leases. Another is the growing number of laws designed to protect the unwary consumer. A third is the concept of the unconscionable contract—the agreement which should not be enforced because it is in some way inherently unfair or unjust (Finn, 1989:88). As a consequence, it is inappropriate to describe modern contract law as a pure strain characterised by its total commitment to individualism. Or, as the Australian jurist Paul Finn (1989:87) has recently observed, 'the older inspiration of self-reliance and individual responsibility is being qualified by a newer concern: that parties deal with each other fairly and in good faith'.

According to the critical legal theorist, Jay Feinman (1983), modern contract law now embodies two competing and conflicting 'patterns of analysis'. One is the individualist strand, 'the heir to the individualist tradition of the classical image'. The other is 'its collectivist opposite'. In this other manifestation, contract law displays a commitment to a world view in which we are interdependent and 'cooperating actors'. The collectivist dimension of contract law is to be seen 'in judicial intervention to correct market imperfections such as ignorance or equality, to deal with unanticipated or unfortunate contingencies, and otherwise to allocate the benefits and burdens of exchange among parties' (Feinman, 1983:843). The competing concerns running through contract law—its commitment to the conflicting principles of individualism and collectivism, or of *Gesellschaft* and *Gemeinschaft*— mean that contract law as a whole does not cohere, according to Feinman (1983:856). Instead it is complex and contradictory.

Notwithstanding the confused priorities of modern contract law, the idea of freedom of contract and the equal capacity of parties is still critical to both the general theoretical foundation and the practice of our law. Its import for our understanding of the legal person is that it tends to conceive of human beings as essentially interchangeable contracting parties, as free and equal owners of commodities who, quite naturally, would wish to barter them in the marketplace. 'Classical contract law and, to a large extent, its modern counterpart treat people as . . . productive units in a complex economy structured by abstract law' (Feinman, 1983:859). It also tends to assume that we are all similarly equipped to engage in transactions which will redound to our personal advantage. Its model for the person is therefore the prudent contractor, making agreements intelligently and wisely in his own interests.

The adversarial form of justice

The *Gesellschaft* legal model may also be seen to display an orientation towards 'the exact definition of rights and duties of the individual through a sharpening of the point at issue' (Kamenka and Tay, 1986:292). This is a reference to the adversarial style of justice, what has been called 'a foundational feature of Anglo-American legal systems'. According to another legal analyst, not only are 'many of the activities in our legal system . . . overtly adversarial' but 'the adversary premise also underlies all of our law and our thinking about law' (Goodpaster, 1987:118).

Again, it must be noted that we are working here with a general model of law, not law in all its details. So while it is true that there is an adversarial orientation throughout the law, it is also possible to identify countervailing trends and influences. For example, in the area of family law, there have been specific attempts to introduce a less combative and more informal type of justice designed to reduce conflict between the parties and to arrive at mutually agreeable resolutions of the dispute. Where this is impossible to achieve, however, the dominant adversary model is brought back into play. Another example of non-adversarial justice is to be found in the operation of neighbourhood justice centres where efforts have been made to resolve disputes through negotiation rather than an open struggle. Such exceptions notwithstanding, it is still appropriate to characterise our law as essentially adversarial in nature.

The 'normative theme' of the adversarial model is one of conflict (Stapleton and Tietlebaum, 1972:98). Its method of resolving disputes between individuals and between individuals and the state is to place the parties in open opposition in a courtroom, as adversaries, and to require them to fight it out. The two parties must advance their own position and try to cast doubt on their adversary's view of the facts. The adversary system entails a contest or struggle in which only one side can win and there is always a loser. It has been depicted as 'a regulated storytelling contest between champions of competing, interpretive stories' (Goodpaster, 1987:120). In the adversary system, the better-armed (the person who can afford the better hired gun) and hence the better-argued is more likely to convince the judge of the justice of their case.

The adversarial process is not just confined to the courtroom but tends to shape the general approach of lawyers towards their work. When advising their clients the message imparted is 'to get as much as you can'. When trying to resolve a dispute the idea is 'to get' the other party on as many points as possible. And when planning transactions, the lawyer is pressing for the most advantageous (as opposed to the fairest) deal. Repeatedly, litigation is cast in terms of a competition over limited resources and the success of the lawyer is judged in terms of maximising the individual gain of the client. 'The conduct of litigation is relatively similar ... to a sporting event', says Menkel-Meadow (1987:51). Thus 'there are rules, a referee, an object to the game, and a winner is declared after the play is over'.

Within the legal profession, there are certain ethics and principles which quite explicitly countenance and justify this competitive style of justice. Most significant is that principle of the profession which holds that 'a lawyer must, within the established constraints upon professional behaviour, maximise the likelihood that the client will prevail' (quoted in Goodpaster, 1987:124). Indeed, professionally, lawyers are not supposed to have a view of the rightness or wrongness of the matter in hand (though they are not supposed to defend a client who openly confesses guilt). Their job is to go into battle using all the skills at their disposal, not to agonise over the morality of the behaviour in question.

What distinguishes adversarial legal systems from other human interactions, says Parsloe (1978:12), is that they leave no room 'for agreeing to differ or being unable to decide'. The starting point of any case is disagreement and in the end one of these views must prevail. To highlight its distinctive character, the adversary approach has been contrasted with the medical model of decision-making. In the latter,

> the doctor confesses that there are some questions to which he has no answers and acknowledges that some matters must be left open to await scientific proof. But no trial court can do that. Eventually, right or wrong, some judge will [have to] say: 'This is the answer; this is the end of the litigation.' The physician can say with honesty: 'I just don't know.' The judge can never say that'. (Hazard, quoted in Parsloe, 1978:12)

The oppositional style of Anglo-American justice contrasts also with the *Gemeinschaft* model which, as we have seen, rejects the basic premises of the adversary system. From the, *Gemeinschaft* perspective, the resolution of difference through an adversarial court battle 'disrupts the "natural harmony" thought to exist in human affairs, relies on coercion rather than moral suasion, and fosters litigious and shameless concern for one's own interests rather than those of society' (Rosenberg, 1988:803).

The more conciliatory *Gemeinschaft* approach to justice contrasts dramatically with the adversarial *Gesellschaft*. Where the former seeks to avoid friction and to find a solution favourable to both parties, the latter places the parties in direct opposition, requires them to go into battle and to use as much pressure and moral suasion as possible and then lets only one of the parties win.

To the Australian legal critic Pat O'Malley (1983: 122), there is a direct parallel between 'adversary justice and the structure of competitive capitalism'. He observes that they 'are sufficiently striking to lead commentators to refer to adversary justice as "a direct transplant of competitive economics into the apparatus of justice".' Malcolm Feeley (1979:123) has also noted the connections between adversarial procedures and the *laissez faire* ideology of capitalism in which each individual is expected to be self-seeking and competitive:

> as with the division of labour and interest in the market, it is expected that the self-interest of the individual parties will be sufficient to ensure that appropriate decisions are made. Efficient solutions are arrived at, not because there are shared goals to which all adhere, but because there are conflicting interests, and the pursuit of those interests is expected to produce fair and efficient results.

Constructing the legal person: the competitive entrepreneur

The official rhetoric of legal impartiality tells us that law prefers no one type of person. In our *Gesellschaft* type of justice, law's person is thought to be an abstract individual, a standard being, a human norm operating anywhere. And yet, at the same time, a consistent and quite particular vision of people and society is implicit within this supposedly universal model of humanity. What we have discovered is that law's abstract person is not anyone. On the one hand, the legal subject possesses certain emphasised and distinguishing characteristics which identify him clearly, posing a direct challenge to the notion of his non-specificness or interchangeability. On the other hand, because of his very abstraction from society, his any-personness, he seems to lack some basic features of humanity—those which are conventionally associated with *Gemeinschaft* values and which are expected of women in the private sphere.

Consistently, the identity suggested is of an autonomous, self-interested, competitive man of property operating in a hostile and competitive society of like-minded people. In this society, individuals are thought to be pitted against each other in a struggle for profit and self-advancement. The scene described is of enterprising men hard at it in the free market; it is the Hobbesian conception of man and society.

In a paper on the liberal conception of citizenship, Mary G. Dietz (1987) has tried to summarise the attributes which seem to typify people in the *Gesellschaft* idea of society. First, human beings are 'atomistic, rational agents whose existence and interests are ontologically prior to society'. By this she means that human beings are not to be defined by their social context. They enter the world with a predetermined set of qualities. Importantly, they are rational beings who possess an essential autonomy. They do not depend on others for the definition of their needs and interests, nor for their satisfactions.

Second, individuals have an inherent right to a large degree of freedom to fulfil their promise. It is vital that they be allowed to discover their own values and ends, regardless of the 'rightness' or 'goodness' of their personal choice. The individual's right to self-determination depends on 'his' having access to a private realm of freedom in which the state is said not to interfere (though in truth, as we have seen, it exerts considerable influence).

A further quality of human beings in the *Gesellschaft* society is their love of competition. In the words of Adam Smith, their 'natural propensity' is 'to trade, truck, and barter' (quoted in Dietz, 1987:4). Mary Dietz (1987:5) encapsulates the essential attributes of this being thus: '[he] must be understood as the competitive entrepreneur, his civil society as an economic marketplace, and his ideal as the equal opportunity to engage, as Adam Smith wrote, in "the race for wealth, honours, and preferments".'

The *Gesellschaft* view of the individual envisages a certain form of society in which this being can be seen to thrive. Scheman (1983:231) offers an illuminating account of this community:

> we exist essentially as separate human individuals ... and any social order has to begin by respecting [this] ... The societies thus envisioned aim at maximally respecting the separateness of their members by providing mechanisms for adjudicating the claims that one member may make against another, while leaving as intact as possible the rights of each to be self-defining.

According to the individualistic ethic of *Gesellschaft* justice, law's task is the arbitration of competing rights, securing the liberty of the individual, promoting property rights, and putting the individual before the collective group. Its emphasis is the liberty of the individual. It is the world-view in which the free, unattached, contracting, commercial person provides the human model. This view of society entails a failure to imagine anyone acting for other than their own ends. It assumes 'a pervasive self-interest'. The morality implicit in its notion of justice 'is that which seeks simply to contain individuals' self-seeking, to provide a framework of legal and moral rules which will ensure that the whole system does not break down through the untrammelled egoism of such self-seeking'. Accordingly much legal doctrine deals specifically with such matters as property and contracts which are designed to limit one's right to interfere with the liberty of another (Grimshaw, 1986:197).

In the *Gesellschaft* model of the individual, we are dealing with someone who is essentially combative and competitive for the purposes of material gain. The legal person, the individual envisaged by the Anglo-American legal tradition, is financially successful, a person of property. And he keeps his hold over his material assets with the law's approval and protection.

The problem of abstraction

To this point, the chapter has addressed the problem of the human model in law. That which the law professes to be universal, its abstract individual, we have found to possess quite particular qualities which mesh well with, and are functional for, the liberal conception of the free-market society. Later we will consider more closely the type of people included in (Chapter 4), and excluded from (Chapter 5), the model, as well as the injustices thus created for the latter group (Chapters 6 and 7): those who fail to fit or who are excluded from the legal model of the person. The final task of this chapter, however, is to address the process of abstraction itself and consider its implications for the legal claim to impartiality.

Specifically, the present intention is to show that significant problems flow from the legal endeavour to abstract people from their social contexts and then to impose on them the character of the legal person. All of these problems raise doubts about the legal precept of impartiality itself which depends so heavily on the process of abstraction to achieve its desired result of equality before the law.

Perhaps the most obvious problem with abstraction is that many regard it as a human impossibility and therefore quite meaningless. People, they say, are inextricably bound up with their particular social environments and it is vital, for fairness, that they be viewed within these contexts. A second problem with legal abstraction is that it ignores vital differences between people, differences which relate not only to their culture but to their real level of power in the world, and imposes on them a spurious sameness and a spurious equality.

A further problem with the *Gesellschaft* process of abstraction is that it imposes on people priorities, values and interests with which they might fundamentally take issue, given the chance. Indeed it is likely that *Gesellschaft* law's depiction of the standard person as an automaton, emotionally and physically detached from all around him, engaging only in contractual, profitable relationships with others, fails to reflect much of the experience of most people, and is positively objectionable to many.

The impossibility of abstraction

The legal fiction of the abstracted individual who is able to stand outside the society to which he belongs and, in a detached, dispassionate and, it would seem, disembodied manner, muse upon his place in it has attracted criticism from a number of quarters. Political scientists, philosophers and feminists (categories which, of course, are not mutually exclusive) have all raised objections to the concept. One challenge which specifically addresses the ontology of Hobbes comes from the British political theorist Tom Campbell (1981:87). He describes 'the fallacy of thinking that human behaviour patterns exist independently of their social relationships':

> If not only language, and hence thinking, but all the emotional states and activities about which rule-governed standards apply, are moulded by life in society, then the idea of a fixed and universal specific human nature abstracted from a particular social setting is a

nonsense. Whatever disclaimers may be made about the hypothetical and unhistorical status of the social contract, thinking in these terms at all is a dangerous encouragement to the mistaken notion that man's nature is independent of his social existence.

The feminist philosopher Alison Jaggar (1983:40) has pointed out the biological problems raised by, or rather omitted from, the concept of the abstracted, pre-social person of the *Gesellschaft*. She says that as soon as one takes account of 'the facts of human biology', such as reproduction and the needs of small children, it becomes obvious that we are all utterly dependent on society for our survival. 'Human interdependence is thus necessitated by human biology.'

Jaggar (1983:42) is also of the view that the type of people that we are is very much a result of our social experiences. Our priorities and our interests, she says, are all a function of the social context in which we are nurtured and from which we derive our values. Human beings, declares Jaggar, are therefore never pre-social.

In a specific challenge to the Rawlsian conception of the abstract individual, Jeremy Sandel pursues this point that we are always a part of, and are never outside, our social context. In particular, he takes issue with Rawls' idea that we would be able to make important moral decisions, such as what is the just society, from the pre-social 'original position'. To Sandel (1982:179) our morals do not precede our place in the social world but flow out of our conceptions of ourselves as particular persons with particular social connections. Thus 'we cannot regard ourselves as independent in this way without great cost to those loyalties and convictions whose moral force consists partly in the fact that living by them is inseparable from understanding ourselves as the particular persons we are — as members of this family or community or nation'.

One of the most vociferous critics of the notion of the abstracted human being, however, is the political philosopher Robert Wolff (1976). In a pithy and humorous attack on the concept, wryly called 'There's Nobody Here but us Persons', he explains why he feels it is absurd ever to talk about human beings as if they were fixed, abstract identities — as if they did not change over the course of their lives but were always, inevitably, rational, able-bodied subjects. To Wolff (1976:130), what he describes as 'the facts of the human condition' are inescapable and are therefore 'philosophically fundamental' to the understanding of human beings as political actors. We are all, at some stage, constrained by the limitations of our wills and the restrictions of our bodies. Death is not simply an 'accident of man's nature''; childhood is not an inessential stage of our lives; babies are not 'ignorant spastics'.

What makes the theory of the abstract individual unsatisfactory to Wolff (1976:132), is that it seems to assume that as soon as we have acquired motor skills and some basic knowledge of the world we are ready 'to launch out on the public world and start making self-interested bargains in pursuit of private satisfactions'. The human 'facts' that we are nurtured to this state of public personhood are set aside in the *Gesellschaft* conception of society: certainly the role of the parent (who in practical terms is usually the mother) is rendered invisible and therefore inessential. The net result is an image of the political world as 'a timeless or static community of adults, met together to transact their collective business' (Wolff, 1976:133).

Imposing sameness and equality

Implicit in the *Gesellschaft* concept of law is the idea that we are formally equivalent and equal. Accordingly, such important aspects of our lives as our race, our sex, our age or level of wealth do not matter. The legal intention of this setting aside of our human and social differences, this abstraction of ourselves from our particular contexts, is a commendable one. It is the legal ideal of equality of treatment, regardless of these distinguishing characteristics: that is to say, justice dictates that they should not hamper us. In the public world of the law, colour, creed, class and sex are therefore deemed to be inessential components of our selves. They may make a difference to our private lives but they do not provide an appropriate basis for legal distinctions. For the express purpose of law is to dispense justice 'without fear or favour' and 'without affection or illwill'.

There are several problems with the legal ideal of non-discrimination or equality sought through the process of abstraction. One is that it fails to address the real needs and priorities of those people who least fit the legal notion of the abstracted person (a problem which will be taken up in later chapters). To give just one brief and simple example, the abstracted legal person does not appear to experience pregnancy or raise children, but most real women do. As a consequence those concerns and interests which arise in women out of the maternal processes, which are to do with social responsibility and human interdependence, are not centrally addressed by *Gesellschaft* law, which assumes that people are independent and detached from others. Constrained by the notion of the abstract individual, the most that the *Gesellschaft* model of justice seems able to achieve are some special provisions (such as maternity leave) which tend to regard pregnant women as human aberrations with a curious disability.

Another problem with legal abstraction and the assumption that the law should be the same for all, regardless of social difference, is that it rules out of court any discussion of the power differences caused by these social differences. Put differently, the failure of *Gesellschaft* law to deal with those aspects of the person which cause them disadvantage—that is, those aspects which depart from the legal model of the person—imposes a spurious equality and sameness on people and therefore bypasses the problem of structural social inequality.

True, one can identify countervailing influences informed by the *Gemeinschaft* strain of law—influences which indicate the strains and tensions within the *Gesellschaft* model. These entail specific legal endeavours to compensate particular individuals and groups whom society deems to be disadvantaged and generally take the form of welfare provisions, supplementary benefits and concessions designed to bring the status of such persons closer to that of the abstract individual. But these efforts are peripheral in the sense that they do not go to the heart of law's approach to the world. They do not fundamentally alter the most basic assumptions about the nature of the individual implicit in our *Gesellschaft* type of law. Instead they are specific and piecemeal efforts to ameliorate some of the harsh effects of the *Gesellschaft* ethic of competitive individualism and individual responsibility. They are a limited acknowledgment that the fiction of the abstract individual is just that: that it does not work for all, though *Gesellschaft* law assumes that it does.

It is also true that social differences associated with disadvantage (such as gender and race) may be made the subject of specific laws designed to address the problem of discrimination on just these grounds. But again such initiatives do not rebut the *Gesellschaft* assumption that we can be treated as interchangeable abstract and equal individuals. Instead, the purpose of such anti-discrimination legislation is not to incorporate human diversity into law, but rather the opposite: to have the differences excised. They must not be used as a basis for less favourable treatment of the person, but nor must they be made a basis for preferential treatment. In other words, equality must be assumed and differences must be ignored.

Imposing values

A final problem with legal abstraction in its *Gesellschaft* form is that it imposes on individuals values and priorities with which they might well fundamentally disagree, given the opportunity. We have already seen the type of objections raised by feminists to the values which are thought to inhere in law. The second-phase feminists, in particular, were eloquent on the subject. To Ann Scales (1986:1391), for example, law describes 'a pretty grim view of life on the planet'. In the abstracted legal vision, individuals are regarded as 'isolated monads, as natural adversaries who must each stake out his own territory and protect it with the sword/shield mechanisms called "rights"'.

Legal feminists have also begun the task of describing a better social vision as a basis for legal thinking, one which takes a kinder view of human nature—one which meshes well with the *Gemeinschaft* conception of justice. In this view, the focus is on 'the preservation of human relationships', not social conflict (Scales, 1986:1381). The endeavour of feminist legal writers to produce a different, more humane, model of individual and social relationships is one which will be returned to at the end of the book when we consider some possibilities for legal change.

Social philosophers have also brought a critical eye to bear on the abstract individual and the values he is thought to represent. To Alison Jaggar (1983:45), 'the egoistic model of human nature is unable to acknowledge the values intrinsic to participating in an affective, a productive or a rational community because these values involve, by definition, a concern for individuals other than oneself'. In a similar fashion, Tom Campbell (1981:83) identifies the critical oversight of the social vision implicit in the *Gesellschaft*. What it fails to realise is that people may actually derive satisfaction from acts of altruism, without being kind simply to derive selfish pleasure for themselves.

The scene excluded from the *Gesellschaft* vision of abstracted humanity is that of human kindness and human frailty, of inter-dependence and nurture, what Wolff (1968:184) has called 'the social values of community'—the values of the *Gemeinschaft*. This is the side of life relegated to the private sphere in the *Gesellschaft* model, what has been regarded as the world of women. It is the world thought to complement (and hence to buttress) the harsh individualism of the legal sphere, though it is not admitted to that more exalted place.

Critical lawyers have also objected to the *Gesellschaft* ethic of abstract individualism. The comparative lawyer H.C. Gutteridge, for example, suggests that law's interests in protecting the rights of individuals to pursue their own interests can only be described as 'the consecration of the spirit of unrestricted egoism'. Erlich wrote criti-ically of law's focus on 'the individual and his property, the individual who has an untrammelled power of disposition over his property, who recognises no superior but the state, and is not bound by anything but the contracts he has entered into'. Weber referred to law's 'community of strangers' (quoted in Cotterrell, 1984:126).

In truth, we all have attachments, emotions, a sense of affinity with others, and we find it difficult to thrive without a network of human relationships. It is certainly difficult to make it to adulthood without some individual or family to nurture us. Indeed the very word conventionally applied to the working man whom the model is intended to fit, that of 'breadwinner', presupposes connections with persons for whom the bread is won, relationships which are supposed to be informed by love, not profit. An important contradiction which lies at the heart of *Gesellschaft* law is that it actually recognises this breadwinning role, with its clear implications of human inter-dependence, while adhering to the fiction of abstraction and separation. Hobbes' abstract individual was a head of a family, while Rawls thought of the person in the original position as a family representative.

The abstract individual of the *Gesellschaft* is therefore both abstract and contextualised. He is isolated in his self-interests and yet he is thought not to exist in an emotional and social vacuum. He is an automaton and yet he is part of a network of family and friends which do not cease to exist when he enters the public sphere. The abstract individual can thus be seen to contain an internal contradiction. On the one hand, he is expected to be a self-seeking hermit. On the other hand, he is believed to have a home life—which does not intrude on the public sphere—from which he derives emotional succour and presumably the motivation to go out and do battle in the public sphere. Thus the abstracted man of law is not only a contested idea of a paradigmatic person, in that many take issue with his values and would like to see others given precedence, but those values themselves contain a fundamental contradiction.

4

Lawyers and the legal paradox

The abstract individual who assumes such a central place in our *Gesellschaft* conception of justice is manifestly a controversial character. As we saw in the previous chapter, he has been challenged on a number of counts from a variety of quarters. And yet this person has endured. It is therefore pertinent to consider why this is so. How has the *Gesellschaft* conception of the individual been sustained in the face of these many objections? Why does our *Gesellschaft* style of law continue to organise around an individual who does not possess universal qualities, but rather the qualities associated with privileged and successful men, and why does it persist in its belief in the universality of those qualities?

The argument of this chapter is that the legal community has played a significant role in sustaining the *Gesellschaft* model of the individual and society. Not only has it failed to examine critically the social model with which it is asked to operate but, by its day-to-day invocation of the model, it has effectively endorsed it. The purpose of this chapter is, principally, to consider why this is the case.

In so doing, this chapter seeks to expose a paradox which is central to legal thinking and legal practice. The paradox is this. Members of the legal community are professionally committed to the pursuit of an ethic of individualism and yet individualism is discouraged within the profession itself. To explain, the job of the lawyer is to protect the interests of individuals against the state, to advance individual rights and impose individual responsibility. According to law's model of the person, which lawyers and judges are called upon to interpret and administer, we stand alone in this society and must be allowed to pursue our individual path, unimpeded by others, so long as we do not impede them. As one writer has observed, 'the legal system as a whole tends to exist for the vindication of individual and not collective rights' (Atiyah, 1983:87). And yet, while lawyers and judges are

84

expected (in principle) to enhance the individualism of others, they are not expected to display this quality themselves.

As we will see below, within the legal community there operates a powerful form of social closure which works against the maverick voice to suppress dissent. And it is this social control exercised from within a profession whose task it is to secure the independent stance of others which constitutes a vital tension in the practice of law. Those who might offer an independent perspective on the legal world stand to be admonished or punished for their difference, while those who endorse the dominant way of doing things stand to be rewarded. Members of the legal fraternity, it will be argued, have good reason not to make waves by criticising the traditional form of law.

This chapter will also suggest that, for many who work with the legal model of humanity, there may be little reason to question it. For them, it may be said, the model is seen to work and hence the model is true. It represents their universe of experience and therefore their view of social reality. In other words, there is a close affinity, almost a kinship, between the legal person and many members of the legal community. The individual who features so centrally in our *Gesellschaft* law can be seen to share a common culture with many of the people who populate the legal world.

A further claim of this chapter is that the durability of the *Gesellschaft* legal model of the person owes much to the immunity of the legal world from effective challenge to its social vision. Those who might be able to demonstrate the limitations of law's idea of humanity, it will be claimed, are not in a sufficiently powerful position to overturn law's truth.

The following study of lawyers and judges does not attempt to be exhaustive. It does not pretend to offer a taxonomy of lawyers, their work and values, in all their diversity. Our task is a more modest one: to examine some of the defining characteristics of those who represent the profession's most influential members in England, the United States of America and Australia. To this end we will consider their social and economic background, how they organise, the sort of concerns they bring to their profession and how they are expected to relate and to defer to each other.

The legal community

In England and in many states of Australia, the legal profession is divided between lawyers who specialise in courtroom matters and lawyers who do the rest of the legal work. The members of the former group, known as barristers, argue cases in court. Professionally, they organise into groups known as Bars. Rather than making their services available directly to the public, barristers receive their court 'briefs' from the other branch of the profession, known as solicitors. It is the solicitor who deals with the client and then instructs the barrister on the nature of the case. Solicitors often associate together in partnerships from which they tend to offer to the public a general legal service, though different partners may specialise in different areas of the law.

In those places where the profession is divided, promotion to the judiciary, or the Bench, is usually from the Bar. Barristers therefore are considered to represent the cream of the profession and exert, accordingly, a considerable influence on its mores and priorities. In the United States, there is no formal division of the profession. There is to be found, nevertheless, a certain degree of specialisation which serves to stratify it. Those lawyers who manage to operate successfully in the world of high finance represent, in effect, the elite of the American legal community. Less influential are the smaller group practices and the lawyers working alone who may in fact be relatively isolated from each other and from the powerful legal houses of the city (Cotterrell, 1984:195).

For the purposes of this study, we will mainly be looking to the Bar and the Bench for our understanding of the profession in England and Australia. For our American evidence on the legal community, we will concentrate on the values and practices of lawyers who service business. To reiterate, this is by no means an exhaustive look at the members of the legal world, whose working lives have been shown by other writers to be both complex and highly stratified (Schur, 1968; Heinz and Laumann, 1982; Tomasic, 1983; Disney, 1986:61). Rather the present focus is on those parts of the legal fraternity which have been found to exercise considerable influence on the practice of law in the three countries under scrutiny.

A detailed social profile of Australian lawyers practising in New South Wales was documented by Roman Tomasic (1978a) in the late 1970s. It revealed a number of striking regularities about the profession. For one thing, the vast majority were men. Among the New South Wales lawyers, women were to be found in their largest numbers among city solicitors, of whom they represented a mere 6.6 per cent. In rural areas, only 0.6 per cent of the solicitors were women. (Although the representation of women has since increased substantially, around the country (to about 17 per cent), they are still in the minority and, perhaps more importantly, as we will see, they are still mainly to be found in the lower echelons of the profession (Australian Bureau of Statistics, 1987)). For purely demographic reasons, then, it is likely that Australian legal men adopt a fairly traditional attitude to women and their role. For not only are the women in their working lives more likely to be their secretaries than their colleagues at the Bar, but it is unusual for their mothers to be members of the paid workforce at all (Tomasic, 1978a:23).

Australian men of law are likely to come from legal families. About half the solicitors in private practice have legally qualified relatives. And whatever their occupation, the fathers of lawyers are likely to be well placed, socially and financially: 'it is most unusual for lawyers ... to have fathers employed in lower status occupational jobs' (Tomasic, 1978a:23). Australian lawyers, not surprisingly, tend to have been private-school boys. 'Less than one in five city and suburban solicitors attended non-selective government high schools, while one in ten barristers ... attended such schools' (Tomasic, 1978a:26). Finally, Tomasic (1978a:28) observes that the vast majority of the profession is politically conservative. He concludes that the profession is still 'tradition bound'. It is 'the embodiment of the values of a parochial and conservative, male-dominated society'.

As Australian lawyers proceed from the Bar to the Bench, so their conservative tendencies are strengthened. A profile of the Victorian Supreme Court judges sitting in 1978 reveals that all were male, 90 per cent had attended private schools, half were members of elite social clubs whose membership excluded women, and the vast majority lived in the most exclusive suburbs of Melbourne. In their review of the social characteristics of the Australian judiciary, Sexton and Maher (1982:6) depict 'a group of men ... from comfortable backgrounds, who have spent almost all of their adult lives in the sheltered world of the bar'. The profession, they claim, possesses 'extraordinarily close-knit qualities'.

Bankowski and Mungham (1976:83) describe a similar situation in England. 'Unlike nearly every other profession', they say, 'the law has preserved an institutional solidarity, a closed caste recruitment ... which has scarcely changed at all in the last half century.' English practitioners have in common with their Australian counterparts 'a high degree of social and cultural homogeneity'. Atiyah (1983:11) confirms this with some simple social statistics on the composition of the English Bench. Nearly all judges, we are told, are middle-aged or elderly men. The greater their seniority, the greater their age, so that few Lords of Appeal are under 60 and many judges are much older. 'Overwhelmingly', judges are drawn from the managerial and professional classes. Over three-quarters have attended public (that is private) schools and have proceeded to Oxford or Cambridge. Politically, it is likely that the vast majority are conservative. In sum, 'those who reach the top posts are usually "mature, safe and orthodox men"', to quote Lord Devlin.

Maureen Cain (1976:237) supplies us with further information on the men of the senior English Bar and the Bench. Of the 105 Queen's Counsels in her sample, '81 went to either Oxford or Cambridge, and most of these were there between 1945 and 1950'. From Cecil's study of the biographies of 45 out of 90 County Court judges she adduces further evidence of the social character of the judiciary:

> Twenty of these were at Oxford University and twenty at Cambridge University. One went to Leeds, one to London, and two had no degree. The biographies of 36 out of 73 Court of Appeal and High Court Judges showed that 17 of the 36 had been to Oxford University, 16 to Cambridge, one to London, one to Manchester, and one had no degree. This indicates greater homogeneity of origin the more powerful the position.

The American profession has also been found to display a distinctive social profile. Heinz and Laumann (1982:187–90) observed in their study of Chicago lawyers that they were disproportionately drawn from the entrepreneurial classes who would be expected to have inculcated such capitalist values as autonomy and individualism. About three-quarters of the Chicago lawyers had fathers working in areas described as 'professional, technical, or managerial'. Also like their Australian and English counterparts, a disproportionately large number of the Chicago lawyers had lawyers as fathers.

Socially, members of the Bar, the elite of the profession, continue to operate much like an exclusive private men's club. This is perhaps not surprising given that lawyers' chambers tend to be concentrated in the one place. 'In Sydney the 800 practising barristers work in five different buildings which are located within an area of two city blocks near the law courts' (Sexton and Maher, 1982:6). In the State of Victoria, only six barristers out of almost 900 had based their practice outside the centre of the capital city, Melbourne. None worked in the suburbs (Disney, 1986:51). In London, 'nearly all barristers ... have their chambers in a small part of the town—the Temple, Lincoln's Inn, Gray's Inn and the surrounding area' (Atiyah, 1983:30). As a result, they get to know each other well, they lunch together and generally 'develop a camaraderie which is probably unmatched by any other professional group' (Atiyah, 1983:30). Bankowski and Mungham (1976:85) describe the English Bar as 'an insulated professional community'. Podmore and Spencer (1982:355) speak of 'the intensive formal and informal interaction that lies at the heart of professional life'.

Although the profession in the United States of America tends not to be as concentrated geographically, a trend has been observed away from dispersed solo practices towards the large consolidated firm

(Heinz and Laumann, 1982). A limited parallel can therefore be drawn between the legal milieu of parts of London and Sydney and that of the huge American law firms in which over 100 lawyers may now practise together. What have come to be known, facetiously, as the 'law factories', whose principal task is to service business and commerce, now play an important role in setting the priorities of the American legal fraternity (Griswold, 1972:278). Theirs is also the most prestigious sector of the profession, to be contrasted with the poor relations of the legal world: lawyers who service individual clients, 'especially clients from lower socio-economic groups' (Heinz and Laumann, 1982:127). As we will see, the large American law firms generate working communities of lawyers which operate with a shared goal: to facilitate the transactions of the business and financial sector. 'This common experience', according to Heinz and Laumann (1982:43), must inevitably generate 'a community of common fate and purpose'.

A unity of outlook

The legal outlook, in particular what will be claimed is the willing-ness of the legal fraternity to accept and endorse the status quo, is not simply a function of social homogeneity: the fact that at the senior levels of the profession we find like types working closely together in a tightly knit social world. It is also constituted by the type of work lawyers do and the type of clients with whom they deal for much of the time. Though an increasing number of lawyers dedicate themselves to the practice of law for the poor, (as we will see, there have been substantial changes to the profession in recent years) it is probably true to say that the majority of the profession spends most of its time advancing the financial interests of the most wealthy sections of the community. As a consequence, like deals with like: affluent lawyers advise affluent clients about the best ways of aug-menting their economic position. The nature of much legal practice thus tends to reinforce, rather than to challenge, the existing priorities of the profession and to reinforce the legal ethic of free-market individualism.

Margaret Hetherton (1981) presents some startling statistics on Victorian lawyers, showing this to be the case in Australia. The results of her Melbourne survey of barristers and solicitors conducted in 1975 indicated that nearly a third of respondents had dealings with an economically disadvantaged client 'either never or not more than once a year'; another third estimated the extent of their contact with such a person as perhaps once a month. 'The overall picture confirms the impression that the work of practising lawyers for private clients is concentrated on service to middle and high rather than low income groups in the community' (Hetherton, 1981:19).

A similar situation prevails in Britain. According to Atiyah (1983:87), despite the increase in legal aid which has brought larger numbers of disadvantaged people into the legal system, the general picture is still one of the privileged advising the privileged.

The most successful Australian law students, according to Sexton and Maher (1982:10), go on to work in the area of commerce. This is where the money and prestige is to be found. As corporate lawyers, they give advice on such matters as takeovers, share issues, contracts and advertising. This commercial orientation of the profession has been reinforced over the past few decades by the substantial growth of foreign investment in Australia.

A parallel trend has occurred in the United States. As early as 1933, Karl Llewellen said of the metropolitan Bar: 'Most of its best brains, most of its inevitable leaders, have moved ... out of a general practice akin to that of the family doctor, into highly paid specialization in the service of large corporations' (Heinz and Laumann, 1982:18). The expansion of corporate legal work has continued to the point that it now seems to shape the general orientation of much of the profession. In their exhaustive study of Chicago lawyers, Heinz and Laumann (1982:54) found that the bulk of legal work related to corporate matters. Indeed, the profession was observed to display an overall preoccupation with capital, 'with business transactions, transfers of wealth, and the defence of property rights'.

The Chicago study also revealed the remarkable insularity of lawyers from the problems of the poor, a finding which tends to confirm the view of President Jimmy Carter that Americans are 'over-lawyered and under-represented' (Sexton and Maher, 1982:11). Heinz and Laumann (1982:54) discovered that less than half of their sample of Chicago lawyers had anything at all to do with what they termed 'the alleviation of personal plight', and even with these practitioners it constituted a minor part of their work. As explanation, these authors note that 'the personal plight fields' have little prestige among the profession and are largely the province of part-time (and one assumes less career-minded) lawyers.

Smigel's (1969) investigation of lawyers on New York's Wall Street confirms that, as in Australia, it is the legal men of commerce who represent the elite of the profession. The vast commercial law firms of the City—the 'mega-firms'—can afford to take their practitioners from the best law students in the top universities (Cotterrell, 1984:195). They proceed to exercise a good deal of influence, both within the legal profession and in the business community, in their provision of 'prudential and technical assistance to the management of the private sector of the economy' (Grace and Wilkinson, 1978:146). Good commercial lawyers are expected to extend themselves beyond the traditional lawyer's role of legal advisor and become, in effect, corporate men. They must steep themselves in the world of business, develop 'inside knowledge', 'economic experience' and 'organisational know-how' (Cotterrell, 1984:205).

Sexton and Maher (1982:11) suggest that the obvious result of the business orientation of commercial lawyers is a strong identification with the aims and style of commerce to the point that there develops a 'symbiotic relationship between the business and legal worlds'. Commercial and corporate lawyers are apt to perceive the world in terms of the needs and goals of corporations whose sole concern is maximising their dividends. In the legal world of finance, competition, money and profit all loom large.

Dispensing patronage and stifling dissent

Community of outlook is not conditioned merely by commonality of origins. Nor is it just a matter of workers engaging in the same sort of work with the same sort of clients. In addition, it is a nurtured thing. That is to say, there are positive rewards for those who comply with the accepted *modus vivendi* and punishments for those who depart from it. In England, this process of patronage and punishment among the Bar and the Bench has been documented by Maureen Cain.

'The world of the successful barrister', according to Cain (1976:241), 'may be both closed and close. Long hours of work and an esoteric education encourage the former, while the intimate conviviality can be described no other way'. Within this 'legal hothouse', reputations are swiftly made or broken. And it is not skill alone which singles out the young man for promotion. Rather, it is the ability 'to think congruently on technical legal matters'. Thus when compiling the law reports (the summaries of significant judgments which form the common law), the young barrister must be sufficiently *au fait* with legal mores to choose the right cases—that is those entailing the right (the important) barristers and judges.

Those who do not think in the same way, the right way, may well find themselves demeaned in the public forum of the court. Cain (1976:241) gives as an example of judicial wrist-slapping the following comment from the Bench to a young barrister: 'I notice, gentlemen, that you are deeply moved by that beautiful peroration to which you have just listened. I am not surprised. I am also moved, every time I hear it!' By contrast, those who are 'reasonable', who are helpful and cooperative, may receive approbation from the judge for their 'brevity and simplicity' or their 'economy'. To Cain, the individualism of the Bar is necessarily a constrained and limited thing. The junior barrister is allowed to be 'stimulating'—to engage in 'amiable' disagreements with his senior colleagues, but he must do so in the same language and with the same understandings. What he must not do is issue a fundamental challenge to the dominant mode of thinking.

A recent decision of the English Court of Appeal also demonstrates these points about the Bar and the Bench—that they represent a closed shop and that within that shop, what is expected is a common approach and understanding of the job, not dissenting voices. In the 1985 case of *Abse* v. *Smith*, the court was asked to consider whether solicitors should have a right of audience before the court. Sir John Donaldson (1986:354) and his fellow judges decided that they should not and gave the following reasons: 'These high standards of skill and probity [of the Bar] are not capable of being maintained without peer leadership and peer pressures and appropriate disciplinary systems and the difficulty of maintaining them increases with any increase in the size of the group who are permitted to practise advocacy before the courts.'

In Australia, we may also observe a similar system of social control at work among the men of the Bar. In the eastern States, where the profession tends to be divided between solicitors and barristers, it is the Supreme Court which ostensibly acts as the body to discipline barristers and regulate their conduct. In practice, however, this work is left to the Bar associations (private companies or unincorporated associations of barristers) which are able to exercise effective control over their own membership. Such organisations issue clear rulings about the appropriate conduct of a barrister, 'embracing not only the association's specific code but also more elusive unwritten principles of conduct, described by one association as "the spirit and tradition of the Bar"' (Disney et al., 1986:43). Though such rulings operate with statutory force in the State of Victoria, in other places they function effectively without legislative sanction. 'Generally, in the smaller, cohesive communities of barristers, these rules, the interpretive powers and the informal sanctions of group opinion are powerful moderators of professional behaviour' (Disney et al., 1986:44).

The internal pressures for conformity among the Australian legal profession have been remarked upon by other legal writers in the context of debate about whether the two branches of the profession should fuse. This is a proposal which has been staunchly resisted by the profession, which has employed its considerable powers to sanction non-conforming voices. Thus we are told by Forbes (1979) that in 1965, when a solicitor advanced the view that a separate counsel was not required in divorce cases, he was warned by the president of his professional society that 'an experienced practitioner would not make such a statement'. Forbes goes on to conclude that 'there is much self-censorship among lawyers on the subject of fusion', particularly from the Bar which is more closely knit and can therefore apply more 'peer group pressure'.

In the United States, Heinz and Laumann (1982) have described a similar set of social forces for conformity operating among the powerful legal men who advise the corporate and business sector. Here the pressures emanate from still another source, however: they stem from clients of enormous wealth who evince a sophisticated understanding of the legal aspects of their business. Eve Spangler (1986:16), who has conducted more recent investigations into the work of the American corporate lawyer, observes that such clients can often be regarded as patrons in relation to their lawyer. They set the goals and pay the bills. 'The depth of the client's pocketbook', says Spangler (1986:64), is 'a significant factor in structuring the lawyer–client relationship.' This is particularly the case with the recent boom in law graduates, which means that 'lawyers are selling their services in a buyer's market'. It follows that 'they are in no position to challenge or subvert their client's goals'. Any note of dissent is likely to lead to their replacement by a willing competitor for a place in a big firm. In short, the wealthy client (or employer) can call the lawyer's tune; the indigent, by contrast, have no basis from which to question the quality of their counsel and so are obliged to take what they can get, as we will see in Chapter 6.

In the case of the large private law firms which service the corporate world, pressures for salaried lawyers to be cooperative and compliant also issue from the senior partners of the firm. Thus Spangler (1986:39) comments on the 'highly effective series of technical and social controls' developed by the partners which are specifically designed 'to shape the behavior of associates and, ultimately, of individual partners as well'. These entail a guild-like system in which young associates are taken on by more senior lawyers who act as their patrons and mentors. Similarly in the in-house law departments of corporations, another major employer of American lawyers, resort is had to a system of 'mentoring' and 'peer pressure' which produces a compliant and willing legal staff.

In each of the situations described, in each of the three countries under scrutiny, we find powerful reasons for the most successful members of the legal profession to demonstrate compliance rather than individualism. The way to the top is through cooperation, not dissent, and once at the top there are few incentives to speak with a dissonant voice. From this pinnacle of the profession, the dominant, traditional legal model of 'man' and society is even more likely to appear as both natural and functional.

A changing profession?

None of this is to suggest that the legal profession is static. In fact, there are several indicators of change within the legal community which may well contribute to the development of a more critical stance within legal thinking. For one thing, from Australia there is evidence of a broadening of the social base of the profession, though the change is not a dramatic one (Tomasic, 1983). The sheer volume of lawyers is also expanding. In America this has led one writer to comment on 'the recent spectacular growth in the number of lawyers', a trend which is also reflected to different degrees in the other two countries under study (Spangler, 1986:2). Still another change to the profession is the growth of legal aid services—that is, services for the poor—particularly in the 1970s. Recently, however, there have been suggestions that the provision of law for the poor is coming under threat (Spangler, 1986:145). But perhaps the most significant change to the profession in recent decades is the rising number of women entering the law (Disney et al., 1986:174; Menkel-Meadow, 1986).

What has been described as the 'feminisation' of the Bar represents an important change to what has been a remarkably masculine occupation. If we take, for example, the percentage of women graduating from Australian universities from the early 1970s to the early 1980s, we find a dramatic shift. In 1970, women represented 13 per cent of law graduates at the University of Adelaide. In 1981, they were 38 per cent of graduating students. Equivalent figures for the Australian National University are 16 per cent and 39 per cent. Moreover, in 1982, in at least one law school, young women represented over half of the entry-year students (Matthews, 1982:634).

Though statistics such as these are heartening, they give a misleading view of the sex of the profession as a whole. While it is true that women are coming into the law schools in large numbers, they do not sustain this high degree of representation when they go into legal practice, nor do they tend to advance to the higher echelons of the profession. Thus it is still true to say that law is a male-dominated profession, particularly in the more prestigious sectors of the legal community. Accordingly women lawyers still lag behind men in their earnings, in their status and hence in their degree of influence on professional values (Kay, 1988).

In England, Podmore and Spencer (1982) have documented the experience of the woman lawyer. They observe that in 1979 and 1980 there was only one woman out of the 70 lawyers on the governing body of the Law Society. In 1980, out of the 555 partners in fifteen leading London firms, only five were women. In the same year there were only nine women among the 537 'Benchers of Gray's Inn, Lincoln's Inn, and the Inner and Middle Temples', while only thirteen of the 720 Queen's Counsels were female. To Podmore and Spencer (1982:343), such data 'suggest a massive underrepresentation of women in the highest ranks of the barristers' branch of the legal profession'.

In this same study, interviews with English women lawyers revealed that a significant impediment to success was the exclusive nature of 'the men's club' which still characterises the profession. As one woman lawyer expressed the problem:

'The difficulty comes when you try and socialise during working hours, because they all tend to go down to the pub for a drink at lunchtime and they don't really want a woman there because, you know, they go home to their wives in the evening and they get away from them during the day, they don't really want *you* there.' (Podmore and Spencer, 1982:355)

In Australia, Judge Jane Matthews (1982) has also found substantial obstacles confronting women lawyers, in particular the traditional notion that women are 'primarily suited for child-bearing and home-making', not life at the Bar. Writing in 1982, she observed that to date only four women had ever made Queen's Counsel. Furthermore, women tended not to receive general partnerships, another strong indicator that they were not regarded as suitable for promotion to the senior levels.

In America, Cynthia Epstein (1981) has commented similarly on the sex-stereotyping of women lawyers, which has the result that they tend to be channelled into the less remunerative and less prestigious areas of family and government law, as well as public interest and defender work. For those women who manage to climb to the top rungs of the profession, their means of acceptance by their peers, according to Epstein, is to assume the male pattern. What this suggests quite clearly is that the small number of women who have succeeded in the legal world have not been in a strong enough position to introduce a different voice or perspective to legal thinking. Instead, the closed social nature of the Bar, what has been called 'the men's club', has meant that women have had to slot themselves into existing frameworks of legal thought and practice.

Overall, it would seem that recent changes undergone by the profession have not achieved a radical restructuring of the legal fraternity. In particular, the evidence on the experience of women endeavouring to make their way in the profession suggests that the legal world can still be characterised by its social closure rather than its willingness to invite new members and possibly new perspectives.

The implications of the imbalance of power

We have seen that law is dominated by a particular type of person: powerful, conservative men, many of whom are of a commercial bent. It is their social vision, indeed their professional experiences, which we find mirrored in our *Gesellschaft* conception of justice. It is their paradigm which the law reflects. Put differently, there is an obvious congruence between the social world of the men who people the legal community and the view of the social order implicit in *Gesellschaft* law. This is particularly so in the case of lawyers who work in the business and corporate sector which is composed of competitive, profit-minded, entrepreneurs. This commonality of vision, this 'unity of subjectivity', to borrow Peller's (1985:1283) term, may do much to explain the durability of the *Gesellschaft* model of society. Missing from this conception of humanity are the views from below: the views of the powerless—the men and women who depart from the legal ideal of the person, whose relation with the law will form the subject of later chapters.

The imbalance of power we see manifested in our legal system is crucial in at least three respects. In the first place, it skews the perceptions of those who administer the legal view of the world (Harding, 1984:45). The legal model of the individual is congruent with their social vision in that it describes a position of privilege which in many ways parallels their own experience. For those who might offer a competing or different voice, for those for whom the model is not true, their relative position of disadvantage undermines their ability to offer an effective challenge and renders them largely impotent when they themselves must come before the law (as we will see in Chapter 6).

As P.S. Atiyah (1983:18) has remarked about the English Bench, the considerable prestige which attaches to senior judges also does not conduce to 'an attitude of humility'—an attitude which might open a window to a different view on the world. Indeed, because judges do tend to get the final word on any matter (only subject to appeal to a higher court) they may well come to see themselves as 'infallible oracles'. In the legal community, they remain unaccustomed to any form of challenge which might cast doubt upon the fairness and justice of the law. So insulated are they from dissenting views, as

Cain (1976) and Peller (1985) have argued, that their way may well come to be perceived as the only, the natural, the inevitable way. So singular is the thinking, so 'unitary' are the 'ways of legal understanding' that they cease to become a way of thinking (Cain, 1976:238). Theirs is the way which is not a way because it is the dominant, the accepted way.

All parties in the courtroom, it would seem, have a vested interest in pleasing the presiding judge. For he determines the success of their endeavours and is in a 'strategic' position to dispense patronage (Cain, 1976:243). What is more, the high degree of formality which continues to characterise the operation of the courts largely involves obeisance to the Bench, both in language ('If your Honour pleases') and gesture (the required bow to the judge whenever he enters court or rises). Again, judicial authority is reinforced and any skewed perceptions are allowed to stand and to dominate the operation of the law. Indeed, as Cain (1976:241−42) has argued, so strong is the pressure within the courtroom for congruent thinking, that lawyers who fail to comply may well be demeaned, while those who co-operate receive approbation.

The power imbalance inherent in law is important for another reason. It not only ensures the perpetuation of a singular and hence unidimensional image of humanity—that of the *Gesellschaft*—but also positively harms those who must deal with the law but who are not in a position to challenge its interpretation and operation: those who do not fit the legal model of the person. While lawyers and judges may think one way and less privileged men and women as legal users another, it is the former, more powerful group whose viewpoint fits the existing way of doing things. As Jean Grimshaw (1986:99−100) observes:

> Theories, ideas and ideologies are not only ways of 'making sense' of the world. They may also be means by which one group of people may dominate or exercise control over another. And the fact that one group has power over or exploits another, cannot be reduced to anyone's belief that this is so; nor does the fact that someone does not understand their experience in terms of oppression or exploitation necessarily mean that they are not exploited or oppressed.

Women, and less privileged men, the less powerful groups, are poorly placed to ensure that the law is attuned to their world-views. Their 'other knowledge gleaned through other discourses and other metaphors for articulating social life [is] marginalized' (Peller, 1985:1156). The result is that women, for example, do not encounter the law as a neutral force. Instead they often confront a law which casts them in a subordinate domestic role, which is deemed both natural and functional in the patriarchal legal vision. As we will see in subsequent chapters, notwithstanding the history of women's resistance to discriminatory laws, a sexist ideology may still be seen to inform the law and its institutions.

A further implication of the power imbalance in law is that the powerful have less incentive to understand and accommodate the view of the powerless than vice versa and therefore may have a poorer grip on social 'reality'. Indeed the very ideal which judges are expected to pursue—that of impartiality conceived as detachment and neutrality—countenances and sanctions this state of ignorance. It obliges judges to maintain a healthy distance from those they judge, to stay clear of any 'improper' influences. Or as Maureen Cain has argued, for members of the Bar and the Bench to retain their sense of legal purity of thought, their intellectual certainty, it is essential that they not be contaminated by competing views. For this would expose the legal mode as only one of many; it would introduce uncertainty to a law which professes to be certain. For judges to maintain their integrity (their distance from competing styles of thought), for them to be certain of their certainty, they must remain 'necessarily out of touch' (Cain, 1976).

In effect, such judicial homogeneity and detachment is likely to insulate the men of the Bench from the harsh realities of life for those individuals from other classes who come before them and whose actions they must judge. Working-class men, single mothers and unemployed teenage girls are therefore likely to remain a mystery to the judiciary.

The result may be that women, for example, as members of a weaker group, may end up with a better appreciation of the social world, in all its rich diversity. For them, the world is less monolithic, more heterogeneous. Second-phase feminists made this point. They maintained that women, in their position of underdog, are likely to have less distorted perceptions of the way the social world works because they must make it their business to get to know the ways of the powerful. That is to say, they must not only have an appreciation of their own situation (and probably thus an appreciation of the situation of other underdog groups), but they must also acquire a knowledge of the needs, the likes and the dislikes, of the dominant group.

The literature on the characteristics of socially inferior groups supports the notion that the weak make it their business to find out how those who wield authority operate in order to accommodate to their needs and to survive (Harding, 1984). By adapting their behaviour to the expectations of the controlling group, by fitting in with the view of the powerful, rather than offering a challenge which may well have costly consequences, the perceptions of the dominant are allowed to persist. In the following chapters we shall examine the effects of these skewed legal perceptions of humanity on those who are excluded from the legal model of the world: the dispossessed, the powerless.

5

The man of law

The person who forms the subject of the *Gesellschaft* conception of justice has been described as a competitive entrepreneur, a successful market individual who fosters his own interests and has an eye to the main chance. In this chapter, this legal individual is subjected to further scrutiny. The central question now posed is, whose interests are mirrored and served by this human model and who is omitted from the legal view of humankind?

The defining characteristics of the legal person, we observed in the previous chapter, are closely related to the world-view of the socially powerful. Included within the membership of this elite—indeed exemplifying its very character—are the judiciary and the top echelons of the legal profession: they may be viewed as prototypical members of the dominant group. Simply, this group is white, educated, affluent and male. Law's institutions and principles, its general orientation, may all be seen to reflect and reinforce the priorities of those who interpret and administer the law. Law's sense of the social order and the nature of people is, in many ways, their sense of the natural order. The legal person—the natural inhabitant of the legal landscape in the *Gesellschaft* model of law—therefore possesses a set of values and a public role which is remarkably similar to, indeed mirrors and reflects, the moral and social priorities of these most powerful of persons and hence is perceived as unproblematic.

The abstract individual of *Gesellschaft* law therefore is not a prototypical person, as he is alleged to be. Rather, he is an idea of humanity, what will be described below as a Weberian 'ideal type'. He has the social and physical characteristics and the moral qualities considered ideal by those who find themselves reflected in his image. The 'ideal type' of legal person, we will see, possesses at least three essential qualities which match those of the socially powerful. One pertains to sex, a second to class, a third to gender. The legal model of the person, it will be argued, is a man, not a woman. He is a successful middle-class man, not a working-class male. And he is a middle-class man who demonstrates what one writer has termed a

100

form of 'emphasised' middle-class masculinity. In short, he is a man; he is a middle-class man; and he evinces the style of masculinity of the middle classes.

This is not to say that the man of law is simply a creature of the imagination of a few old legal men at 'Patriarch Headquarters', to borrow a term from Franzway and colleagues (1989:29). As the previous chapters have shown, the provenance of the legal model of the individual lies outside the law, in liberal political philosophy, and is part of a larger social vision of what constitutes the good life in the free-market society. This vision may in turn be viewed as the product of a complex interaction between groups and structures, rather than the work of certain instrumental key figures conspiring together for their own selfish purposes. In other words, the liberal vision of society which underpins much of our law may be traced to the concerns and interests of the rising middle-class men of the *Gesellschaft*—whose lives were envisioned by Hobbes—as well as to a set of more impersonal social and economic forces which stimulated the rise of free-market society (McPherson, 1962).

From this it follows that this book is not a search for individual villains within the legal establishment. It is not a witch, or rather a wizard, hunt. Though the characteristics of the legal person may well mesh with the beliefs and the values of a small number of key men who are most influential in the law, those for whom the social and economic status quo in fact works well—which may do much to explain its durability, as the last chapter sought to argue—the legal person is not their brainchild.

Nor should the present argument be taken to mean that the legal person, here described, is always and necessarily the central organising character of all of the law and all of its practices. For he is by no means translated into law in a perfect fashion. As we have already seen, countervailing *Gemeinschaft* tendencies are to be found throughout the law. The cool-headed, entrepreneurial rational agent of the *Gesellschaft* is sometimes given second place to a more socially connected being whose actions may be attributed to his place in the social world. (For example, we observed the operation of *Gemeinschaft* principles in the juvenile sphere of criminal justice where the courts take into account the social and economic circumstances of young offenders.)

This book thus endorses the point of the third-phase feminists: that while law professes to be internally coherent and certain, to organise around clear and rational principles (such as the need for us all to be treated as free, autonomous and rational beings), it is in fact shot through with contradictions (so that sometimes it perceives us as determined and dependent, as not fully in charge of our actions).

Though law projects an image of consistency and uniformity of intention, it in fact operates by fits and starts and may often be seen to display a multiplicity of purposes rather than a single overarching goal.

The following discussion of the legal person therefore addresses a dominant motif in the law and legal thinking which we have seen to be constituted by a variety of principles and practices. It is not the only organising concept; nor does it permeate all areas of the law—as feminist writers from both the first and third phases have ably demonstrated. In fact the legal history of women's rights considered in this book is largely a story of progress, so that today, within the law, there are positive benefits to be had for women. The man of law does not always take centre stage. And yet, as Smart (1984) has stressed, and as we will see below, the law still plays an important role in reproducing the existing patriarchal order. More specifically, law's characterisation of the person often serves to render women (and many men) marginal in the eyes of the law.

As a man

To identify the sex of our legal person, it is useful to return to basics and examine more closely the assumptions about men and women and their proper place in the social order implicit in the original theorists of the social contract. Much of this work has already been done by the American political scientist Susan Moller Okin (1979) in her volume *Women in Western Political Thought*. There she scrutinises the writings of Hobbes and Locke for their views of the sexes and concludes that the sort of person they had in mind all along in developing their notions of citizenship, of civic personhood, is not an abstract, ungendered individual, as has usually been contended, but a man acting on behalf of a family. We have already considered Okin's analysis of Rawls which highlighted the implicit sexism of his thinking. If we now examine her account of the writings of Hobbes and Locke, we see how she arrives at a similar conclusion about the most prominent theorists of the social contract.

Hobbes grounded his entire theory of politics on the notion that we are all equal, and he explicitly included women in this view. At the same time, however, he sought to justify the actual inequality of the sexes, in particular the rule of families by the fathers, by maintaining that men were the founders of nations and therefore should assume a dominant position. As Okin (1979:198) points out, 'There is clearly something lacking in Hobbes's reasoning, here, for his explanation does not answer the problematical question of how just half of a race of people, all of whom are equal in what is for Hobbes the most important sense, could come to be in a position to found a commonwealth in which they had dominion over all the members of the other half'. Having accepted, without further justification or explanation, that the family is a patriarchal institution, Hobbes simply proceeds with his theorising on the equal rights of all.

From this point on, alleges Okin, the patriarchal family becomes Hobbes' 'primary social and political unit'. Thus Hobbes' solution to the fundamental contradiction posed by the assertion of the equality of all individuals and the social reality of the male-dominated family is simply to substitute the male-headed family for the individual in his ensuing political analysis. In this way he justifies the actual exclusion of women from political activity and their real subjection within families. 'But this solution is paradoxical,' observes Okin (1979:199), 'since the tradition of which Hobbes is the founder is supposedly defined by its founding of politics on the characteristics and rights of individual, atomistic, human beings, and its renunciation of natural hierarchies or groups as the fundamental entities with which politics has to deal.'

Locke finds himself in a similar dilemma, according to Okin. When putting his case for the freedom of individuals from interference from the state, he wishes to treat the sexes as equals. Ultimately, however, he reneges on his commitment to the equal rights of women by maintaining that there is indeed 'a Foundation in Nature' for the subordination of wives by husbands. When husband and wife are in conflict, 'the Rule . . . naturally falls to the Man's share, as the abler and the stronger' (quoted in Okin, 1979:200). Again the husband-father is invoked as the holder of rights: he decides the fate of the family and represents it in the public sphere. As with Hobbes, the fundamental subject of political analysis becomes the man at the head of a family in which women are clearly inferiors.

Another feminist who has commented on the sexist paradox inherent in the story of the social contract is the political theorist Carole Pateman (1988). She too observes that, at one and the same time, the foundation theorists of the social contract sought to secure the equal rights and freedoms of all while implicitly assigning a subordinate status to women. Pateman explains this paradox in terms of a prior, hidden contract which underpins the official social contract though it is not acknowledged. This is the 'sexual contract', a contract not of freedom but of subordination, a contract between men and women. In this earlier sexual contract, or what we see daily in its modern form, the marriage contract, a man gains legal access to a woman who will bear him children.

According to Pateman (1988:111), the classic theorists of the social contract assumed that male dominance achieved through marriage was part of the natural condition. 'Marriage, or the orderly exchange of women, which gives equal sexual access to all men, is the original exchange that constitutes culture or civilisation.' Axiomatic to the theorists of the social contract was that men should enjoy 'the natural "superiority of their sex"' and when women married it was considered only natural that they thereby agreed to subjection to their husbands. With the formation of the social contract, this natural state of male dominance was simply carried over through the marriage contract. That is to say, both before and after the social contract, it was assumed that men would exercise sexual rights over an obedient woman.

Why this sexual contract of subordination has of necessity remained hidden in the official story of the social contract is that it indicts the traditional view that the social contract confers freedom on all and that women too are a party to that contract. For the real effect of the sexual contract, to Pateman, is to make women the sexual property of their husbands. The sexual contract confers on men what are euphemistically referred to as 'conjugal rights' which, though they may not be an explicit part of the story of the social contract, were nevertheless considered natural and necessary by the theorists of the notional first contract and were also (as we shall see) sanctioned by the laws of the day. The fetters imposed on women upon marriage were therefore both built into and sanctioned by the story of the social contract which was nevertheless presented as a story of human freedom, not of slavery.

To writers such as Okin and Pateman, the function of women in the *Gesellschaft* vision of society would appear to be the enablement of the legal subject, who is implicitly assumed to be a man. Woman's task is to enable the legal man: she makes it possible for him to spring forth into the public sphere, fully nurtured, full-grown, emotionally nourished, and unencumbered by children, but with the means (that is, herself) to reproduce and care for them. Woman's role in the story of the social contract is to make of men the free and equal beings envisaged by the *Gesellschaft*: the rugged and able-bodied individualists who will pursue their interests by making contracts with similar beings. Woman's place, by contrast, is in the home, as care-giver, as child-bearer and -rearer, as repository of emotions—the haven in a heartless world, the guardians of the *Gemeinschaft* values. Women's place is to sustain the paradox of the *Gesellschaft*. They nurture the human side of the abstract man, care for his children and make him fit to go out into the hostile, public world where he must then maintain the appearance of a free, independent and self-sufficient agent of his own (and his family's) interests. He must be the free, mobile, healthy worker and political being. She stays behind the scenes, maintaining the health and independence of the male worker.

This 'systematic divorce of the private from the public realms of social life', as Robert Wolff (1976:135) has described it, this 'steady draining away from the public realm of the human dimensions of the human condition' is a highly functional arrangement from the point of view of industry. It may also help to account for the success and tenacity of the *Gesellschaft* vision. As Wolff explains: 'This depersonalization of the world of work and public life has its roots in the rational imperatives of industrialization. Industrial production and management require the standardization of labor as well as the standardization of products. [Thus] the demands of the market invade the natural rhythms of human existence.'

The reality of the inequality of the sexes, both denied and yet justified by Hobbes and Locke, was reflected and countenanced by the law of the day. Indeed until well into the nineteenth century, married women were not regarded as persons in law with civil rights, and as we will see shortly, even today women are not invested in all respects with complete civil standing. In a quite literal sense, for legal purposes, the public person was (and remains) a man.

William Blackstone (1978:442), writing in the eighteenth century, was pithily eloquent on the legal position of the wife.

> By marriage, the husband and wife are one person in law: that is, the very being or legal existence of the woman is suspended during the marriage, or at least is incorporated and consolidated into that of the husband: under whose wing, protection, and *cover*, she performs every thing; and is therefore ... said to be *covert-baron*, or under the protection and influence of her husband, her baron, or lord; and her condition during her marriage is called *coverture*.

In this statement we are told just who the law took to be the legal person: it was the husband-protector who subsumed his wife's being into his own for the purposes of the law. Through the doctrine of 'coverture' he was said to cover her existence and she, in effect, disappeared. Her role was to be an invisible one, within the family. She was domestic and care-giver, not free person. The autonomy of the individual, so central to the *Gesellschaft* vision of society, was explicitly reserved for the male.

There were several important consequences of the doctrine for married women. For one thing, they were unable to possess property. Upon marriage, their land passed into the possession of the husband and they could deal with it only with his consent. Also under the doctrine, a married woman was prevented from seeking redress for any legal grievance without the concurrence of her husband (O'Donovan, 1982:347). By contrast, the benefits of coverture to the husband could be considerable in that he personally was entitled to the full income from his wife's land and received the whole of her personal property, including her earnings, as an absolute gift (Mac-Kinolty, 1979:68−69). Virtually all that women retained in their own right was their jewellery and their beds.

In Blackstone's (1978:445) account of the effects of marriage on women, he attributed to law the most honourable of motives in its failure to recognise the wife's legal personality. His view was that 'even the disabilities, which the wife lies under, are for the most part intended for her protection and benefit. So great a favourite is the female sex of the laws of England.' To feminist legal critics, however, what the law was in truth preserving was not so much female sensibilities as a traditional, domestic role for women. In other words, the law was keeping women in their place: in the family and out of the male domain of the public sphere—of the *Gesellschaft* (Sachs and Wilson, 1978; Smart, 1984).

Other legal theorists have been more candid about their belief in female inferiority as the basis for women's legal subjection. They have made it plain that the reason why the wife's personhood was absorbed into that of her husband was simply because she was not his equal. According to Bracton, 'Women differ from men in many respects, for their position is inferior to that of men'. Glanvill insisted also on 'the wife's subjection to the husband'. As Katherine O'Donovan (1985:31) explains, 'The couple were, in the eyes of the law, united in the person of the male'.

The passage of the Married Women's Property Acts in England from 1870 to 1882 (in New South Wales, Australia, in 1879) removed many of the legal disabilities of wives resulting from the principle of coverture. And yet well into the twentieth century, the English judiciary were committed to the remarkable view that women were not 'persons'. We know this from a series of judicial decisions which specifically considered the meaning of this term. The 'persons' cases were employed in Chapter 2 to demonstrate the inconsistency of the Bench. These cases also represent a famous part of the history of women's struggle for legal rights, for they were the direct result of the considerable efforts of various women to enter the public sphere in the capacity of doctors and lawyers and voters. Finding themselves denied entry to the public sphere, these women went to the courts for legal redress. There they received little joy.

Under English law, there was a clear statement to the effect that 'persons' who possessed the necessary qualifications were entitled to enter the professions, to have access to public office and to vote. The courts were therefore called on to decide whether appropriately qualified women were to be regarded as persons under English law, with all the rights and privileges attracted by this term. Repeatedly the English Bench declared that they were not and therefore could not exercise these fundamental rights of citizens (Sachs and Wilson, 1978).

In their history of women's legal battle to enter the public arena, Sachs and Wilson (1978:10) explain the type of judicial thinking which supported this view of women as non-persons. Members of the judiciary, they observe, were convinced that women lacked the essential human qualities necessary for public life. These were a 'loftiness of mind, a capacity for reverence, and the ability to indulge in abstract thought'. While men were thought to be well endowed in each of these respects, women were considered incapable of impartiality, of working from abstract principles. Women's place, in the legal view, was the domestic sphere where law's dispassionate intellectual style was not only unnecessary but could even be dysfunctional.

In the manner of Blackstone, however, the holders of judicial office tended to couch their opposition to women's rights in terms which sought to flatter women while keeping them firmly in their place. In declining to grant women public privileges, judges usually referred to women's natural delicacy and decorum which suited their essentially domestic function as wives and mothers. In truth, argue Sachs and Wilson (1978:11), the motives of the men of law were less honourable: 'upper-middle-class men shared an interest in keeping women as head servants at home and keeping them out of the ranks of competitors at work. In other words, men had and still have a material stake in resisting the emancipation of women.' Sachs and Wilson depict the problem for women in terms of a male monopoly, with the men of law striving to keep women out of public positions, and women striving to break in.

To illustrate their theory of the male monopoly, Sachs and Wilson note the vehemence with which the English legal profession opposed the admission of women to the Bar, a position they successfully maintained until the end of the First World War. They also remind us that it was Parliament, not the judiciary, which, in 1918, enfranchised English women and in 1919 finally 'removed all disabilities on women from holding public office' and that it was not until 1929 that the Privy Council (the highest court in England) finally admitted that women were 'persons' in the eyes of the law (Sachs and Wilson, 1978:38, 40). 'What emerges from a perusal of the male monopoly cases', conclude Sachs and Wilson (1978:50), 'is that the judges serenely ignored not only the natural meaning of the word "person" but also factual and historical evidence which demonstrated that the legal status of women was one of subordination rather than elevation.'

Though Sachs and Wilson adduce ample evidence of legal men acting in an apparently self-serving and anti-female fashion, it is too simple to construe the problem for women as essentially a male conspiracy to reduce competition in the public sphere. Other feminists suggest that the story was, and remains, more complex than this (Smart, 1984). Such legal endeavours to exclude women from public life, they suggest, should not be conceived as a simple plot to keep women out of public positions. Rather, they are more appropriately interpreted as an effort to constitute a particular domestic and nurturing role for women in the private sphere which was regarded as both natural and desirable. In other words, they can be understood as a means of reproducing what Smart (1984:21–22) calls 'the existing patriarchal order'.

In this order, women's assigned task was (and still is) to hold together the 'private', more human, *Gemeinschaft* side of life which was thought to be extraneous to public and hence male decision-making. This legal interpretation of women's place was by no means eccentric. It reflected and reiterated the prevailing belief about the appropriate roles of men and women. In this view, it was deemed only right and proper, as natural, that the family should have the father at its head, as family representative in the public domain, and the mother as its heart. Katherine O'Donovan (1985:11–12) describes the respective roles assigned by law (and society) to the sexes in the following terms:

> Men who pass freely between public and private, but who are primarily located in the public, are socially expected to act as rational, calculating economic individuals, whose actions are guided by self-interest. Women, who are seen primarily in the context of reproduction, home and family are expected to retain the values of *Gemeinschaft*. The private, regarded in legal ideology as unsuitable for legal regulation, is ordered according to an ideology of love.

As feminists such as Smart and O'Donovan have also pointed out, the legal ideology of the sanctity of the domestic sphere (and the natural place of women within it) was more idea than fact. While the theory was that law did not enforce duties and responsibilities within the family, the reality was that the law did intervene, that it made quite positive and specific endeavours to define and enforce a subordinate, domestic role for women within the home. Indeed considerable legal efforts were made to ensure that the legal person of the public place was to be thought of as a man and that there was quite another place and role for women.

One of the clearest demonstrations of the positive legal construction of a role for women as domestic and care-giver—one which gave rise to a legally enforceable male right—is the law of consortium. Right up to the 1980s in England and in the Australian State of New South Wales, a husband whose wife was injured negligently by a third party could sue for loss of consortium (Pateman, 1988:127). This was defined in law as 'housework and childcare' as well as the wife's 'love, affection, companionship, society and sexual services' (Weitzman, 1981:60).

The ongoing right of husbands in most jurisdictions to enforce their conjugal rights to their wives' sexual services demonstrates the continuity of this legal idea of women's domestic place. In law, women are still constituted the subordinates of their husbands who may require of them the traditional female functions of love (sex) and domestic duties. This is deemed to be the enforceable male right and the concomitant female responsibility (Pateman, 1988:124).

Further evidence that law actively assigns a domestic role to women is supplied by protective legislation which seeks to control the activities of women in the public sphere, supposedly for their own health and safety. An example of this type of law is the English Mines Act which states that women cannot work underground as coalminers. As Katherine O'Donovan has observed, if we trace the history of this type of legislation we see that the specific concerns of the state were with the procreative powers of women. Women should not work in hazardous places, where a man might, because it was more important that they be healthy mothers than free workers. 'Protective legislation', maintains O'Donovan (1985:165), is 'imbued with beliefs about the primacy of women's domestic role'.

It will be the task of a later chapter to examine more carefully the practical implications for women of law's quite particular construction of their role as domestics and nurturers: as guardians of the *Gemeinschaft*. There we will consider the type of justice received by women at the hands of a law which defines them in terms other than that of the legal person. For the moment, it is sufficient to note law's assignment to women of a role which is not that of the free, public legal subject—a position reserved for men. In our *Gesellschaft* law, the man is deemed to be the natural inhabitant of the public sphere; the woman is accorded a more constraining domestic role. For another contemporary illustration of this point—that the legal person still has a sex and that he is male—we turn to the United States and consider the evolution of the law governing eligibility for jury service.

Over the course of a series of decisions in the 1930s and the 1940s, the American Supreme Court made it clear that when a State assembly 'used the word "person" in connection with those ... liable to jury service, no one contemplated the possibility of women becoming so [liable]' (quoted in Sachs and Wilson, 1978:123). In 1966, a Federal District Court maintained, however, that 'jury service on the part of the citizens of the United States is considered under our law in this country as one of the basic rights and obligations of citizenship' (quoted in Okin, 1979:261). And yet it was not until 1973 that women were granted the right to sit on juries in every American State and even then provision was made for their voluntary exemption.

The reasons given for the exclusion of women from juries, right up to the late 1960s, were the usual ones. Courts referred to 'women's special delicacy and domestic functions' (Okin, 1979:262). As recently as 1966, the Mississippi Supreme Court held that 'the legislature has the right to exclude women so they may continue their service as mothers, wives and homemakers, and also to protect them (in some ways they are still upon a pedestal) from the filth, obscenity, and noxious atmosphere that so often pervades a courtroom during a jury trial' (quoted in Okin, 1979:262). The clear implication of the American jury decisions is that judges have perceived the citizen to be a man, not a woman. Grand statements about the inviolable rights of Americans as public persons to judge their peers have not included women in their sweep.

A different type of evidence of the sex of the legal person can be derived from closer scrutiny of the qualities ascribed to this individual in a previous chapter. There he was described as a free, mobile, detached, atomistic individual who negotiates with others in the public realm for reasons of personal advantage. This style of existence most closely approximates that of the male worker who is not directly responsible for young children: the man who moves freely between the public and private spheres. It least resembles the experience of many women who are wives and mothers, who engage in paid public work only to the extent that their domestic duties allow, and who assume full responsibility for the daily care and nurture of children.

In other words, the characteristics of the legal person seem to connect with the experience of many men, but far fewer women. This, of course, is no legal or historical accident. Instead it is, in large part, a function of the way in which law has helped to reproduce the dominant social order by assigning to men a public role in which they are expected to be free, detached and mobile and by assigning to women a private role in which they are supposed to take care of the family.

From this reading of the story of the original social contract and of recent historical developments in the legal concept of personhood, it is clear that the omission of the experience of women from our *Gesellschaft* type of justice is neither an innocent oversight nor a conscious male conspiracy against women. Rather, it would seem to be a function of a positive and genuine commitment on the part of law and its agents to a traditional view of the sexes. In the *Gesellschaft* vision, there is a clear sexual division of labour in which it is thought only natural that men are the holders of public office and women are responsible for the family. And as we have also seen, this legal attitude to the sexes and their complementary roles is not comprised simply of empty rhetoric. Repeatedly, the law has put its theories into practice by upholding, indeed sanctifying, the public status of men while relegating women to the home. When the (male) inter-preters of our law have thought of the legal subject, they have thought of men, not women, whom they have consigned to what they have perceived to be a lesser but nevertheless vital role in the private sphere—as helpmate to the man of law, as guarantor of his public freedom.

As a middle-class man of the market

While the connection between law and sex has tended to assume a blatant form (such as the express denial of public rights to women and the negation of their personhood), considerable efforts have been made by those who defend the Rule of Law to persuade us of its essential class-neutrality. As we have seen, the way that it does this is through the invocation of the universal legal subject: the notion that the law does not deal in categories of person but serves the needs of anyone, anywhere, whatever their social status. The argument of this volume is that there is a clear relation between law and class and that the legal ideal of neutrality itself displays a class bias—in favour of the status quo—in that it sanctions wilful blindness to existing differ-ences (that is, inequalities) between people.

The class character of law may be seen to take a number of forms. Perhaps its most obvious manifestation of a class preference is its preoccupation with the rights of property-owners. Blackstone (1978:138), for example, gave primacy to the private possession of property. He saw it as an absolute right, 'inherent in every English-man': it consisted 'in the free use, enjoyment, and disposal of all ... acquisitions, without any control or diminution, save only by the laws of the land'. Thus the social contract depicted by Blackstone was 'a contract of the propertied' (Coltheart, 1986:114). Blackstone's owner of natural rights was therefore not only thought to be a man, but a man of a certain status. The 'sacred and inviolable rights of private property' were quite obviously only inviolable when prop-erty had actually been acquired. Though Blackstone (1978:140) declared that such rights 'appertain to every Englishman', they were in fact meaningless to the unpropertied. Blackstone himself seems to concede this when he speaks of the need of 'every man of rank or property' to know and consider his natural rights.

It is the strong identification of law with the rights of the propertied which has led some writers to posit a direct relation between law and class. In the previous chapter we found that lawyers are themselves fairly uniformly drawn from the middle to upper-middle classes and this is the sort of person with whom they prefer to, and generally tend to, deal. The most prestigious and profitable legal work is done for clients with substantial commercial interests and is concerned with the maintenance and improvement of those interests. And as we saw, a surprisingly large proportion of the profession has either little or no contact with the poor.

'In England', according to Cotterrell (1984:201), 'the primary identification of lawyers seems to be with property interests in general.' He also makes the interesting point that as conveyancing (the transfer of land) represents a substantial part of solicitors' work, there is a 'traditional identification of the profession with individual property owners' interests'. In Australia, Sexton and Maher (1982:11) have commented on the closeness of the relationship between the business and the legal communities. In America, the main identification of lawyers has also been observed to be with business interests (Cotterrell, 1984:201). The common factor in the bulk of legal dealings in all three countries is thus the class character of the client. That person is a propertied individual. In the words of the German sociologist Max Weber (1954:318), the legal profession is 'a group which is active in the service of the propertied, and particularly capitalistic, private interests and which has to gain its livelihood from them'.

The sheer expense of litigation supplies further evidence that law mainly addresses the concerns of the haves, not the have-nots. The adversary process is slow and costly. Its time-consuming and intricate nature demands that participants must be able to marshal substantial material resources to go into battle. 'For such reasons', observes O'Malley (1983:123), 'the association between the competitive free-enterprise model of justice and the interests of the propertied and especially capitalist classes [was] clear to classical sociologists.'

In this relatively uncomplicated interpretation of legal bias, law is depicted as a specific instrument of the capitalist classes in that it specifically represents their interests in property. It guarantees their right to monopolise the means of making money, the means of production, by ensuring the security of their transactions and their property. It secures their freedom to make profit and then to enjoy that profit, free from interference—no questions asked about the uses to which it is put or the equity of the social arrangements which produced it (Cotterrell, 1984:114).

Other writers posit a more subtle and complicated relation between law and class, perceiving it as a complex amalgam of the form law assumes, the way it conceives the legal subject and the way that it presents and justifies itself as essentially a fair institution. The current analysis draws from this tradition of critical legal analysis and more particularly from the work of the Soviet jurist Evgeny Pashukanis (1978), and his assessment of the relation between capital and the form of law.

For Pashukanis, the class character of law is fundamental. It resides in the very form of our law which, as we have seen, is individualistic and rights-based. That is, it treats us all as separate, individual, and interchangeable holders of rights and duties who are all equal before the law. Why we are considered to be equal in the eyes of the law is that we are all assumed to be the owners of commodities. Blackstone, as we saw, was entirely frank about this. Our individual freedom which is protected by law is primarily our freedom to truck and barter these commodities in the marketplace. Pashukanis calls this the commodity form of our law. 'Thus legal relations are fundamentally the relations of commodity owners in the market' (Cotterrell, 1984:124). Or as another writer puts it, 'the individual legal subject is essentially the bearer of commodities, the owner of economic assets producing a revenue' (Picciotto, 1979:172).

In reality, however, we are not similarly situated individuals in terms of the market. Again, Blackstone was quite candid about this when he spoke of the law's concern with the rights of men of a certain rank. We are not equal owners of commodities and so the idea of equality before the law contained in the commodity form is only an ideal, not a reality. Its important purpose, according to Pashukanis, is to obscure the fundamental structures of inequality which support it (Cotterrell, 1984:124).

Because there is an uneven distribution of property in society, the real effect of the legal ideals of freedom and equality implicit in the commodity form is to preserve the existing rights of people who do own property to quiet possession of that property, and to engage in profitable transactions, while conferring a quite meaningless right to negotiate in the market and to freedom from interference with their property on those who have little with which to interfere. According to this reading of law, our legal subject is not a universal man, as he is alleged to be, but a commercial man of the marketplace. He is a man of property, a commodity-owner, who uses his financial ingenuity to further his material interests and, in so doing, receives the law's full support and imprimatur.

As a masculine man

The masculinity of law forms the focus of much of the feminist writing in the discipline. The second phase of feminist writers, in particular, spoke of the maleness of the entire legal approach to the world. They associated a number of the characteristics of law with masculinity. Law's competitive adversarial style was thought to exemplify a male way of doing things. Its aggressive, competitive form was said to be masculine, not feminine. They believed that law's preoccupation with individual rights reflected a male tendency to pursue one's own interests at the expense of others. According to the second-phase feminists, law's division of the social world into isolated, mutually disinterested atoms coming together solely to press their own advantage, reflected the male and not the female experience of the world. It mirrored the life of the adult, male, worker in the public sphere, where interactions were for profit, not for love or pleasure. It failed to address the conditions of women's lives, particularly those women responsible for dependent children, whose existence was both constrained and enriched by family demands.

Law's presentation of itself as objective, fair and rational, argued the second-phase feminists, was a sham. It represented a male defence of an unfair and an unfeeling law which failed to consider and reflect the situation of this other (supposedly female) sphere of existence. It invoked principles deemed important by men, but which law, in truth, failed to exemplify. Law might be said to be objective and dispassionate. In reality its self-proclaimed objectivity was a political device for obscuring the partial perspective of law: it represented the male, not the female, view of the world.

Feminists have also taken issue with the concept of objectivity itself, as we saw in Chapter 2. There is no such thing, they say, as a perfectly neutral position, a distanced, dispassionate stance, from which it is possible to witness the single truth of any matter. Instead, there are many understandings of the world which are informed by the particular location of the observer in time and place and culture. Indeed participation in life, not distance, is thought to be a better way of arriving at a meaningful understanding of life's rich complexity (Gregg, 1986).

A problem with the second-phase feminist depiction of law is that it treats men and the male culture as a job lot. Men, as a sex, are seen to be law's beneficiaries. Men and the law are one and women, and their perceptions of the world, are excluded, deemed irrelevant. Men are invariably the legal oppressor, women the legal victim. Mac-Kinnon, in particular, stresses the victimisation of women as a group by a legal system which is of men and for men, which conducts its business in a male way for the edification of men, not women.

The Australian sociologist R.W. Connell (1987:61) has commented recently on the limitations of this style of feminist thinking. It makes of men, he says, the 'omnipresent enemy'. It treats them as an 'internally undifferentiated general category' when in truth men, as well as women, come in many cultural forms. Feminists, such as MacKinnon, who object to the treatment of women as a homogeneous group—who object to women's objectification— may be repeating the errors of the sexists whom they criticise by themselves treating men in just this way. According to Connell (1987:63), we must recognise that there are 'multiple masculinities'. We need therefore to disaggregate the concept of 'the male' as a powerful being, to break it down into its component parts, and consider more carefully the specific types of male and masculinity to which we object.

In line with Connell, the argument to be advanced here is that it is misleading and unhelpful to regard men as a homogeneous sex which stands always to benefit from law, never to lose. Notwithstanding the limitations of their analysis, the early feminist critics of law, especially Sachs and Wilson, were sensitive to the fact that it was a particular type of male, not all men, who wielded legal power. They referred to the white, middle-class men of the law. The feminists of the third phase, notably Smart, were also aware that law did not benefit one group in a consistent and uniform fashion. This view, however, was developed to the point that a general theory of law was abandoned as inappropriate. In the present volume, the case to be argued is that one can discern in law a certain male style but that it does not represent the style of all men or even of the majority. Law, it will be argued, embodies a middle-class style of masculinity. The man of law is a middle-class man whose masculinity assumes a middle-class form. He is therefore at some remove from his earthier, working-class brother who, as a consequence, may well find the law an alien institution (as we shall see in the next chapter).

The man of law is an interesting blend of characteristics, all of which, however, cast him in the mould of our society's view of the superior male. On the one hand there is the Hobbesian component. This aspect of the individual is 'acquisitive, competitive, tough, active and individualistic' (Coltheart, 1986:116). In this respect he is a hard-driving individualist: thick-skinned and assertive, a man with a purpose, an agent not a victim. It is this concept of human nature advanced by Thomas Hobbes in the seventeenth century, and endorsed by John Locke, which according to Coltheart (1986:113) 'remains the model of the liberal citizen'. And it is this liberal model of the public person which has been directly imported into law by theorists such as Blackstone and Rawls.

The man of the social contract, the man of the marketplace, is nobody's fool. He is aware that the public sphere is a battleground and that only the best man will win. The man of law competes, pushes his own suit and succeeds. He flourishes in a legal system which is essentially adversarial, in which there are winners and losers, which is based on conflict. In this mould, our man of law might be seen as the archetypal tough-minded businessman—the entrepreneur: a John Elliot, a Rupert Murdoch.

But there is also another side to the man of law which complements his rugged image of masculinity and demonstrates his cultural superiority. This is the man of reason: the prudent maker of contracts, advancing his own interests, with rational calculation. His is a highbrow, cultivated form of masculinity which depends on an ability to think and act intelligently, not with brute force. And his is a middle-class intellectual conception of masculinity in the sense that middle-class, male intellectuals have tended to find these qualities in themselves. It calls to mind a comment of Sachs and Wilson (1978:10) on the judicial view of the male sex: 'If anything, the judges attributed to men a superior spirituality rather than a greater physical prowess, as reflected in loftiness of mind, a capacity for reverence, and the ability to indulge in abstract thought.' It also reminds us of the style of thinking cultivated in our law schools and valued in the courts. This is the intellectual, rational mode of debate in which legal problems are conceived of in the abstract as fine, almost algebraic equations. An ability to reason dispassionately and articulately is deemed essential in legal man.

The qualities of the man of law closely resemble the attributes identified by Frances Olsen (1984a) as those which have been considered most desirable in western liberal thought. This intellectual tradition, she declares, has consistently exalted a particular type of individual as the human ideal and then associated men, not women, with these ideal characteristics. According to this liberal view, the preferred person is active and powerful (such characteristics describe the Hobbesian man) but he is also rational, cultivated and objective, an abstract thinker (exemplified by the lawyer or jurist). Women, by constrast, have been deemed to possess all the antithetical qualities and therefore have been thought incapable of exercising fundamental public rights. The early legal writers—Blackstone, Glanvill and Bracton—all regarded women as unsuited to the rigours of citizenship, and therefore ideally suited to the less demanding but nevertheless critical domestic role of wife and mother. This is a legal view which has held well into the nineteenth century, as we saw in the jury decisions.

Feminist writers, from several disciplines, have confirmed this male analysis of human nature. In philosophy, Carol Gould (1983) and Genevieve Lloyd (1983) have noted that human nature has been described in terms of a certain abstract form of intellectual rationality generally thought to be the exclusive possession of men. In psychology, Carol Gilligan (1982) has identified the operation of similar sexist assumptions. Moral maturity, she observes, has been interpreted as an ability to reason in a conceptual fashion, a state of human advancement said to be achieved by a few superior men, but hardly any women.

What is interesting about this view of the ideal person is its consistency across intellectual disciplines. Philosophy, psychology, sociology and political theory have all been found by feminists to assume as their intellectual starting point an ideal type of male who is juxtaposed with a less ideal individual who is assigned an antithetical set of qualities which are associated with females (Olsen, 1984a:1). 'From antiquity to the present day', according to Harding (1983:44), 'women have been claimed less capable of abstract and systematic thought than men, less capable of developing a mature sense of justice than men, more ruled by the emotions, the passions, and the appetites than men, and more inclined toward subjective assessment and less toward objective ones than men.'

Women consistently fare badly in this sexist conception of humanity. Women's thinking is said to be too emotional, too confined to the particular, and should therefore be confined to the private sphere — not the public, legal world which requires a more expansive, more conceptual, more male type of intellect. In Freud's (1977:342) now famous words on women: 'Their superego is never so inexorable, so impersonal, so independent of its emotional origins as we require it to be in men. [Women] ... show less sense of justice than men ... they are less ready to submit to the greater exigencies of life ... they are more easily influenced in their judgements by feelings of affection or hostility.' Or in the words of another writer on the subject of women's nature:

> What moves men to action are emotions which have been transformed by the requirements of reason into channels of efficiency and consistency; feminine emotions, devoid of reason, are everywhere infected by excess and particularity, hence the lack of proper regard for what is due to impersonal and unknown others; the lack of a sense of justice, which has — notoriously — been supposed to be characteristic of women. (Poole, 1985:22)

The model of rational masculinity with which women are being contrasted in these accounts is an elevated one. Women are being distinguished from men not in terms of their physical inferiority but because of a lack of mental refinement. Indeed, if anything, women are deemed inferior because of their closeness to nature, and men are superior because of their high degree of cultivation. The dominant idea is that the more rational, the more abstract, the more removed from particular and physical circumstances, the more advanced and the more masculine. 'The traditional view, in short, is that women are more closely associated with nature and men with culture; women with the body and men with the mind'. (Jaggar, 1983a:46).

Women menstruate, lactate, and give birth: all rather earthy, but nevertheless creative, functions. Again, this makes women ideally suited to their assigned tasks of child-rearer, general domestic and loving wife in the private sphere. 'Men', by contrast, 'are thought to express their creativity through the creation of "culture"' (Jaggar, 1983b:23). It is therefore only right that they should assume the role of family head and representative in the public sphere, which, with their superior mental skills, they are able to do with little difficulty. Such tasks might be beyond the ken of a woman, whose very nature confines her to the limited and more particular tasks of the home. But they draw on the essential qualities of a man: his capacity for larger thoughts which extend beyond the confines of the domestic sphere.

It is not only women, however, who fare badly in this view of humanity. Jaggar (1983a:46) has noted that 'it is easy to see how men, *at least men of a certain class*, would be likely to place supreme value on "mental" activity and to ignore the fact that such activity would be impossible without the daily physical labor of women' (my emphasis). She might also have added that the mental exertions of those men who have shaped our ideas of human nature would be impossible without the daily physical labour of another class of less privileged men.

The masculinity of the man of law is not the masculinity of all men. To borrow Connell's terms, it is an 'emphasised' and a 'hegemonic' form of masculinity, a masculinity considered desirable by a dominant, middle-class type of male who is able to earn a living through his intellect rather than with his hands. There is nothing of the bar-room working-class male culture in this conception of human nature. Nor are we talking about a male ethic of mateship, or of comrades in arms. There is nothing crude, earthy, coarse or physical about the man of law. Instead his is a distinctive masculinity shaped by the circumstances, expectations and priorities of the men of his class: this is a masculinity of the boardroom or the legal chambers, not of the football club.

The man of law is a middle-class man who demonstrates his masculinity by being assertive, confident, rational; he is firm in his negotiations; he advances his own cause, perhaps aggressively, but in a cool-headed manner, not through his physical prowess. He is willing to make enemies if the situation demands it, he is independent; he proceeds alone. He is an individual who does not need to run with the pack. He is the shrewd commercial client we saw in the last chapter, who puts the law to his own profitable uses. He is the skilful maker of bargains envisaged by classic contract law.

The legal person as an ideal type

The man of law, we have observed, is not every man but a man of a certain class who has assumed a middle-class style of masculinity. In still another sense, our man of law is not a typical man. For not only does he fail to represent the humanity of working-class men but he is in fact like few real middle-class men, though he appears to be cast in their image. He is a myth of masculinity, not male reality. Pure reason, pure detachment, pure objectivity, pure self-interest, absence of emotions, may describe a middle-class male ideal, but few actual men. The man of law, the prudent and canny maker of contracts, is an idealised man, a model male, invoked as a powerful metaphor by our legal systems to vindicate such key legal concepts as the freedom of contract. He is, however, at some remove from the multifarious men, even middle-class men, we encounter in our daily lives.

Weber's notion of the ideal type may help us to understand the relationship between this highly stylised 'man of law', the actual men who work in the law, and the rest of the male community. Weber conceived of the ideal type as a conceptual shorthand, a way of 'arranging certain traits, actually found in an unclear, confused state ... into a consistent ideal construct by an accentuation of their essential tendencies' (Weber, 1971:64).

The ideal type helps us in a number of ways to comprehend the nature of the man of law. In the first place, it serves to highlight the distinction between the man of law, a highly contrived and stylised human being, and the true diversity and complexity of male (and female) humanity. The legal view of human nature is based on an ideal type of individual, not typical flawed men. It represents an ideal type in the sense that it invokes an organising concept of the person: it brings together what are thought to be men's essential tendencies and presents them as an internally consistent human model. The 'ideal type' of man implicit in legal thought is true to the Weberian concept in its failure to reflect real people's inconsistencies, contradictions and complexities.

There is still another way in which the man of law can be understood as an ideal type. He is ideal in the sense that he has been invested with a set of qualities which both *Gesellschaft* law and consequently the legal community which invokes that law implicitly interpret as right and good, as ideal. The legal individual is thus a model person to those who interpret and administer the law; and in a more critical but impersonal sense, he is ideal as the central justifying character of the *Gesellschaft* concept of justice, an observation which will be explained more fully below. True to the Weberian concept, the legal concept of the person 'contain[s] what, from the point of view of the expositor, should be and what to him is "essential" in [the type] ... because it is enduringly valuable. If this is consciously or—as it is more frequently—unconsciously the case, [the ideal type] ... contain[s] ideals to which the expositor evaluatively relates [the type]' (Weber, 1971:66).

In other words, the legal viewpoint idealises the attributes of the man of law because these are the qualities which are regarded as highly functional in the *Gesellschaft* society which our law assumes. Such qualities are considered important, valuable and necessary in public-legal life which is characterised by contractual rather than 'fraternal' bonds. Indeed, for a man to get on in the cut-throat world of freely negotiated contracts, the world envisaged by *Gesellschaft* law, it is considered vital that he assume this persona. The man of law is therefore ideal in the sense that he is imbued with the preferences and assumptions of those members of the legal community who invoke him daily (one might think of the *Gesellschaft* values which necessarily order the working life of commercial lawyers and their commercial clients described in the previous chapter). But more significantly, he is ideal in that he possesses the qualities which equip him so well for life in the *Gesellschaft*, qualities which enable him to rise to the demands of the contractual, market society (again, this point will be further explored below).

In all these ways, the legal person may be regarded as an ideal type. He represents a cultural norm of male behaviour, with which many men may wish to identify (many lawyers included) because this set of human qualities historically has been accorded a central place in the liberal vision of the free market which underpins our law. The legal man is quintessential man of the *Gesellschaft*. Men may well want to emulate him given his perceived success in the marketplace. For men who are seen to exemplify the model appear to function best in the public world in which dog is expected to eat dog. Thus the John Elliots and the Rupert Murdochs seem to offer a successful, and much-feted, model of masculinity.

The legal person is thus an idealised, not a typical man. Few men, and fewer women, are as materially and culturally advantaged as the man of law. The economic and intellectual assets of the legal person depend on conditions available only to a small minority of the population. Most people fall well short of this ideal. Nevertheless, the legal person has a way of life and qualities which more men than women will approximate because of the sexual and economic division of labour. That is to say, it is more feasible for men to realise a successful life in the public sphere, unencumbered (unenriched) by human attachments which demand their time and attention.

The relation between real men and women and the characteristics identified as masculine and feminine is therefore complex. Olsen (1983) suggests an analysis of this relation. A male-dominated culture, she says, has split up humanity into two sets of opposing qualities. Men have identified themselves with the set which has been deemed superior. They have said that the ideal man has these qualities — which happily equip him for the rigours of public life — and the ideal woman has the other, inferior set, which is thought to fit her for life in the domestic sphere as helpmate to the man. Our culture therefore rewards men and women who come closest to the ideal but at the same moment tells women their ideal qualities are inferior: the female Catch 22. Because they are ideal types, men and women are unlikely ever to embody their gender ideals perfectly. However, men are likely to strive for the ideal (as are women) because of the cultural rewards, and the result will be a tendency for men in general to be more like the male ideal type than women in general, and vice versa. Men are also likely to suppress those qualities in them which approximate the female ideal type, further accentuating the impression of sex difference.

Though few men may even approximate the ideal of the legal person, our culture ensures that even fewer women do. Not only are there cultural inducements for men to be like the masculine, legal ideal but the qualities associated with this fictitious creature flow out of the experiences associated with the traditional ideal male public role. It is, however only an ideal, a liberal idealisation of male public life in the market. The reality, as Olsen stresses, is that there is little real freedom for most men in the market.

In sum, the qualities of the ideal type of legal person flow out of the experiences of a few socially advantaged men. In truth, very few men even roughly approximate the independent, unemotional, self-interested, unencumbered 'man' of law in their social relations, though one might want to argue that this ideal lends its support to men acting as if they do (for example, it might lend legitimacy to the deserting husband). In reality, supposedly male and female characteristics overlap; human lives are a mixture of freedom and interdependence. Few men and women have the real economic or social freedom implicit in the *Gesellschaft* concept of the person. Law's freely contracting man of the market, negotiating profitable transactions, describes few of us.

The net effect is that *Gesellschaft* law envisages a person who is largely a fiction. It organises around a mythical male who is educated, affluent, and over 21 (the qualities of law-makers), who functions in the public sphere without reference to the demands of a family— even though he is paradoxically assumed to be at the head of one (a tension in the model described earlier); who is not seen to benefit from the emotional and physical services of a caring wife (though the law endeavours to ensure that he will have access to such a person); who is fully severed from the life of the heart (because a woman is taking care of this side of things); who is entirely self-interested.

My claim therefore is that there is indeed a positive association between the qualities of the legal person and a certain style of masculinity, but that it is not the one described by the second-phase feminists. The man of law is more a male ideal than male reality. The ideal legal individual embodies the set of values and the lifestyle aspired to by a certain style of male: the educated, middle-class man. This is not the lifestyle or values of most men who, as a consequence, (as we shall see) do not reap the benefits of its inherent sexism. It is even a distortion of the lives of the men who most closely approximate the man of law. Legal thinking invokes an idealised male, not real men.

Why law needs the legal man

Though the man of law is an idealised fiction of a man—in no way a typical person, or even a typical man—it is vital for the legal scheme of things that he be seen to be typical. For in the role of everyman, as the human prototype, he becomes the very justification of law's approach to the social world and the linchpin of its claim to fairness and impartiality.

The reason is this. As we saw in an earlier chapter, law claims to be universally applicable—not to prefer any one type of person in its principles, its priorities or in its methods—but it rests this claim on the belief that we are all constituted in the form of the man of law so that if his needs are served, so are everyone's. Law therefore generally assumes, for legal purposes, that we are all healthy, wealthy, wise and competitive and able to cope well in a society thought to be comprised of similarly able-bodied and competitive men. There are important exceptions, as we saw in an earlier chapter, exceptions which highlight the inability of law to sustain a single, overarching organising principle. For example, juvenile criminal justice acknowledges the particular needs of children, while in civil law the concept of the unconscionable contract implicitly recognises the notion of the vulnerable contracting party. But on the whole *Gesellschaft* law takes us to be similarly enabled. This legal view of the world meshes well with the needs of the competitive market, which law envisages, in that it provides a legal model of the public man or worker as free, mobile, able-bodied and self-sufficient.

Law's assumption of the universality of the qualities of the legal man may be seen to justify the adversary system. Indeed, only if people all tend to flourish in adversity, only if direct opposition brings out our best fighting instincts, as it does with the man of law, can the adversary system be said to be a fair and desirable system for all of us. The assumption that the man of law is the human prototype equally justifies the principle of individual rights and responsibilities. Indeed, only if we are separate, independent atoms—as free and detached as the man of law—does it make sense for law to operate upon a principle that we must each carry the can for our own, but for no one else's, actions.

The assumption of the legal man's typicality, as we saw above, is also the necessary justification for the contractual form of law. Indeed, only if we are able to look after our own interests in the harsh world of the marketplace in the manner of the man of law is it fair to conceive of human relations in terms of an endless series of freely made and therefore legally enforceable contracts. In each of these cases, law is said to serve all of us equally well because we are all assumed (and yet not assumed in the case of women, hence the paradox alluded to by Okin and Pateman) to have the qualities of the legal man: to do well in open conflict; to function independently of others; to have the opportunity and means and the inclination to press our own suit.

For the law to be regarded as a fair, impartial, non-arbitrary and universal system, it is essential that it be seen to invoke a universal person. The fiction of the equality and essential sameness of all before the law, the idea that the man of law is in fact a human prototype, is thus the very basis of the ideal of the Rule of Law. The legal person's very abstractness, his paradigm quality, serves to show that the legal approach is not an approach in fact but an inherently neutral way of organising and arbitrating relations between human beings. By his any-personness, the man of law demonstrates the appropriateness and essential rightness of the law's particular approach to the world—the way that is not a way. The legal man is thus proof of the law's impartiality, and so to question his status as a paradigm person, as we have done here, is to question, at a most fundamental level, the fairness and therefore the justice of law.

6

The sacrificial men

A newcomer to the criminal courts will probably be struck by the uniformity of the defendant population. Our observer will find that those who form the object of the court's attention tend to be young, poor, uneducated and male. Indeed the overall maleness of the courtroom as a whole is readily apparent. The judge is more likely than not a man; so is the prosecutor; and so is the defence counsel. But while the courtroom personnel share their sex with the accused, they seem to have little else in common. Indeed an enormous social gulf appears to separate those who are doing the processing from those who are processed.

The large majority of people who are dealt with by the criminal justice system appear before the lower courts. And it is here, in particular, that we find the sacrifices of the legal process, the failed men. In the introduction to his study of the operation of a lower court in Connecticut, New Haven, Malcolm Feeley (1979:4) offers a useful summary of the typical defendant. 'By conventional standards nearly all of the defendants are failures, both in life and in crime. They are poor, often unemployed, usually young, and frequently from broken homes. Most of them lack self-esteem, motivation, skill, and opportunity.' What Feeley omits to mention in this passage is that the large majority of criminal defendants are male.

The principal intention of this chapter is to demonstrate the poorness of fit between the prevailing notion of the man of law and the role accorded the real men who are brought before the criminal courts. A second aim is to show why this generates problems for accused persons in their bid to extract justice from the law. The perceived failure of the defendant to live up to the legal idea of the articulate, reasoning and forceful individual, capable of defending his position in an adversary setting, means that he is open to manipulation. It is perhaps this disparity between the ideal legal person and the criminal defendant which, as we will see, encourages a belief among legal experts that the accused person is unable to cope with the complexities of the legal system (unlike, say, the more sophisticated

124

commercial client who more closely approximates the quintessential legal person), that he is out of his depth and that it is only right that control of his legal affairs should be in the hands of the lawyer.

In the following discussion of the plight of the sacrificial men of law, those men who appear before the criminal courts, two perspectives will be explored: that of the lawyer and that of the defendant. These might be called the view from above and the view from below. Together they demonstrate the costs incurred by ordinary men as a result of the idea of the man of law.

The view from above

The basic principle of legal practice is that the lawyer must obey the directions of the client. 'The lawyer must not "substitute his own judgement for the specific instructions of his client", even if he believes his own judgement is more likely to operate in the client's best interest' (Disney et al., 1986:637). Discussions between lawyers and their clients are therefore referred to as 'the taking of instructions'. The general idea is that the client explains the nature of his problem to the lawyer, receives advice about its legal implications, and then instructs the lawyer about how he would like to proceed in the light of this advice. When the lawyer appears in court he (as we have seen, the lawyer is more likely to be a man) is said to act on behalf of his client and repeatedly refers to 'his instructions'. If it should transpire during the course of a case that the lawyer is unsure of the wishes of his client, he is required to obtain further directions, not to proceed independently. In theory, then, the lawyer is the servant of the client. He is there to interpret the law and represent the client's interests, to act according to the client's view of the matter, not his own.

The idea that the lawyer is the professional servant of the paying client, that the lawyer is the one who takes orders, meshes well with the ideal of the man of law. It assumes that the client is a sentient, rational being who knows his own mind and, with the assistance of a legal expert, will be able to defend his interests. It vests control of the vital decisions in any legal proceeding with the client, not the lawyer. The lawyer is to explain the law and may advise on tactics, but the wishes and intentions represented in court are said always to be those of the client.

The notion that lawyers are in the service of their clients may also be seen to accord with the legal profession's idea of itself— as impartial, neutral and dispassionate in its legal dealings. The lawyer does not take sides or express a moral or personal view of the matter.

In fact, it can be a breach of ethics to do so. He does not act in his own interests, or according to his personal convictions; rather he acts in the interests of his client according to the client's view of things and according to the client's instructions. The lawyer's sole concern is to provide the best advice possible and to represent the client's version of events in court.

What is wrong with the service model of the lawyer—client relationship is that, in many instances, it does not accord with legal practice. Indeed, as we shall see, there is evidence to suggest that when it comes to representing people in the criminal jurisdiction— who are, in the main, the socially disadvantaged—many lawyers regard their clients as incapable of making sensible decisions and so proceed to take control of the case. There is also evidence that lawyers do not always present themselves in court in a neutral fashion, as the client's representative, but seek to establish a social distance between themselves and the individuals who hire their services. Indeed, it has been observed that lawyers in the criminal courts seem at times to identify not with their clients, their social inferiors, but with the other members of the court (Blumberg, 1967; Carlen, 1976; Bankowski and Mungham, 1976).

One can point to a number of reasons why lawyers might not grant their clients the full status of the legal person. One is the implicit acceptance among many lawyers that their superior knowledge of the law makes it only sensible that they should take the reins. As Tomasic (1978a) has shown in his study of New South Wales lawyers, the dominant legal cultural value is one of cynical realism in that lawyers acknowledge that their clients are powerless. Though the service ideal is meant generally to guide the work of legal practitioners, one can find professional support for the view that lawyers should at times assume full command of their client's cases, particularly when those clients are thought incapable of acting wisely.

In a recent Australian publication directed at practitioners, for example, clear recognition is given to the lawyer—client relationship which employs the 'lawyer-control' model, as opposed to the 'client-control' or the 'co-operative' model. Its justification, we are told, is that 'the lawyer has the training and the expertise to assess what is in the client's best interests'. The acknowledged cost of the lawyer assuming full control of the relationship, however, is that it may fail to preserve 'the autonomy, responsibility and dignity of both parties' (Basten, 1986:23). In other words, it sacrifices the ideal of the legal subject as an intelligent and independent individual.

A recent appraisal of the American lawyer—client relationship also stresses the value of the more participatory model, but notes its limitations. Based on a study of New York City practitioners, it observes that when clients are allowed to take an active role in their case, more satisfactory results are achieved. The same writer, however, concedes the professional problems of giving clients too much control. Notably, the lawyer may lose the ability 'to restrain clients from taking immoral, illegal or simply unfortunate actions'. In other words, there are times when the lawyer knows best and should secure his authority over the wayward client (Rosenthal, 1974). Moreover, it is not always possible for the client to grasp 'the complexities of technical language' nor to deal with 'uncertain, multifaceted decisions'. The service ideal which vests authority in the client as a rational legal subject, it seems, is fine in theory but not always feasible.

Other commentators on the lawyer's role believe that, from the outset, authority should be wrested from the client. Such lawyers suffer no illusions about the autonomy or intellectual faculties of the client. Simply, the client is perceived to be a dependent person with little command of the situation. For example, the perceived ineptitude of the client is described in the most candid of terms in the following opinion of a Canadian Queen's Counsel on lawyers in the criminal jurisdiction (who, by nature of their work, deal mainly with the less privileged members of the community). Defending counsel, we are told, should assume 'total control and responsibility over the defence'. This should be done kindly but firmly since the defendant is likely to be 'a rather frightened and bewildered man [who] is looking for help'. Thus 'some time, quite early in the process, you should tactfully let him know that you are in charge' (Martin, 1969:282).

Clearly, some members of the legal community defend their right to take full charge of their clients' cases. Others favour a more egalitarian relationship. Though the lawyer-dominated model of legal practice tends to cast the client in a dependent relationship, it is not regarded by the legal community as inappropriate behaviour. Witness Halsbury:

> When counsel is instructed, then, subject to his duties to the court, and subject to his right to advise another course of action, he must accept and adhere to the instructions given by or on behalf of his client, but counsel is entitled to insist, and as a general rule, ought to have complete control over how those instructions are carried out and over the actual conduct of the case. (Quoted in Disney et al. 1986:639)

Indeed if one looks closely at the ethics laid down for advocates one can see that they are a bundle of contradictions. Though lawyers must take instructions, they are also expected to be in control.

Though they must obey the wishes of their client, they must not
identify with their client's claims. In fact the case law shows that
lawyers are more in danger of 'professional misconduct' if they go
too far when criticising other lawyers than if they assume too com-
manding a role in the lawyer—client relationship (Disney et al.,
1986).

Where lawyers have attracted criticism, however, is in those instances where they have been observed to treat the client as purely
incidental to the business of the court or, more worrying still, when
they have been thought to act more in their own than in their client's
interests. In such cases, the threat to the client extends beyond his
autonomy as legal subject.

A swingeing critique of the treatment of defendants by English
lawyers has been advanced by Bankowski and Mungham (1976). In
their volume, *Images of Law*, they characterise the treatment of
defendants in English magistrates' courts as a 'degradation ceremony'.
This expression is borrowed directly from Garfinkel (1955:420), who
defines it as 'any communicative work between persons, whereby
the public identity of an actor is transformed into something looked
on as lower in the local scheme of social types'. The purpose of such
courtroom degradation, according to the authors, is to subdue and
pacify the defendant so that he will cause as little difficulty as
possible.

The 'arcadian sketch' of the courtroom, in which 'skilled and
articulate advocates' protect the interests of their clients, is therefore
expressly challenged in this analysis of English justice. Instead, the
situation described by Bankowski and Mungham is one in which
lawyers coopt the identity of their clients, refer in open court to the
intimate details of their private lives, without reference to the clients
themselves, who are treated as the non-participating objects, not the
subjects, of the legal process. Lawyers, they claim, speak in a technical language which specifically excludes the layperson. What is
more, little effort is made to involve or engage the client, to ensure
that he knows what is happening to him. Rather, it is simply
assumed that he is neither able nor inclined to understand. Consistently,
he is seen to be the recipient of whatever is deemed by the court to
be appropriate for him (Bankowski and Mungham, 1976:89).

The English criminologist Pat Carlen (1976:91) presents a similar
view of the treatment of accused persons. Indeed her observations of
the operation of a magistrates' court led her to conclude that the
dominant attitude to defendants was that they were ' "pretty dim",
"rather pathetic creatures" who had "never had a chance" '. The
lawyer's response to this sorry assessment of the defendant was to
make him over, to tell the accused, before he got into the courtroom,
what he should say and how he should say it.

This finding again puts paid to the traditional notion that it is the client who invariably informs the lawyer what he wants done for him in the form of 'instructions'. While clients may well call the lawyer's tune in the lucrative sphere of commercial law, as we saw in Chapter 4, in the criminal courts, where the poor predominate, the reverse would seem to be true. It is more a matter of the lawyer instructing the client than the client instructing the lawyer. As another commentator on English justice describes this process:

> The lawyer takes down those facts that he considers relevant to the client's case; he tells him how to plead; he decides what aspects of the defendant's character and background to emphasise before the magistrates, whether to challenge the police or probation officer and what sentence to propose to the court. In most cases it is clear that the lawyer is in charge. Defendants tend to follow advice and obey instructions. (King, 1981:118)

To make matters worse, there is a variety of ways in which the status and contribution of the defendant can be further diminished once he enters the court, to the point that he ultimately becomes, according to Carlen (1976), merely a 'dummy player'. All professional members of the courtroom, Carlen informs us, use signals, gestures, language as well as legal procedures to ensure that the defendant does not take an active part in proceedings. A bad defendant, from the point of view of all professional players in the legal drama, lawyers included, is one who steps out of line and attempts to offer an independent and unorchestrated challenge to the court. But it is not difficult to quell the recalcitrant defendant, according to Carlen, by ruling his comments inappropriate and inadmissible.

The Canadian criminologists Ericson and Baranek (1982:3) present a view of North American justice which meshes well with that offered by the English critics. In the course of an ambitious longitudinal study of accused persons, from encounter with the police to court disposition, they interviewed 100 defendants about their experiences of the law and also, where possible, spoke to their legal counsel. Their general conclusion was that the accused was a dependant in the criminal process. He was caught up in a legal web not of his own design, subject to the orders of others, his freedom to make choices that might serve his own interests 'clearly circumscribed, and often foreclosed'.

The common opinion of lawyers interviewed in this study was that the lawyer should make the main decisions affecting the case because the accused did not appreciate the processes of the law. As one lawyer put it: 'No, I really have a tendency to decide myself which is better for the client and I don't say, well, these are the avenues, because I don't think they understand enough of what I'm

talking about. I don't think they're capable of me explaining everything to them because it took me a long time to learn what the
different avenues meant too' (Ericson and Baranek, 1982:96). To
another legal representative, a precondition of his defending an accused
person was that the client should fully surrender control of his
affairs. In the opinion of this learned counsel, 'any lawyer who's
worth his salt tells his client how to dress, how to have his hair cut,
how to have it combed, how to behave, how to answer questions'
(Ericson and Baranek, 1982:98). Again, there is little evidence here of
our knowing and assertive man of law who calls the shots.

Though writers such as Bankowski and Mungham and Carlen
have been highly critical of lawyers who dominate their clients, other
writers have at times found more noble motives informing just this
sort of lawyer–client relationship. Eve Spangler (1986:167–68), for
example, writing about members of the American profession who
provide services to the poor, has observed that 'in taking over the
decision-making process, lawyers are trying to honour the intentions
of their clients'. Thus:

> When people come to us, they're in immediate crisis. They
> literally come in, 'My God, what is going to happen to me and
> my four-year old [who] is lead poisoned, and me, who has
> emphysema and 85 per cent over-weight and can't walk up the
> stairs?' We're people who have a lot of clients die on us. There
> are all these questions and choices they have to make, and
> they're crying during the whole time that you talk to them and
> they just say, 'Will you please do what you think is best? You're
> the lawyer. I don't want to have to do this. You do it.' So you
> take the cue from them.

Good intentions, however, can also work against the client, when
they lead to the lawyer supplanting the client's wishes for his own.
Spangler (1986:168), for example, remarks on the practices of certain
legal aid lawyers whose personal opinion of what is best for their
clients, what is in their clients' own good, may lead them to use their
superior knowledge to subvert their clients' goals.

Whatever the intentions of legal counsel, whether they be altruistic
or self-interested, it is possible to observe a clear distinction between
their relations with the indigent client (discussed here) and their
dealings with the wealthy (described in Chapter 4). In the former
case it is the lawyer who is in a position to make the critical decisions
while in the latter case, the client assumes command (Heinz and
Laumann, 1982; Spangler, 1986). The degree of fit between the social
location of the client and the social character of the man of law
therefore makes a difference to his treatment by the legal profession.
Wealthy, commercial clients closely approximate the legal model of

the person and accordingly retain control of the legal process. Socially disadvantaged clients depart from the model in most respects and so have little say over what is done to them in the courts.

The view from below

In *The View From the Boys*, the English sociologist Howard Parker (1974) offers a vivid account of the courtroom experience from the point of view of the young men who are brought before the law. It serves well to demonstrate the disparity between law's idealisation of the legal person—what it conceives as the rational, forceful and articulate juridical subject—and its approach to the actual working-class males who come before the courts on criminal charges. There is small chance, here, of confusing the man of law with the men who appear in the criminal courts. Between the two there is a massive cultural divide. Where one is respected, the other, according to Parker, is treated with disdain, a fact which is not lost on the recipients of criminal justice.

As Parker (1974:171) makes clear, the defendant plays a small part in the legal drama. Indeed the principal actors—judicial officer, defence and prosecution—tend to proceed as if he were not even there. The effect, we are told, is to instil in the defendant a sense of powerlessness as well as a conviction that any endeavour to influence the course of events will be taken as a sign of disrespect. And as Parker also observes, this may indeed be the truth of the matter since the entire orientation of the courtroom is one of intimidation, 'with the procedure quietly emphasising—you may not be guilty this time, but you're one of them, you look and speak like one of them and you'd better respect the Court and take home your experience as a warning'.

The passivity and non-participation of the accused in his own defence has been remarked on by a number of writers, from both sides of the Atlantic. To Ericson and Baranek (1982:191), for example, writing of the Canadian experience, the court is a place to be feared, an institution 'that is deferred to rather than used by the accused'. This is well illustrated by the comments of the defendants they interviewed:

> Well it's not—a place you go very often . . . It's a very forbidding place, you know. The judge sits way up there and . . . you're kind of a low man on the board . . .
>
> I know there were people at the back there but I didn't know—it was all I could do to—thank goodness they had a chair for me to sit down . . .
>
> Well, all I heard was you are charged with and then my mind

sort of went blank. And she asked how I plead and I couldn't even answer. I had to look to [the lawyer] there.

From the viewpoint of the defendant, say Ericson and Baranek, the unfolding of the case is often thought to be a matter for the experts and therefore does not concern him. Indeed, as we have seen, such passivity may well be fostered by legal counsel who feel that the technical language and procedures of the courtroom are beyond the ken of their clients. Instead of monitoring the interpretation of events, as told by the lawyer, the defendant's attention becomes focused exclusively on the official outcome of the proceedings, however it is achieved. To draw again from the Canadian study:

> Q: Did you understand the things that everybody was saying? Your lawyer, the crown attorney, the court clerk?
> A: Ah, not really. Because he's—he used ten dollar words sort of thing.
> Q: Who didn't you understand?
> A: Well the only person I did understand was the judge.
> Q: Would you have felt better if you did understand them?
> A: Well I couldn't really say because—I'm not really listening to what they're saying. I just want to—I'm just waiting for what the judge is going to say.
> Q: OK. Why don't you listen to what they say?
> A: Well, because, uh, I'm more worried about what I'm going to get than what they're saying. (Erikcon and Baranek, 1982:192)

In England, Pat Carlen (1976:32) has also commented on the non-involvement of defendants in proceedings, focusing in particular on the conduct of magistrates' courts. She emphasises the readiness with which accused persons slip into their assigned role as deferential observer rather than active participant.

> Most defendants, cause no trouble in the courtroom. After a long wait in the corridors of the waiting-room, many of them make an initial attempt to hear and follow the proceedings and then visibly give up the pretence of understanding and stare restlessly around the courtroom until the policeman, touching them on the arm, indicates that the formalities are over.

Like their North American counterparts, English defendants appear not to engage with the processes of justice, as knowing agents, as holders of legal rights. Instead they tend to be the objects of the law who have justice done to them.

This is not to imply, however, that the defendant will necessarily feel or express dissatisfaction with his treatment in the courtroom. Notwithstanding his relegation to the status of passive and uncomprehending object of the proceedings, other research has revealed a surprisingly high level of satisfaction with legal representation

(Tomasic, 1978b:132). The problem with drawing too much from such findings is the very powerlessness and helplessness which characterises the position of the accused. To put it simply, the defendant may not be in a position to judge the value of legal representation, to know whether he is getting his due (Ericson and Baranek, 1982:185). As Carlen (1976:69) notes, 'the defendant, as dummy player, is kept sufficiently in the dark as to the exact nature of the procedural rules that usually he cannot act to prove whether formal justice has been done or not'.

Another reason why defendants may not question the quality of the assistance they receive from their advocate is that the latter has at his disposal a number of tools which are capable of enhancing his value in the eyes of the client. Significantly, in the criminal jurisdiction (in England and Australia), he is in a position to use the known disparity between penalties for offences nominated in legislation and the actual sentences handed down for such crimes to convince an accused that he would have been worse off without representation. In other words, any sentence obtained which is less than the nominated maximum can be made to appear a bonus which has been successfully fought for by learned counsel. In the civil sphere, Sarat and Felstiner (1986) have shown that lawyers in divorce cases gain control over clients by stressing the random and error-prone nature of the legal system. Thus their insider knowledge gives them the upper hand.

This is not to say that defendants are incapable of smelling a rat. Though one can point to evidence of client satisfaction with legal services, there is also ample documentation of the discontented, not to say the incensed, client. As one of Howard Parker's (1974:172) 'boys' was reported to observe, 'the law's on the law's fuckin' side'. Indeed one of the most widely quoted and controversial studies of English justice from the defendant's perspective, conducted by Baldwin and McConville (1977), has revealed strong and well-articulated dissatisfaction with the legal profession.

The heated debate which surrounds this study arose out of its exposure of a well-developed practice of informal plea bargaining between defence lawyers and prosecution, a practice traditionally frowned upon by the English Bench and the Bar (in contrast to its widely accepted role in American criminal justice) and therefore generally denied and denounced. Plea bargaining may take a number of forms, but in general it entails an offer of various concessions by the prosecution in exchange for an admission of guilt from the defendant. Its perceived advantage for both prosecutor and defence counsel is that it is quick and efficient, saving the considerable time and effort needed for a full-blown trial. It also minimises conflict between the prosecutor and the defending lawyer who, as a number of critics of the system have observed, may be officially professional adversaries but are also working colleagues who wish to maintain good continuing relations (Blumberg, 1967; Cotterrell, 1984:203).

Through their survey of 121 defendants appearing before the Birmingham Crown Court, Baldwin and McConville (1977:25) not only brought to light this unofficial practice of plea bargaining but showed that defendants were perfectly aware of what they considered to be an unacceptable degree of lawyer collusion with the opposition and a concomitant disregard of their own wishes. As Case 29 was noted to observe,

> the barrister who's defending and the one who's prosecuting have got it pretty nearly sewn up. They're in the law courts every day and they know what's going on. They brow-beat many people [into pleading guilty]. When they've got a long indictment, they talk between themselves like a couple of carpenters saying 'We'll cut that piece to that length.' It's just a job for them.

Or in the words of Case 68: 'Barristers always say things like "If you plead guilty to this, then I'll ..." and it's all hush-hush. They won't come out with what has gone on behind the scenes. It's all on the grape-vine and they only let you hear a little bit' (Baldwin and McConville, 1977:34).

Still more worrying was the finding that in certain cases, lawyers were perceived to be positively bullying and overbearing. Witness the comments of Case 134:

> I was really forced to plead guilty. I was feeling pleased because the witnesses didn't say much about me in their evidence ... But then my barrister and solicitor took me down below and they said 'Look, you've got no chance, so you will plead guilty.' I said, I don't want to plead guilty, they are very bad charges against me and I didn't assault her and it was only a few quid.' The barrister then said, 'If you're found guilty you will get about 10 or fifteen years but if you plead guilty you will get 4 or 5 years.' I was really shocked. I was so scared, sweating and nervous and he frightened me with this 10–15 years stuff and saying I had no chance. They then talked to my mother and frightened her as well ... I agreed to plead guilty but it wasn't my decision. I had no choice about it. I was very frightened by everything. (Baldwin and McConville, 1977:49–50)

This was one of the worst cases identified by Baldwin and McConville, who were at pains to stress, from the outset, that only a small minority of the lawyers described in their study were found to engage in such unprofessional conduct. Nevertheless, the overall picture presented by the authors is of a profession which tends to make the critical decisions for clients who, as a consequence, often feel vulnerable and unable to control the events of their case.

A recent survey of client perceptions of Queensland lawyers tells a similar story. Here, young people who had sought the assistance of a lawyer in relation to a number of legal matters were asked to report their experiences. In response to the proposition 'your lawyer is always on your side', over a third indicated their disagreement, while another third were uncertain. Moreover, the majority of respondents found both lawyers and legal matters difficult to understand. The discouraging conclusion of the authors was that 'the law is perceived as complex, abstract and hence, inaccessible' (O'Connor and Callahan, 1988:16).

The problem for the dissatisfied defendant of giving vent to his discontent is that it does not necessarily help his case. Especially in the courtroom, what is expected of the good accused is remorse and obeisance, not criticism and challenge. He must subordinate himself to his lawyer and to the Bench. Ideally, he should be entirely silent and let his lawyer do his talking, leading to curious tripartite conversations in which the judge questions the lawyer about the defendant and then the lawyer asks those same questions of his client and then returns the information to the Bench — as if the defendant were not really there to answer for himself. Indeed, as Doreen McBarnet (1981:135) concluded from her observations of English and Scottish courts, 'defendants may not play the role of the confident punch-pulling advocate because it clashes not only with the incompetence and deference routinely demanded of the lower-class people who dominate the courts, but because it clashes with the role expected of the defendant'.

In short, it is considered inappropriate for the working-class defendant in the criminal courts to display those very characteristics which we have found to be implicitly attributed to the man of law. While our classic legal person (that is, the wealthy commercial client) is expected to be forceful, confident, articulate and assertive — such attributes providing the necessary vindication of our adversary system of justice — those who appear before the criminal courts are required to abandon these qualities if they want to receive a favourable hearing. While our distinguished man of law may assume a central place in both the rhetoric of Anglo-American justice and in the privileged legal world of commerce, he is not expected to inhabit the less salubrious regions of the criminal courts. And those defendants who attempt to invoke their rights as legal subjects in the manner of the man of law are likely to find themselves admonished, rather than rewarded, for their efforts.

7

Keeping women in their place

Over the last century, women's engagement with the law to improve their public standing has been a difficult and painful one, as the first-phase feminists record. And at first blush, it would seem, the battle has been largely successful. Today, in most respects, women appear to be treated as formal equals with men. They are now recognised to be citizens with almost the same rights as men (there are some residual areas of discrimination such as industrial protection legislation which applies differently to the sexes). If we consider the law on the books, it would seem that women may now inhabit the public world and advance their own cause in much the same manner as our self-interested legal person. So is this virtually the end of the struggle for women?

As feminists of the second and third phase have shown us, formal legal rights for women are not enough. Though deleterious references to women have been expunged from most laws, there are several indirect ways in which the law still reaches into the lives of women and controls and limits their day-to-day existence. Carol Smart (1982; 1983; 1984a; 1984b), for one, has concentrated on the way the law has helped to constitute a particular form of the family in which women are cast in the role of dependent wife and mother. Catherine MacKinnon (1982; 1983; 1985; 1987) has focused on the sexism of laws which ostensibly constrain male violence against women but in substance allow such violence to continue. Katherine O'Donovan (1985) has argued that the reticence of law to be seen to enter the private sphere has tended to support the traditional view that a man's home is his castle and that he represents the law in his own home.

The aim of this book has been to reinforce the arguments of these latter-day feminists and show that looks can be deceiving. The specific claim of this volume is that while the law may appear to offer roughly equal rights to men and women, in truth the law organises around a particular individual who is both male and masculine. The

136

legal person is still very much a man, not a woman, and the law still reserves another place for women: as other than the man of law.

In this chapter, the intention is to look at some of the ways in which the law and legal practice continue to advance a traditional view of women: as the antithesis of the man of law. To this end, we will observe the efforts of the courts both to reward women who are perceived to be good as women and to punish those who are perceived to be bad. In both sets of practices, the message to women is that they should be in the home, caring for husbands, nurturing children and providing a moral force for stability and family values. In this legal view, it is considered unseemly for women to step outside the boundaries of acceptable feminine behaviour, let alone assert themselves in the public world.

A second purpose of this chapter is to consider how the maleness of the legal person affects those women who insist on their formal legal rights to inhabit the public world, unimpeded by sexist sentiments and practices. The argument here is that women who try to use anti-discrimination laws to get fair treatment in the public sphere can only get satisfaction if they model themselves on the man of law. That is to say, for women to get legal recognition as equals in the public world, they must satisfy the law that they are really just the same as men. They cannot get satisfaction on their own terms as a distinctive but still valuable resource. To restate the immortal words of Professor Higgins, here the question posed by the law is 'Why can't a woman be more like a man?'. Equality, it will be claimed, is for those women who can demonstrate their resemblance to the man of law; it is not for women who deviate from this legal paradigm.

Rewarding the good women

The good woman, in the legal view, is by now a familiar character. She is the female counterpart of the man of law identified in earlier chapters. She is the woman who manifests a form of emphasised femininity: she is loyal and loving, compliant and altruistic. But whereas the man of law finds his freedoms fostered and nurtured by the law and its institutions, good women can be distinguished by their abandonment of their own interests and their overriding concern for the interests of family members. The good woman is a faithful wife and mother whose sphere is the home, not the competitive arena of the marketplace.

Feminist criminologists from both sides of the Atlantic have produced convincing evidence of the tenacity of the legal view of 'the good woman'. They have done so in the context of a wider debate within criminology about whether women are the beneficiaries of a chivalrous criminal justice system. What has emerged from these investigations is that women, overall, are not accorded greater leniency and indeed that the law is not consistent. Rather, different types of women receive different treatment. Those who are deemed to be too free in their behaviour, who are therefore unfeminine may be treated more punitively than men. Where women are perceived to be good wives and mothers, or where they are simply located in a suitably dependent relationship however, they may well draw a more positive response from the court, though this would seem to be insufficient to tip the scales significantly in their favour. There is also evidence to suggest that often the sexes are now treated much the same (Naffine, 1987:1).

One of the more imaginative comparative studies of men and women before the courts is that conducted by the English criminologist Mary Eaton (1986). The focus of this inquiry was a London magistrates' court where, over a period of two years, material was compiled on 210 male defendants and 111 women. Eaton's chief concern was the mode of depiction of the sexes in the courtroom. She considered whether men and women were presented to the court in essentially the same manner or whether there were important differences in the rendition of their social histories to the court. To this end she examined lawyers' pleas in mitigation as well as social inquiry reports (reports on the social and economic circumstances of defendants prepared by probation officers). She also scrutinised the pronouncements of magistrates on the men and women who came before them.

A traditional view of women and their role in the family emerged in a number of ways. In pleas of mitigation for both men and women, the nuclear family was presented as a stabilising and controlling influence on the defendant. In the social reports of probation officers, a clear picture emerged of the respective roles expected of men and women in a stable and therefore desirable family. Not surprisingly, it was considered normal and appropriate that the man provide financially for family members and the woman assume responsibility for childcare and housework. But women were expected to do more than this. On home visits to male defendants, the wife was expected to demonstrate an understanding of her husband's behaviour (though a reciprocal understanding was not expected of men), to monitor and sustain the 'emotional situation' of the home and to demonstrate a suitable 'home-like atmosphere': in short, they were expected to be dutiful and caring wives. Where women were themselves the defendant, however, the focus became the quality of their housewifery. As Eaton (1986:66) observes: 'to learn more about a woman it is sufficient to visit her home, but to learn more about a man, one must see the individuals who share his home.'

In what she refers to as 'magistrates' talk', the comments on defendants issued from the Bench, Eaton gleaned further evidence of the legal view of women. Not only did her magistrates envisage and endorse a traditional sexual division of labour, but they also expected the man of the household to assert himself as head of the family. As one magistrate observed reprovingly: 'most people on the Bench look to the woman to maintain the standards of the home ... [but] it says something about the man—the fact that he is indifferent to, or can tolerate, or *does nothing to encourage an alteration of these standards*' (Eaton, 1986:74, original emphasis).

Another British study has revealed similar attitudes to women among members of the Bench. In her interviews of Scottish sheriffs (judges), Pat Carlen (1983) observed a disinclination to imprison women who were thought to be good mothers. As one sheriff put it: 'If she's a good mother, we don't want to take her away. If she's not a good mother, it doesn't matter.' Like the London magistrates, Carlen's sheriffs also had faith in the husband as a disciplinarian. Thus: 'If she has a husband, he may tell her to stop it.' And: 'Not many women with steady husbands or cohabitees commit crime. They're kept occupied' (Carlen, 1983:67).

From the United States of America has come a somewhat different approach to the question of what courts think of women, an approach which has yielded compatible results. With access to the probation files of over 1000 women convicted in California for various crimes—from disturbing the peace to assault—Candice Kruttschnitt set out to discover the main influences on the sentencing decision. For most offence categories, the economic dependency of the defendant emerged as the primary factor determining the severity of the sentence. From the comments of probation officers, it transpired that dependent women were regarded as safer bets because their family was thought to exert a degree of control over their behaviour and guide them into better ways. Kruttschnitt (1982a:507) illustrates her point with the following excerpt from the report of a probation officer:

The court is asked to consider the case of [this defendant]. [This defendant] was 21 at the time of her marriage [and] the couple did not establish their own residence, but instead ... moved into her parents' home. Following her divorce she moved out of that environment and for the first time lived outside her parents' home ... When she finally got her own apartment she not only began to lead a freer life but one that was marred by poor judgements ... [However] because of the defendant's basically clean past record ... a commitment to the state penitentiary is not being recommended at this time. Since she has never experienced probation before, it can be beneficial to her, replacing to some degree the parental guidance and controls that she lived with for so long and apparently still is in need of.

Such findings, to Kruttschnitt (1982a:510), suggest 'that the legal system prefers to exert little social control over women whose lives presently contain an indicator of daily social control such as that entailed by economic dependency'.

Two other sentencing studies, one American, one English, throw further light on the legal view of the good woman. In New York, Ilene Nagel (1981) found that being married was of positive advantage to women, but not necessarily to men, at the point of sentencing. In Cambridge, England, Farrington and Morris (1983:246) also found this to be the case. They discovered that 'while some factors ... had an important influence on sentence severity and re-conviction for both men and women, others only had an influence for one sex. In particular, marital status, family background and children were more important for women than for men.'

Together, such findings suggest that the law, through the agency of judicial officers, lawyers and probation officers, at times employs an idea of women in which theirs is a subordinate domestic role. And it is according to their degree of fit with that role that women may draw the court's approval. Ideal women, in the legal view, may be characterised by their dependency, the care with which they keep house, the attention they pay to their husband and children and their ability to create an emotionally stable family atmosphere. In short, they are good wives and mothers.

Enshrining motherhood

The legal notion that women are most importantly mothers is not confined to the criminal jurisdiction but is also echoed in the family courts. Indeed, in the fraught area of custody disputes we find reiterated, time and again, the naturalness and general desirability of full-time mothering. It is here, perhaps more than anywhere else, that we see women being rewarded for being what the courts want them to be.

In her critique of English family law, *The Ties that Bind*, Carol Smart (1984:123) produced the following set of statements from the Bench on the role of women as mothers. These show not only the high esteem accorded the institution of motherhood but also the court's commitment to the traditional idea that women should assume exclusive responsibility for children.

The dictates of nature that the mother is the natural guardian, protector and comforter of very young children, and in particular, of a very little girl [have] not been displaced. (Stamp, L.J., Re K (Minors) (1977), 1 All E2, p. 651, quoting the County court judge who originally heard the case)

[The mother], not as a matter of law but in the ordinary courses of nature, is the right person to have charge of young children. (Sir J. Pennycuick, Re K (Minors), op.cit., p.655)

However good a sort of man [the husband] may be, he could not perform the functions which a mother performed by nature in relation to a little girl. (Stamp, L.J., M v. M (1979) 9 Fam. 1. p.92)

As Smart (1984:124) remarks, such pronouncements are not unusual. Indeed they are the norm and thus show us the degree of judicial support for what Smart terms 'the ideology of motherhood'.

Smart's own research into the attitudes of Sheffield magistrates confirms, yet again, the commitment of judicial officers to a highly conventional view of the appropriate roles of the sexes. When asked what they thought of the idea that men should assume the mothering function, over 80 per cent of the magistrates which formed her sample responded negatively. Smart identifed two strands in the magistrates' thinking. One was a strong conviction that men should be the breadwinners. The other was a belief that if men obtained the custody of children, then they should remain working and employ a woman to perform the labours of childcare. Moreover, two magistrates went further than this, expressing the view that it would unman the father if he were to take on full-time child-rearing, while another two felt that it would damage the children psychologically if they were to witness their father out of the workforce (Smart, 1984:212).

Such sentiments about the proper roles of the sexes are not to be dismissed as harmless musings from the Bench. They represent a real threat to women's independence. Though women have benefited in custody disputes from the traditional belief that women make more natural and therefore better parents, such judicial attitudes have also served to constrain and control women and ultimately to punish those who fail to toe the patriarchal line. Where women have wanted to step out of the role of good and dutiful wife and mother, they have been chastised by the courts. As Smart (1982:142) has noted elsewhere, at the time of divorce and separation working mothers may come under the close scrutiny of judges who feel that mothers with the care of young children should not work.

This places many women who confront the prospect of single motherhood in a double bind. If they stay home, as the courts expect them to do, they may well face poverty. (Indeed, some fathers are now winning custody disputes for just this reason: their traditional role as breadwinner, which the courts tend to approve, means that they are better able to provide financially for the children of the marriage.) If women go out to work to try to provide economic support comparable to that which the father may be able to provide, then they may well be seen to be inadequate mothers.

The question of how to provide and care for children, in a manner which the courts will find acceptable, is not the only problem confronting divorcing mothers. Mothers, in the legal view, should also be chaste and those who engage in adulterous conduct may find themselves punished for their transgressions. In the words of Lord Justice Lawton in the case of *B* v. *B*:

> There might be other women in similar circumstances who thought they would be justified in leaving their husbands. If they took the romantic view that love would triumph over all and there was no danger of losing the children, it was right that it should be brought home to them that there was a grave danger of their so doing. (Quoted in Smart, 1984:121)

Indeed, as we will see below, women who fail to conduct themselves with decorum stand to be actively admonished and sanctioned by the courts.

Punishing the bad

In some ways, 'bad' women may be regarded as the counterparts of law's sacrificial men, though in the eyes of the law they would seem to be considerably worse. Bad women are women gone astray. They are women who, in one way or another, have abandoned their femininity and hence their right to be given the law's protection or favour. Where good women may attract the sympathies of the court, a positively censorious approach may be taken to women who are thought to be bad. Indeed there is ample evidence of the agents of the law punishing women who have had the impudence to challenge the legal view of their role.

A substantial portion of the literature on the law's discriminatory treatment of females before the courts specifically addresses the situation of girls charged with status offences (Datesman and Scarpitti, 1977; Sarri, 1983; Hancock and Chesney Lind, 1985; Chesney Lind, 1982; 1986; 1988; Bailey-Harris and Naffine, 1988; Naffine, 1986:122; 1989). As the name suggests, such charges depend on the juvenile status of the transgressor. They refer to behaviour considered by the courts to be inappropriate in children but which is not criminal by adult standards. Status offences go by many names. Depending on the jurisdiction, a child may be said to be 'incorrigible', to be 'uncontrolled', to be 'exposed to moral danger' or to be 'at risk'.

Characteristically, status offences tend not to specify a particular form of anti-social conduct which the potential offender can positively identify and so choose to avoid. Instead the determination of a child's 'incorrigibility' or 'uncontrollability' is largely a matter of value—the court's not the child's. It is up to the court to decide whether any particular child is wayward and so requires the law's intervention.

What has most offended feminist critics of the status offence in its application to young women, however, is not so much its vagueness as its uneven application to the sexes. Repeatedly, it has been shown that girls are far more likely than boys to be charged with these offences and then to receive a harsher sentence for such behaviour (Alder and Polk, 1982:101). This is true despite clear evidence from both official and unofficial sources that girls are far less criminal than boys: that they commit less serious offences less often (Sarri, 1983:354). The allegation of feminist criminologists is that the status offence has been used to control sexually active young women, to punish them for behaviour which is considered to be unfeminine. Similar behaviour in a boy is generally accepted and so does not lead to offical action (Datesman and Scarpitti, 1977).

Though feminists have done much to expose and eliminate such sexist attitudes and practices, to the extent that status offences have been removed entirely from the statutes in some jurisdictions, there is also evidence that the police and the judiciary are resisting such moves and finding alternative ways of controlling young women (Chesney Lind, 1988). The following thoughts on female status offending contained in a speech of the director of the National Center of Juvenile Justice, Hunter Hurst, would still seem to exemplify the legal view of young women who stray:

> The issue is that status offenses are offenses against our values. Girls are seemingly over-represented as status offenders because we have a strong heritage of being protective towards females in this country [the United States of America]. It offends our sensibility and our values to have a fourteen-year old girl [*sic*] engage in sexually promiscuous activity. It's not the way we like to think about females in this country. As long as it offends our values, be sure that the police, the church or vigilante groups, or somebody is going to do something about it. For me, I would rather that something occur in the court where the rights of the parties can be protected. (Chesney Lind, 1988:157)

Even when a woman comes of age, it seems that, in the eyes of the law, she does not obtain the same freedoms as a man. Though the status offence is not available in the adult sphere to punish the wanton woman, there is sufficient discretion in the justice system to allow the agents of the law to show their disapproval of unfeminine activity. One stage of the justice process where this is readily apparent is in the police decision to arrest or report a suspected offender. In an American study of nearly 800 encounters between the police and citizens, for example, the police were observed to respond more positively to women who approximated the stereotype of the 'good woman'. In the author's own words, those female suspects who violated what the author termed 'typical middle-class standards of traditional female characteristics and behaviors'—that is, women who were young, black or hostile—were singled out for less favourable treatment than white, older and submissive women (Visher, 1983: 22–23).

In another American study, Candice Kruttschnitt (1982b) has singled out women's 'respectability' as a significant factor influencing the sentencing decision of the court. After analysing the files of over 1000 female offenders, Kruttschnitt found that severity of sentence was positively associated with a poor employment record, alcohol or drug use or a psychiatric history—in other words with being generally disreputable. Indeed, so powerful was the effect of the social reputation of the offender that it overrode legal factors which legitimately enter into the sentencing decision. Thus 'respectable' women with a criminal record were given more lenient sentences than 'disreputable' first offenders. In short, a woman's social niceness mattered more to the court than her criminality.

The importance of a woman's respectability to the agents of the law is nowhere more evident than in the treatment of women who make a living out of their sexuality. Consistently, research has shown that police harass prostitutes as a matter of course. Occasionally such harassment amounts to positive brutality (Carmen and Moody, 1985; La Fave, 1969). It has also been shown that police do not subject male prostitutes to similarly hostile treatment (Miller and Graczkowski, 1985).

Why can't a woman be more like a man?

Legal rhetoric maintains the equality of all before the law. We have seen here that, notwithstanding the language of equality now enshrined in the law, traditional notions of what is appropriate behaviour for a woman still influence the operation of the law. 'Good' women do better than 'bad' women. Though the theory is that the sex of the person does not impinge upon the deliberations of the courts, the practice is quite another thing. For when that individual is a woman, she may still be expected to display appropriately feminine behaviour and to adopt a highly traditional role. A further point to be made in this chapter is that there is yet another way in which gender shapes the workings of the law and places limits on women in a way which does not mesh with the legal ideal of gender-neutrality. To come out well in their dealings with the law, it will be claimed, women either have to be good as women, as convention defines us, or good as men. We cannot be good on any terms of our own choosing. Again, the options for women are determined by gender stereotypes. To understand this argument it is necessary to return once again to the story of women's struggle for public rights.

The history of women becoming persons may be viewed as a gradual admission by the agents of the law that women should be accorded the same rights as professional men and that they should therefore be admitted to the male public sphere. The judiciary was not keen to do this, as we have seen, but was obliged eventually to respond to social reality. Educated middle-class women were no longer content with being consigned the purely domestic roles of wife and mother and insisted that they had the abilities and therefore the right to enter public, professional employment. (For working-class women, there was not the same battle to enter public life as they were already there, out of financial necessity, performing the more menial tasks of domestic and factory worker.)

The way in which this battle was fought was inevitably influenced by the style of legal reasoning in which feminists were obliged to frame their arguments. As we have seen, legal reasoning is basically reasoning by analogy. It is the notion that like cases should be treated alike. Faced with the social fact that to be male was to have public rights and to be female was to have none, feminists were obliged to couch their arguments for equal treatment in terms of women's similarity to men. They had to show their ability to function like men in the public sphere (Bacchi, 1990).

But it was not just any man that women had to show their likeness to. Women had (and still have) to show that they too could be like the atomistic, individualistic man of law. To show any other face was to show weakness, to admit defeat, to show that they were not really as good as the boys. Feminists therefore have felt constrained to deny the ways in which women do not fit this model, for whenever women have been identified as different from men, it has generally worked to their disadvantage, as Catharine MacKinnon has made clear.

In short, the evolution of the notion of equal treatment for women is inextricably linked with what is ostensibly a gender-neutral legal

notion: that likes should be treated alike. But the model from which
the likeness has been, and continues to be, derived is not some
unsexed, standard person but a man and a man of a certain ilk. It is
still true to say that for women to get equal treatment they must
show that they can free themselves of childcare responsibilities, work
full-time, have no breaks in their career and have the same unbroken
education. Women who are differently placed for social and economic
reasons cannot get equal treatment because there is no male person
with whom to compare them. And in a society which is so fundamentally gender-divided as ours, the chances are considerable that
women's experiences will differ from men's.

'Why can't a woman be more like a man?' is thus the central
question posed by anti-discrimination laws specifically designed to
secure equal treatment for women. What the courts are looking for
when asked to decide whether a woman should be treated the same
as a man is whether she is the same as a man. An excellent elaboration
of this problem confronting women who want a fair deal in the
public sphere is contained in a recent volume by O'Donovan and
Szyszczak (1988).

Under the English Sex Discrimination Act 1975, 'a comparison of
the cases of persons of different sex or marital status ... must be
such that the relevant circumstances in one case are the same, or not
materially different, in the other'. In the United States, 'the jurispru-
dential model for all equal protection analysis under the Constitution
is to compare members of the group discriminated against with the
mainstream group' (O'Donovan and Szyszczak, 1988:44). The notion
of comparing women with the favoured group is also central to tests
of sex discrimination under Australian legislation. In each of these
places, what a woman must do to establish that she has been the
object of discrimination is to prove that she was in a similar situation
to a man at the time and yet received different treatment. 'The
inevitable requirement', in each case, is 'the comparison of the com-
plainant with a male comparator' (O'Donovan and Szyszczak, 1988:46).

What is wrong with anti-discrimination legislation framed in these
terms, according to O'Donovan and Szyszczak, is that its essential
purpose is to make women like men. It therefore ignores the viewpoints of women—those perspectives which distinguish women from
the male model which forms the point of comparison. Practically
speaking, this means that women are denied any legal redress if
they are unable to find a male with whom to compare themselves.
Obvious problems arise therefore when discrimination relates to
pregnancy and a woman must look around for a pregnant man with
whom to compare herself.

In its current form, anti-discrimination legislation also fails to question the rightness of the male standard with which we are all compared. Instead, both sexes are provided with a strong incentive to turn themselves into the type of person who currently provides the ideal of the public person: the non-pregnant, unencumbered, independent man who is able to participate full-time and continuously in the marketplace. In other words, what anti-discrimination laws encourage us all to do is to model ourselves on the man of law. Thus they affirm and validate this model of humanity.

8

Rethinking the law

Critical legal theorists are fond of exposing the duplicity of law. They argue that while law is delivered to the world as rational, objective and fair, it does not, and cannot, sustain these ideals. Though it presents itself as coherent and logical, law is in fact shot through with contradictions. And though it proclaims its essential impartiality and neutrality, in truth it plays a vital role in affirming the legitimacy of the existing, stratified social order (Feinman, 1983: 854). A number of feminists, notably those of the third phase, have endorsed this critique. Law, they agree, is uncertain and often irrational, notwithstanding its claims to be coherent and predictable. But more significantly, from the point of view of women, law is neither neutral nor objective in its dealings with the sexes. Though law is unable to sustain a single and consistent approach either to women or to men, one can still discern in law a dominant tendency to endorse a particular view of the world in which there is a certain, more privileged, place for men and another, less desirable, place for women.

This book owes a debt to both of these intellectual traditions. Indeed it has sought to explore and develop a number of the ideas advanced by both schools of thought. The central message of this volume is that there is a contradiction at the heart of law which resides in its view of humanity. Officially, the legal subject is potentially anyone, anywhere. And it is this any-personness of the legal person which is supposed to ensure that the law is at the disposal of us all, equally—without fear, favour or affection. This book, however, has found the legal subject to be someone with a quite specific set of distinguishing characteristics. But these characteristics do not sit easily together. On the one hand our man of law is assumed to be a freestanding, autonomous creature, rationally self-interested and hard-headed; on the other hand he is a being who is assumed both to have and to need access to the values of *Gemeinschaft*, the family values, though he must not display them in his public, legal *Gesellschaft* life. The legal person described here is thus essentially a paradox.

148

The contradiction which characterises the legal subject is one which has been identified by other writers as central to liberal philosophy—from whence hales our man of law. Davidoff and Hall (1987), for example, observe that the liberal conception of society contains a tension between the values of the free market and the values of community, of belonging to a social group. Benn and Gaus (1983) talk of two 'divergent models' implicit within the liberal view of humanity, which are essentially incompatible. The dominant model is of 'the individualist'—the man of law identified here. The secondary model is 'the organic' one in which our central character is seen to have a life entailing warm, human contact. 'But try to combine the models', say Benn and Gaus, 'and the individual's relation to society certainly will be a puzzle' (1983:61). The argument of this volume has been that the law (and the society which it helps to reproduce) assigns to women the job of holding the two worlds together. (A related argument has been developed by Carol Bacchi (1990) in a new book which considers how the feminist movement deals with some of these questions.) As the courts continue to tell us, the *Gemeinschaft* functions are vital and necessary ones, but they are most appropriately performed by dutiful wives and mothers—not by the man of law.

Women's domestic labours sustain the paradox of the man of law. They make it possible for our legal individual to function in the public sphere without reference to the demands of a family, even though he is assumed to be at the head of one. The invisibility of women's work helps to give credence to the legal view that our legal man is emotionally and physically self-sufficient—even though, at one and the same time, he is assumed to have the right to the offices of a loving, caring wife. Women's efforts of emotional succour in the domestic sphere allow the legal man to appear fully severed from affairs of the heart. For somewhere, in the background, there is assumed to be the good wife and mother doing the loving work and making the efforts of the self-interested male worker all worthwhile. The legal man can appear in public life, physically whole and re-plenished and unencumbered by the demands of those who are less self-sufficient than him if there is the invisible wife caring for the young, the sick and the old. To make it all work, she must take care of the less robust members of the community—including the legal man himself, when he succumbs to emotional or physical ill-health.

This is not to say that law embodies a monolithic male culture, à la second-phase feminism. The present argument in fact poses a specific challenge to the idea that the law simply represents the interests of the male sex: that it is for men and by men and against women. For one thing, it has been argued, the law is not invariably committed to the idea of the atomistic, individualistic legal man, though he is the dominant model of the individual. Of necessity, to make the law a workable institution, our man of law has at times been accorded a secondary role. In his place, a more dependent, a more vulnerable and less assertive individual has assumed centre stage. Thus in the law's treatment of young offenders and in the idea of the unequal bargaining power of certain contracting parties, we have seen positive concessions being made to notions of human weakness, duress and irresponsibility. Indeed, running throughout much of the *Gesellschaft* law of Australia, England and the United States is a countervailing *Gemeinschaft* ethic which many feminists have tended to associate with feminine values (Bacchi, 1990:Ch. 10). And of course, our legal man himself contains this vital tension between the values of *Gesell-schaft* and the values of *Gemeinschaft*.

A further way in which this volume challenges the idea of a monolithic male culture of law is in its claim that few men are like the man of law, who is a highly privileged individual. As a con-sequence, it has been argued, many men, as well as most women, are likely to find the law an alien institution which does not serve their purposes. One should not, therefore, interpret the law as a uniformly masculine institution which is in the service of men. Indeed, often the law can be seen to work to the positive disadvantage of certain men, as we saw in the analysis of young men before the criminal courts. And as Smart has pointed out, it is possible to identify instances of the law preferring women over men, as in custody and maintenance disputes (Smart, 1984:xii).

Though this book has identified a set of victims of the machineries of law, it has not been a search for villains. Indeed, a point made throughout is that the legal ideal of the person is not the creation of certain key legal men bent on their own purposes. Instead, the provenance of this individual was traced to a more impersonal (but nevertheless patriarchal) social vision of what represents the good life: that of liberal political philosophy. The ideal life, in the liberal view, is that of the free market populated by free and unencumbered men. To the extent that the legal person can be seen to serve any one set of needs, those needs are most appropriately characterised as the needs of capital. As Wolff (1976) put it, 'the depersonalization' of working life in the public sphere 'has its roots in the rational imper-atives of industrialization'. What is required for industrial production is the standard, free, unencumbered worker to produce the standard product.

Feminist critics of the liberal idea of the abstracted individual have also noted that it is highly serviceable to capital to have a class of people—that is, women—behind the scenes securing the freedom of the male worker by assuming responsibilty for the encumbrances of family life. Dorothy E. Smith (1977:166), for example, observes how women make it possible for the managerial and professional classes to engage in their intellectual work by freeing such men from the vicissitudes of bodily existence.

> The structure of work in this mode and the structure of career assume that individuals can sustain a mode of consciousness in which interest in the routine aspects of bodily maintenance is never focal, and can in general be suppressed. It is taken for granted in the organization of this work that such matters are provided for in a way which will not interfere with action and participation in the conceptual mode.

To Smith (1977:167), 'it is a condition of a person's being able to enter and become absorbed in the conceptual mode'—what has been identified here as the mode of the man of law—'that attention to the local and bodily remain . . . "horizontal" rather than focal or thematic'. By taking care of the more mundane and routine necessities of daily existence, women make it possible for the man of law to assume the demands of cerebral working life, to the point that he appears almost to be incorporeal.

It is not just in the home that women get on with the tasks of the *Gemeinschaft* and leave the male worker free to pursue his affairs of the *Gesellschaft*. In the legal world itself, women as secretaries and as junior lawyers, many of whom specialise in the more messy affairs of family law, insulate the more exalted men of the profession from the less savoury realities of daily life. It may even be said that the junior women of the law help to make the legal man the human abstraction that he appears to be from the legal viewpoint, by themselves dealing with the less savoury details of their clients' lives. This is seen most clearly when a woman performs the role of instructing solicitor to the more senior male barrister, who will go on to present the legal problem in court. In this event, she deals with the flesh-and-blood clients, hears their sorrows and their woes, extracts the vital legal facts and hands on the abstracted person to the barrister. Professionally speaking, this is regarded as an ideal arrangement as it allows our senior counsel to deal dispassionately and intelligently with the case. Personal dealings with his subject are thought only to muddy the legal waters.

What feminism brings to our understanding of law is not simply an appreciation of the deficiencies of law in relation to women—in particular, their exclusion from the category of legal subject—or even, as we have seen here, in its relations to many men. The value of feminism lies in its recognition of different and dissenting voices which are normally rendered inaudible by the more powerful voice of the man of law. And it is this chorus of dissenting voices, the voices from below, which necessarily calls into question law's most fundamental claims to fairness and impartiality.

All would be well with the law—in its theory, its doctrine and its substance—if we were all the sort of people law takes us to be. If we were all similarly independent, assertive, autonomous, unencumbered and healthy it is likely that a contract-based law which treated us as self-interested bargain-hunters would be fair and equal. Thus would be realised the legal ideal of equality of all before the law. The adversary system would also make sense: indeed it would bring out the best in all of us. But we are not all like this and the law is disingenuous when it assumes that we are. For at the same moment that it constructs the legal person in this fashion, as the paradigm person, it constructs another person as helpmate to the man of law whose task it is to be all those things which the man of law is not: emotional, encumbered and caring.

The contribution of feminism is to expose as a fiction the legal ideal of the equality of all: that we should all be equally free. Women who shoulder the burdens of life in the *Gemeinschaft* and who are encouraged to do so by a law which professes its commitment to equality are in a position to show the spurious nature of that commitment. Indeed, so too are men who depart from the legal model of the person and yet who find themselves judged according to that model and found wanting. Such women and men are ideally placed to show that law's foundation person—the abstract individual—describes few people and therefore provides an inappropriate organising category for our law.

This is not to imply that women as a collectivity have a superior approach to organising social relations, that they offer an alternative and better 'female' version of law and should therefore be called on to continue their good works by giving to law the necessary feminine touch. Though the feminist critique advanced in this book has questioned the legal values of individualism and self-interest and has argued that they conceal, and yet depend upon, a second set of more altruistic values normally expected of women, the suggestion is not that women should now get on with their womanly duty of humanising the law—as many of the second-phase feminists have implied. Frances Heidensohn (1986:296), for example, has discussed the feasibility of a 'woman-centred' justice system informed by 'female' values, one that is 'gentler, more sympathetic', while Menkel-Meadow (1987:55) has considered the possibility that women lawyers may bring to law 'a more co-operative, less war-like system of communication'.

Jean Grimshaw (1986:17), usefully, has identified a number of problems with this notion of 'a typically female point of view': the idea that women, as a social category, possess the panacea for the harsh individualism of 'masculine' institutions such as law. First, there is the danger of 'false universalism'. This is the tendency to treat all women as alike, of diminishing the differences between women created by historical location, class and ethnicity. Another danger is that of idealising and entrenching 'the female perspective'. The proposition that women's oppression generates a typical form of female thinking can lead to a view of women either as inherently virtuous (we all grin and bear it) or as thoroughly degraded, as victims of the patriarchy.

The proposition that women have a 'self-authenticating', 'self-validating' reality, quite separate from the male reality, also, more worryingly, suggests a certain inevitability about this state of affairs. Moreover, it creates an oppositional mentality: women have a better way of doing things; everything that has gone before is corrupted by the male point of view. If women are deemed to be emotional, caring, even irrational, then these qualities are to be valued because they are facets of the female culture. What feminist critics of law have to offer is a challenge to simple dominant sexist paradigms, which should not be replaced with other simple feminist paradigms.

There are still other dangers for women in the proposition that their experiences in their assigned *Gemeinschaft* role improve them and that, as a consequence, women have a better 'feminine' mode of dealing with legal matters—one which fosters connection rather than individuation. As O'Donovan (1985:5) has suggested, women have every reason to be deeply suspicious of their place in the *Gemeinschaft* since it is the site in which they have experienced oppression and lack of choice. Within the domestic hierarchy of the family, women have been accorded a low ranking and have often been obliged to perform their good offices with little real say in the matter. And as Olsen has remarked, it is not always in women's interests to strengthen their relations with others as there are certain relationships which are positively harmful to women. 'Forced community', such as coerced sexual intercourse, she maintains, does not serve women (Olsen, 1984b:393). Kathleen Daley (1989) makes the additional observation that, in the context of the criminal justice system, a free-floating ethic of care could just as well be expressed in terms of an injunction against hurting male sexual offenders or wife abusers, thus entrenching the risk of harm to their female victims.

The project of this book, however, is not to try to set down the details of a law and a legal system which would be satisfactory from the various perspectives of feminism (though it has noted some of the problems associated with the notion of an alternative female ethic of justice). That is quite another enterprise which is beyond the scope of this volume. Rather, the current discussion stops short at the stage of critique. It seeks to make the more modest point that as outsiders (Harding, 1986), women are able to observe the non-inclusive nature of a law which purports to offer a universal, all-embracing service. They can see that the man of law is not what he is said to be—a paradigm person.

Feminism therefore raises uncomfortable questions for law. By questioning the prototypical nature of the man of law it requires jurists to consider the appropriateness of law's central character. And if the members of the legal community are obliged to jettison the abstract man of law, the man without details, as a legitimating device, then they may be obliged to consider the adequacy of legal methods and legal institutions to meet the various and different needs of the various and different members of the community—people whose lives are all detail. Certainly, some of these people would be tough-minded, independent sorts, like the man of law who may be well served by law in its current form (for example, the commercial clients of commercial lawyers). But there would be many others for whom the law is a far from adequate institution.

Some of these people would be single mothers struggling to support and nurture young children. They would be sick old men who live on the streets. They would be unemployed young men and women who turn to petty theft to make a livelihood. They would be the inarticulate, uneducated and indigent as well as the cerebral and the privileged. They would be the homemakers as well as the bread-winners. Each of these lives, each of these viewpoints, would put to the test the adequacy of legal methods and legal values and hence the legal ideal of equality. 'Turning our attention to human experience', as Lorraine Code (1986:603) has suggested, would enable us to con-sider the possibility 'that in instances where experience seems not to fall within the scope of certain theoretical constraints, it is just as possible that the theory might be at fault as it is that the experience is aberrant'. It would also legitimate rather than deny what one writer has referred to as 'the play of differences existing within society' (Minda, 1986:490).

As this book has sought to show, the traditional idea that law is certain, predictable and dispassionately even-handed in its dealings with people very much depends on the exclusion of these other competing voices, these other experiences. Certainty is achievable in an uncertain world only if the group of key thinkers, who invoke and thus perpetuate the dominant paradigm, are sufficiently like-minded. In other words, it is vital to the maintenance of the appearance of law as an essentially fair and impartial institution that the members of the legal world remain 'necessarily out of touch' (Cain, 1976). The man of law can continue to appear to be truly a paradigmatic person only so long as the people who invoke the model themselves approximate that paradigm and mainly deal with similar, paradigmatic types. The admission of different, dissenting voices, such as those of women, would therefore force a Copernican shift in legal thinking. And as Smith (1977:183) tells us:

> The significance of Copernican innovations was less that the sun rather than the earth was declared to be the center of the solar system than that the position of the observer was no longer fixed and could no longer be disattended in interpreting observations. [The observer] had no longer a fixed, central position but had to be seen as located in a position itself in motion in relation to what [was] observed.

Bibliography

Alder, C. and K. Polk (1982) 'Diversion and Hidden Sexism' *Australian and New Zealand Journal of Criminology* 5, p.100

Atiyah, P. S. (1983) *Law and Modern Society* Oxford University Press

Atkins, S. and B. Hogget (1984) *Women and the Law* Oxford: Basil Blackwell

Australian Bureau of Statistics (1987) Census Data, unpublished

Bacchi, C. (1990) *Same Difference: Feminism and Sexual Difference* Sydney: Allen & Unwin

Bailey-Harris R. and N. Naffine (1988) 'Gender, Justice and Welfare in South Australia: A Study of the Female Status Offender' *International Journal of Law and the Family* 2, p.214

Baldwin J. and M. McConville (1977) *Negotiated Justice: Pressures to Plead Guilty* London: Martin Robertson

Bankowski, Z. (1979) 'The Social Context of Juvenile Justice in Scotland' in P. Brown and T. Bloomfield *Legality and Community: the politics of juvenile justice in Scotland* Aberdeen: Peoples Press

Bankowski, Z. and G. Mungham (1976) *Images of Law* London: Routledge & Kegan Paul

Barker, D. L. (1978) 'The Regulation of Marriage: Repressive Benevolence' in G. Littlejohn et al. *Power and the State* London: Croom Helm

Basten J. (1986) 'Control and the Lawyer—Client Relationship' *Journal of the Legal Profession* 6, p.17

Benn, S. and G. Gaus (1983) 'The Liberal Conception of the Public and the Private' in S. Benn and G. Gaus (eds) *Public and Private in Social Life* London: Croom Helm

Berman, H. J. (1972a) *Talks on American Law* Harvard: Voice of America

—— (1972b) 'The Historical Background of American Law' in *Talks on American Law*

—— (1972c) 'Philosophical Aspects of American Law' in *Talks on American Law*

Bersoff, D. N. (1976) 'Representation for Children in Custody Decisions: All that Glitters is not Gault' *Journal of Family Law* 15, p.27

Blackstone, W. (1978) *Commentaries on the Laws of England* New York: Garland

Blum, L. A. (1982) 'Kant's and Hegel's Moral Rationalism: A Feminist Perspective' *Canadian Journal of Philosophy* 12, 2, p.287

Blumberg, A. S. (1967) *Criminal Justice* New York: New Viewpoints

156

Bottomley, A. (1985) 'What is Happening to Family Law? A Feminist Critique of Conciliation' in Brophy and Smart *Women in Law: Explorations in Law, Family and Sexuality*

Bottomley, A. S., S. Gibson and B. Meteyard (1987) 'Dworkin; Which Dworkin? Taking Feminism Seriously' in P. Fitzpatrick and A. Hunt (eds) *Critical Legal Studies* Oxford: Basil Blackwell

Boyd, S. B. and E. A. Sheehey (1986) 'Canadian Perspectives on Law' *Journal of Law and Society* 13, 3, p.283

Braybrooke, E. K., D. A. Sinclair and J. A. Sonneman (1976) *Ignorance is No Excuse* Melbourne: Longman Cheshire

Brophy, J. and C. Smart (1985) *Women in Law: Explorations in Law, Family and Sexuality* London: Routledge & Kegan Paul

Broughton, J. M. (1983) 'Women's Rationality and Men's Virtues: A Critique of Gender Dualism in Gilligan's Theory of Moral Development' *Social Research* 50, 3, p.597

Burton, C. (1985) *Subordination* Sydney: Allen & Unwin

Cain, M. (1976) 'Necessarily Out of Touch: Thoughts on the Social Organisation of the Bar' in P. Carlen (ed.) *The Sociology of Law* Sociological Review Monograph 23, Staffordshire: University of Keele

—— (1986) 'Realism, Feminism, Methodology and the Law' *International Journal of the Sociology of Law* 14, p.255

Campbell, T. (1981) *Seven Theories of Human Nature* Oxford: Clarendon Press

Carlen, P. (1976) *Magistrates' Justice* London: Martin Robertson

—— (1983) *Women's Imprisonment: A Study in Social Control* London: Routledge & Kegan Paul

Carlen, P. and A. Worrall (1987) 'Gender, Crime and Justice' in P. Carlen and A. Worrall (eds) *Gender, Crime and Justice* Milton Keynes: Open University Press

Carmen, A. and H. Moody (1985) *Working Women* New York: Harper & Row

Cass B. (1985) 'Rewards for Women's Work' in J. Goodnow and C. Pateman (eds) *Women, Social Science and Public Policy* Sydney: Allen & Unwin

Cavers, D. F. (1972) 'Legal Education' in Berman *Talks on American Law*

Chambliss, W. and W. Seidman (1971) *Law, Order and Power* London: Addison-Wesley

Chesney-Lind, M. (1982) 'Guilty By Reason of Sex: Young Women and the Juvenile Justice System' in B. R. Price and N. J. Sokoloff (eds) *The Criminal Justice System and Women* New York: Clark Boardman

—— (1986) 'Women and Crime: The Female Offender' *Signs* 12, 1, p.78

—— (1988) 'Girls and Status Offenses: Is Juvenile Justice Still Sexist?' *Criminal Justice Abstracts* 20, 1, p.144

Code, L. B. (1983) 'Responsibility and the Epistemic Community: Woman's Place' *Social Research* 50, 3, p.537

—— (1986) 'Stories People Tell' *New Mexico Law Review* 16, 3, p.599

Cole, D. (1984) 'Strategies of Difference: Litigating for Women's Rights in a Man's World' *Law and Inequality* 2, 33, p.51

Coltheart, L. (1986) 'Desire, Consent and Liberal Theory' in C. Pateman and E. Gross (eds) *Feminist Challenges: Social and Political Theory* Sydney: Allen & Unwin

Conference Editorial Collective (1986) Introduction to Special Issue: 'Feminist Perspectives on Law' *International Journal of the Sociology of Law* 14, 3—4, p.233

Connell, R. W. (1987) *Gender and Power* Sydney: Allen & Unwin

Constantinople, A. (1973) 'Masculinity-Femininity: An Exception to a Famous Dictum?' *Psychological Bulletin* 80, 5, p.389

Cooke, R. (1987) 'The New Zealand National Legal Identity' *Canterbury Law Review* 3, p.171

Cotterrell, R. (1984) *The Sociology of Law: An Introduction* London: Butterworths

Daley, K. (1989) 'Criminal Justice Ideologies and Practices in Different Voices: Some Feminist Questions About Justice' *International Journal of the Sociology of Law* 17, p.1

Datesman, S. and F. Scarpitti (1977) 'Unequal Protection for Males and Females in the Juvenile Court' in T. N. Ferdinand (ed.) *Juvenile Delinquency* Beverley Hills: Sage

Davidoff, L. and C. Hall (1987) *Family Fortunes: Men and Women of the English Middle Class 1780—1850* St Paul: West Publishing Co.

Dawson, J. P. (1972) 'The Functions of the Judge' in Berman *Talks on American Law*

DeCrow, K. (1975) *Sexist Justice* New York: Vintage Books

Derham, D., F. Maher and L. Waller (1986) *An Introduction to Law* North Ryde, NSW: The Law Book Company

Dicey, A. V. (1959) *Introduction to the Study of Law of the Constitution* 10th edn, London: Macmillan

Dietz, M. G. (1987) 'Context Is All: Feminism and Theories of Citizenship' *Daedalus* 116, 4, p.1

Donaldson, J. (1986) Abse v. Smith *All England Reports* 1, p.350

Eaton, M. (1985) 'Documenting the Defendant: Placing Women in Social Inquiry Reports' in Brophy and Smart *Women in Law: Explorations in Law, Family and Sexuality*

—— (1986) *Justice for Women? Family, Court and Social Control* Milton Keynes: Open University Press

Ehrlich, I. (1936) *Fundamental Principles of the Sociology of Law* 1975 edn, New York: Arno Press

Eisenstein, H. (1985) 'The Gender of Bureaucracy: Reflections on Feminism and the State' in J. Goodnow and C. Pateman (eds) *Women, Social Science and Public Policy* Sydney: Allen & Unwin

Epstein, C. F. (1981) *Women in Law* New York: Basic Books

Ericson, R. and J. Baranek (1982) *The Ordering of Justice: A Study of Accused Persons as Dependants in the Criminal Process* University of Toronto Press

Erika, S. (1986) 'Patriarchy and the State' *Australian Journal of Law and Society* 3, p.53

Evans, M. (ed.) (1982) *The Woman Question: Readings on the Subordination of Women* Oxford: Fontana

Farrington, D. and A. Morris (1983) 'Sex, Sentencing and Reconviction' *British Journal of Criminology* 23, 3, p.229

Fasteau, B. (1971) 'Law and Women' in J. Black *Radical Lawyers* New York: Avon Books

Feeley, M. (1979) *The Process is the Punishment* New York: Russell Sage

Feinman, J. M. (1983) 'Critical Approaches to Contract Law' *UCLA Law Review* 30, 4, p.829

Finn, P. (1989) 'Commerce, the Common Law and Morality' *Melbourne University Law Review* 17, p.87

Fitzpatrick, P. and A. Hunt (1987) 'Critical Legal Studies: Introduction' in P. Fitzpatrick and A. Hunt (eds) *Critical Legal Studies* Oxford: Basil Blackwell

Flanagan, O. J. and J. E. Adler (1983) 'Impartiality and Particularity' *Social Research* 50, 3, p.576

Flew, A. (1979) *A Dictionary of Philosophy* London: Pan Books

Forbes, J. R. S. (1979) *The Divided Profession in Australia: History, Rationalization and Rationale* Sydney: Law Book Company

Franzway, S., D. Court and R. W. Connell (1989) *Staking a Claim: Feminism, Bureaucracy and the State* Sydney: Allen & Unwin

Freiberg, A., R. Fox and M. Hogan (1988) *Sentencing Young Offenders* Canberra: Australian Government Publishing Service

Freud, S. (1977) *On Sexuality* ed. A. Richards, Pelican Freud Library vol. 7, Harmondsworth: Penguin

Frug, G. E. (1988) A Critical Theory of Law, paper presented to the Law Schools Association Conference, Sydney University

Fuller, L. L. (1969) 'Human Interaction and the Law' *American Journal of Jurisprudence* 14, p.1

—— (1971) 'Mediation: Its Forms and Functions' *Southern California Law Review* 44, p.305

Garfinkel, H. (1956) 'Conditions of Successful Degradation Ceremonies' *American Journal of Sociology* 61, p.420

Garland, D. (1985) *Punishment and Welfare* Aldershot: Gower

Gelsthorpe, L. (1986) 'Towards a Sceptical Look at Sexism' *International Journal of the Sociology of Law* 14, p.125

Gibson, D. (1987) 'Blind Justice and Other Legal Myths: The Lies that Law Lives By' *Dalhousie Review* 66, 4, p.431

Gilligan, C. (1982) *In A Different Voice: Psychological Theory and Women's Development* Cambridge, Mass.: Harvard University Press

Glennon, L. M. (1979) *Women and Dualism: A Sociology of Knowledge Analysis* New York: Longman

Goodpaster, G. (1987) 'On the Theory of American Adversary Trial' *Journal of Criminal Law and Criminology* 78, 1, p.118

Gordon, R. W. (1984) 'Critical Legal Histories' *Stanford Law Review* 36, p.57

Gould, C. C. (1976) *Women and Philosophy: Toward a Theory of Liberation* New York: G. P. Putnam's

—— (1983) 'Private Rights and Public Virtues: Women, the Family, and Democracy' in C. C. Gould (ed.) *Beyond Domination: New Perspectives on Women and Philosophy* New Jersey: Rowman & Allanheld

Grace, C. and P. Wilkinson (1978) *Sociological Inquiry and Legal Phenomena* London: Collier Macmillan

Graycar, R. (1986a) 'Yes, Virginia, There is Feminist Literature: A Survey of Some Recent Publications' *Australian Journal of Law and Society* 3, p.105

—— (1986b) 'Feminism Comes to Law—Better Late than Never' *Australian Feminist Studies* 1, p.115

Gregg, N. (1986) 'It Doesn't Affect Me': Reflections on the Feminist Critique of Objectivity, presented at the 36th Annual Conference of the International

Communication Association, Chicago, 22–26 May 1986

Gregory, J. (1979) 'Sex Discrimination, Work and the Law' in B. Fine, R. Kinsey, J. Lea, S. Picciotto and J. Young (eds) *Capitalism and the Rule of Law* London: Hutchinson

Griffiths, A. (1986) 'The Problem of Informal Justice: Family Dispute Processing Among the Baluvena—a Casestudy' *International Journal of the Sociology of Law* 14, p.359

Grimshaw, J. (1986) *Feminist Philosophers: Women's Perspectives on Philosophical Traditions* Brighton: Wheatsheaf

Griswold, E. N. (1972) 'The Legal Profession' in Berman *Talks on American Law*

Gutteridge, H. C. (1983) 'Abuse of Rights' *Cambridge Law Journal* 5, p.22

Hancock, L. and M. Chesney-Lind (1985) 'Juvenile Justice Legislation and Gender Discrimination' in A. Borowski and J. M. Murray (eds) *Juvenile Delinquency in Australia* Sydney: Methuen

Handler, A. B. (1988) 'The Judicial Pursuit of Knowledge: Truth and/or Justice *Rutgers Law Review* 41, 1, p.1

Handler, J. F. (1988) 'Dependent People, the State, and the Modern/Postmodern Search for the Dialogic Community' *UCLA Law Review* 35, p.999

Harding, S. (1983) 'Is Gender a Variable in Conceptions of Rationality? A Survey of Issues' in C. C. Gould (ed.) *Beyond Domination: New Perspectives on Women and Philosophy* New Jersey: Rowman & Allanheld

—— (1986) *The Science Question in Woman* Ithaca: Cornell University Press

Harris, A. R. (1977) 'Sex and Theories of Deviance: A Functional Theory of Deviant Type-Scripts' *American Sociological Review* 42, 1, p.3

Harris, J. W. (1980) *Legal Philosophies* London: Butterworths

Harris, M. K. (1987) 'Moving into the New Millennium: Toward a Feminist Vision of Justice' *The Prison Journal* 67, p.27

Harrison, R. and F. Mort (1980) 'Patriarchal Aspects of Nineteenth Century State Formation: Property Relations, Marriage and Divorce, and Sexuality' in P. Corrigan (ed.) *Capitalism, State Formation and Marxist Theory* London: Quartet

Hart, H. L. A. (1958) 'Positivism and the Separation of Law and Morals' *Harvard Law Review* 71, p.533

Heidensohn, F. (1986) 'Models of Injustice: Portia or Persephone? Some Thoughts on Equality, Fairness and Gender in the Field of Criminal Justice' *International Journal of the Sociology of Law* 14, p.287

Heinz, J. P. and E. O. Laumann (1982) *Chicago Lawyers: The Social Structure of the Bar* New York: Russell Sage

Hetherton, M. (1981) *Victoria's Lawyers: The Second Paper* Victoria Law Foundation

Hobbes, T. (1966) *Leviathan* (in *The English Works of Thomas Hobbes of Malmesbury*) Aalen: Scienta Verlag

Howe, A. (1986) Social Injury Revisited: Towards a Feminist Theory of Social Justice, paper presented to 4th Australian Law and Society Conference: 'Law and Political Justice', Brisbane, December 1986

Hudson, B. (1987) *Justice Through Punishment* London: Macmillan

Hunt, A. (1987) 'The Critique of Law: What is "Critical" About Critical Legal Theory?' in P. Fitzpatrick and A. Hunt (eds) *Critical Legal Studies* Oxford: Basil Blackwell

Jaggar, A. (1983a) *Feminist Politics and Human Nature* New Jersey: Rowman & Allanheld

—— (1983b) 'Human Biology in Feminist Theory: Sexual Equality Reconsidered' in C. C. Gould (ed.) *Beyond Domination: New Perspectives on Women and Philosophy* New Jersey: Rowman & Allanheld

Johnson, K. and A. Scales (1986) 'An Absolutely, Positively True Story: Seven Reasons Why We Sing' *New Mexico Law Review* 16, 3, p.433

Kairys, D. (1983) 'Legal Reasoning' in D. Kairys (ed.) *The Politics of Law: A Progressive Critique* New York: Pantheon

Kamenka, E. and A. E-S. Tay (1975) 'Beyond Bourgeois Industrialism: the contemporary crisis in law and legal ideology' in E. Kamenka and R. Neale (eds) *Feudalism, Capitalism and Beyond* London: Edward Arnold

—— (1986) 'The Traditions of Justice' *Law and Philosophy* 5, p.281

Kanowitz, L. (1973) *Sex Roles in Law and Society: Cases and Materials* Albuquerque: University of New Mexico Press

Kay, J. S. (1988) 'Women Lawyers in Big Firms: A Study in Progress Toward Gender Equality' *Fordham Law Review* 57, 1, p.111

Kearns, D. (1984) 'A Theory of Justice—and Love: Rawls on the Family' in M. Simms (ed.) *Australian Women and the Political System* Melbourne: Longman Cheshire

Kennedy, D. (1979) 'The Structure of Blackstone's Commentaries' *Buffalo Law Review* 28, 4, p.205

Kenny, S. (1986) 'Reproductive Hazards in the Workplace: The Law and Sexual Difference' *International Journal of the Sociology of Law* 14, p.393

Kingdom, E. (1980) 'Women in Law' *M/F* 4, p.75

—— (1985) 'Legal Recognition of a Woman's Rights to Choose' in Brophy and Smart *Women in Law: Explorations in Law, Family and Sexuality*

Klare, K. E. (1978) 'Judicial Deradicalization of the Wagner Act and the Origins of Modern Legal Consciousness, 1937—1941' *Minnesota Law Review* 62, p.265

Kruttschnitt, C. (1982a) 'Women, Crime and Dependency: An Application of a Theory of Law' *Criminology* 19, 4, p.495

—— (1982b) 'Respectable Women and the Law' *Sociological Quarterly* 23, 2, p.221

Kruttschnitt, C. and D. McCarthy (1985) 'Familial Social Control and Pretrial Sanctions: Does Sex Really Matter' *Journal of Criminal Law and Criminology* 76, 1, p.151

Kuhn, T. (1970) *The Structure of Scientific Revolutions* 2nd edn, University of Chicago Press

La Fave, W. (1969) 'Arrest: The Decision to Take a Suspect into Custody' in L. M. Friedman and S. Macaulay (eds) *Law and the Behavioral Sciences* Indianapolis: Bobbs Merrill Co.

Levinson, S. (1983) 'Escaping Liberalism: Easier Said than Done' *Harvard Law Review* 96, p.6

Locke, J. (1960) *Two Treatises of Government, A Critical Edition with an Introduction and Apparatus Criticus by P. Laslett*, New York: New American Library

Lloyd, G. (1983) 'Reason, Gender, and Morality in the History of Philosophy' *Social Research* 50, 3, p.490

—— (1984) *The Man of Reason: 'Male' and 'Female' in Western Philosophy* London: Methuen

Mackie, J. L. (1977) *Ethics: Inventing Right and Wrong* Harmondsworth: Penguin

McBarnet, D. (1981a) 'Magistrates' Courts and the Ideology of Justice' *British Journal of Law and Society* 8, p.181

—— (1981b) *Conviction: Law, the State and the Construction of Justice* London: Macmillan

McCann, K. (1985) 'Battered Women and the Law: The Limits of Legislation' in Brophy and Smart *Women in Law: Explorations in Law, Family and Sexuality*

MacKinolty, J. (1979) 'The Married Women's Property Acts' in J. MacKinolty and H. Radi (eds) *In Pursuit of Justice: Australian Women and the Law* Sydney: Hale & Iremonger

MacKinnon, C. A. (1979) *Sexual Harassment of Working Women: A Case of Sex Discrimination* New Haven: Yale University Press

—— (1982) 'Feminism, Marxism, Method, and the State: An Agenda for Theory' *Signs* 7, 31, p.515

—— (1983) 'Feminism, Marxism, Method, and the State: Towards a Feminist Jurisprudence' *Signs* 8, 4, p.635

—— (1985) 'Feminist Discourse, Moral Values and the Law—A Conversation' *Buffalo Law Review* 34, p.11

—— (1987) *Feminism Unmodified: Discourses on Life and Law* Cambridge, Mass.: Harvard University Press

MacPherson, C. B. (1962) *The Political Theory of Possessive Individualism: Hobbes to Locke* Oxford: Clarendon Press

Maine, H. S. (1959) *Ancient Law* London: Oxford University Press

Martin, G. A. (1969) Problems in Ethics and Advocacy in Defending a Criminal Case, special lecture to the Law Society of Upper Canada

Martin, R. (1985) *Rawls and Rights* Lawrence, Kansas: University Press of Kansas

Mason, A. (1987) Future Directions in Australian Law, the Wilfrid Fullagar Memorial Lecture, Monash University, 25 August

Matthews, J. (1982) 'The Changing Profile of Women in the Law' *Australian Law Journal* 56, p.634

Matsuda, M. (1986) 'Liberal Jurisprudence and Abstracted Visions of Human Nature: A Feminist Critique of Rawls' Theory of Justice' *New Mexico Law Review*, 16, Fall, p.613

Menkel-Meadow, C. (1986) 'The Comparative Sociology of Women Lawyers: the "Feminization" of the Profession' *Osgoode Hall Law Journal* 24, 4, p.897

—— (1987) 'Portia in a Different Voice: Speculations on a Women's Lawyering Process' *Berkeley Women's Law Journal* 39

Mensch, E. (1982) 'The History of Mainstream Legal Thought' in D. Kairys (ed.) *The Politics of Law: A Progressive Critique* New York: Pantheon

Mercer, J., (1985) *The Other Half: Women in Australian Society* Harmondsworth: Penguin

Midgley, M. and J. Houghes (1983) *Women's Choices: The Philosophical Problems Facing Feminism* London: Weidenfeld & Nicolson

Mill, J. S. (1910) *On Liberty* Everyman's Edition, London: Dent

Miller, E. and G. S. Graczkowski (1985) Gender, Sex and Money: A Comparative Analysis of Female Heterosexual and Male Homosexual Prostitution, paper presented at the annual meeting of the American Society of

Criminology, San Diego, California, 16 November

Minda, G. (1986) 'Phenomenology, Tina Turna and the Law' *New Mexico Law Review* 16, 3, p.479

Mitchell, J. (1974) *Psychoanalysis and Feminism* Harmondsworth: Penguin

Mossman, M. J. (1986) 'Feminism and Legal Method: The Difference it Makes' *Australian Journal of Law and Society* 3, p.30

Naffine, N. (1985) 'The Masculinity-Femininity Hypothesis: A Consideration of Gender-Based Theories of Crime' *British Journal of Criminology* 25, 4, p.365

—— (1986) 'Women and Crime' in D. Chappell and P. Wilson (eds) *The Australian Criminal Justice System* Sydney: Butterworths

—— (1987) *Female Crime: The Construction of Women in Criminology* Sydney: Allen & Unwin

—— (1989) 'Towards Justice for Girls' *Women and Criminal Justice* Spring

Naffine, N. and F. Gale (1989) 'Testing the Nexus: Crime, Gender and Unemployment' *British Journal of Criminology* 29, 2, p.144

Nagel, I. (1981) 'Sex Differences in the Processing of Criminal Defendants' in A. Morris and L. Gelsthorpe (eds) *Women and Crime* Cropwood Conference, Cambridge: Institute of Criminology

Nicholas, S. C., A. M. Price and R. Rubin (1979) *Rights and Wrongs: Women's Struggle for Legal Equality* New York: Women's Press

O'Connor, I. and M. Callahan (1988) 'Youth, the Law and Legal Services: Patterns of Legal Need' *Australian and New Zealand Journal of Criminology* 21, p.5

O'Donnell, C. and J. Craney (1982) *Family Violence in Australia* Melbourne: Longman Cheshire

O'Donovan, K. (1981) 'Before and After: The Impact of Feminism on the Academic Discipline of Law' in D. Spender (ed.) *Men's Studies Modified* Oxford: Pergamon

—— (1982) 'The Male Appendage: Legal Definition of Women' in Evans *The Woman Question: Readings on the Subordination of Women*

—— (1984) 'Protectionism and Paternalism' in M. D. A. Freedman (ed.) *State, Law and the Family* London: Tavistock

—— (1985) *Sexual Divisions in Law* London: Weidenfeld & Nicolson

O'Donovan, K. and E. Szyszczack (1988) *Equality and Sex Discrimination Law* Oxford: Basil Blackwell

Okin, S. M. (1979) *Women in Western Political Thought* Princeton University Press

—— (1987) 'Justice and Gender' *Philosophy and Public Affairs* 16, 1, p.42

Olsen, F. E. (1983) 'The Family and the Market: A Study of Ideology and Legal Reform' *Harvard Law Review* 96, 7, p.1560

—— (1984a) The Sex of Law, transcript of speech given at UCLA Law School

—— (1984b) 'Statutory Rape: A Feminist Critique of Rights Analysis' *Texas Law Review* 63, 3, p.387

—— (1985) 'The Myth of State Intervention in the Family' *University of Michigan Journal of Law Reform* 18, 3, p.835

O'Malley, P. (1983) *Law, Capitalism and Democracy* Sydney: Allen & Unwin

Pannick, D. (1987) *Judges* Oxford University Press

Parker, H. (1974) *View from the Boys* Newton Abbott: David & Charles

Parker, S. (1985) 'The Legal Background' in J. Pahl (ed) *Private Violence and*

Public Policy: The Needs of Battered Women and the Response of the Public Services London: Routledge & Kegan Paul

Parker, S. J. and P. Drahoss (1989) Formalism ... Indeterminacy ... Conventionalism, paper in progress, Australian National University

Parsloe, P. (1978) *Juvenile Justice in Britain and the United States: The Balance of Needs and Rights* London: Routledge & Kegan Paul

Pateman, C. (1986) 'The Theoretical Subversiveness of Feminism' in C. Pateman and E. Gross (eds) *Feminist Challenges: Social and Political Theory* Sydney: Allen & Unwin

—— (1988) *The Sexual Contract* Cambridge: Polity Press

Peller, G. (1985) 'The Metaphysics of American Law' *California Law Review* 73, 4, p.1151

Phillips, R. (1987) 'Unequal Before the Law' in G. Zdenkowski, C. Ronalds and M. Richardson (eds) *The Criminal Injustice System* Sydney: Pluto Press

Picciotto, S. (1979) 'The Theory of the State, Class Struggle and the Rule of Law' in B. Fine, R. Kinsey, J. Lea, S. Picciotto and J. Young (eds) *Capitalism and the Rule of Law: From Deviancy Theory to Marxism* London: Hutchinson

Piven, F. (1985) 'Women and the State: Ideology, Power and the Welfare State' in A. Rossi *Gender and Life* New York: Aldine

Podmore, D. and A. Spencer (1982) 'Women Lawyers in England: The Experience of Inequality' *Work and Occupations* 9, 3, p.337

Polan, D. (1982) 'Towards a Theory of Law and Patriarchy' in D. Kairys (ed.) *The Politics of Law: A Progressive Critique* New York: Pantheon

Poole, R. (1985) 'Morality, Masculinity and the Market' *Radical Philosophy* Spring, p.39

Rawls, J. (1971) *A Theory of Justice* Cambridge, Mass.: Harvard University Press

Rhode, D. L. (1983) 'Equal Rights in Retrospect' *Journal of Law and Inequality: A Journal of Theory and Practice* 1, p.1

—— (1985) 'Ethical Perspectives on Legal Practice' *Stanford Law Review* 37, January, p.589

—— (1986) 'Feminist Perspectives on Legal Ideology' in J. Mitchell and A. Oakley (eds) *What is Feminism?* Oxford: Basil Blackwell

Rifkin, J. (1980) 'Toward a Theory of Law and Patriarchy' *Harvard Women's Law Journal* 3, p.83

—— (1984) 'Mediation From a Feminist Perspective: Promise and Problems' *Law and Inequality* 2, p.21

Riseley, A. C. (1981) 'Sex, Housework and the Law' *Adelaide Law Review* 7, 4, p.421

Rosenberg, M. (1988) 'Resolving Disputes Differently: Adieu to Adversary Justice?' *Creighton Law Review* 21, 3, p.801

Rosenthal, D. E. (1974) *Lawyer and Client: Who's in Charge?* New York: Russell Sage

Rubin, G. R. and D. Sugarman (eds) (1984) *Law, Economy and Society, 1750–1914: Essays in the History of English Law* Oxford: Professional Books

Ryan, A. (1985) 'Reinventing Ethics: Why John Rawls is the Most Argued-About Philosopher of the Century' *Australian Society* 4, 4, p.15

Ryan, K. and J. Ferrell (1986) 'Knowledge, Power, and the Process of Justice' *Crime and Social Justice* 25, p.178

Sachs, A. (1976) 'The Myth of Judicial Neutrality: The Male Monopoly Case' in P. Carlen (ed.) *The Sociology of Law* Sociological Review Monograph 23, Staffordshire: University of Keele

—— (1978) 'The Myth of Male Protectiveness and the Legal Subordination of Women' in Smart and Smart *Women, Sexuality and Social Control*

Sachs, A. and J. H. Wilson (1978) *Sexism and the Law: A Study of Male Beliefs and Legal Bias in Britain and the United States* Oxford: Martin Robertson

Sadurski, W. (1986) 'Equality Before the Law: A Conceptual Analysis' *Australian Law Journal* 60, March, p.131

Sandel, M. J. (1982) *Liberalism and the Limits of Justice* Cambridge University Press

Sarat, A. and W. L. Felstiner (1986) 'Law and Strategy in the Divorce Lawyer's Office' *Law and Society Review* 20, 1, p.93

Sarri, R. (1983) 'Gender Issues in Juvenile Justice' *Crime and Delinquency* 29, p.381

Scales, A. C. (1980–81) 'Towards a Theory of Feminist Jurisprudence' *Indiana Law Journal* 56, 3, p.375

—— (1986) 'The Emergence of Feminist Jurisprudence: An Essay; *Yale Law Review* 95, p.1373

Scheman, N. (1983) 'Individualism and the Objects of Psychology' in S. Harding and M. Hintikka (eds) *Discovering Reality: Feminist Perspectives on Epistemology, Metaphysics, Methodology and the Philosophy of Science* Dordrecht: D. Reidel

Schur, E. M. (1968) *Law and Society: A Sociological View* New York: Random House

Scutt, J. A. (1985) 'In Pursuit of Equality: Women and Legal Thought, 1788–1984' in J. Goodnow and C. Pateman (eds) *Women, Social Science and Public Policy* Sydney: Allen & Unwin

Segal, L. (1987) *Is the Future Female? Troubled Thoughts on Contemporary Feminism* London: Virago

Seidenberg, F. A. (1971) 'The Submissive Majority: Modern Trends in the Law Concerning Women's Rights' in J. Black *Radical Lawyers* New York: Avon Books

Sevenhuijsen, S. (1986) 'Fatherhood and the Political Theory of Rights: Theoretical Perspectives of Feminism' *International Journal of the Sociology of Law* 14, p.329

Sexton, M. and L. W. Maher (1982) *The Legal Mystique: The Role of Lawyers in Australian Society* Sydney: Angus & Robertson

Simpson, B. (1986) 'The Common Law and Legal Theory' in W. Twining (ed.) *Legal Theory and Common Law* Oxford: Basil Blackwell

Smart, C. (1976) *Women, Crime and Criminology: A Feminist Critique* London: Routledge & Kegan Paul

—— (1981) 'Law and the Control of Women's Sexuality: The Case of the 1950s' in B. Hutter and G. Williams (eds) *Controlling Women: The Normal and the Deviant* London: Croom Helm

—— (1982) 'Regulating Families or Legitimating Patriarchy' *International Journal of the Sociology of Law* 10, p.129

—— (1983) Patriarchal Relations and Law: An Examination of Family Law and Sexual Equality in the 1950s, research paper, University of Sheffield

—— (1984a) *The Ties That Bind: Law, Marriage and the Reproduction of Patriarchal Relations* London: Routledge & Kegan Paul

—— (1984b) 'Marriage, Divorce, and Women's Economic Dependency: A Discussion of the Politics of Private Maintenance' in M. D. A. Freeman (ed.) *The State, the Law and the Family* London: Tavistock

—— (1985) 'Legal Subjects and Sexual Objects: Ideology, Law and Female Sexuality' in Brophy and Smart *Women in Law: Explorations in Law, Family and Sexuality*

—— (1986) 'Feminism and Law: Some Problems of Analysis and Strategy' *International Journal of the Sociology of Law* 14, p.109

Smart, C. and J. Brophy (1985) 'Locating Law: A Discussion of the Place of Law in Feminist Politics' in Brophy and Smart *Women in Law: Explorations in Law, Family and Sexuality*

Smart, C. and B. Smart (1978) *Women, Sexuality and Social Control* London: Routledge & Kegan Paul

Smigel, E. O. (1969) *The Wall Street Lawyer* Bloomington: Indiana University Press

Smith, D. E. (1977) 'A Sociology of Women' in J. A. Sherman and E. T. Beck (eds) *The Prism of Sex: Essays in the Sociology of Knowledge* University of Wisconsin Press

Snare, A. and T. Stang Dahl (1978) 'The Coercion of Privacy' in Smart and Smart *Women, Sexuality and Social Control*

Spangler, E. (1986) *Lawyers for Hire: Salaried Professionals at Work* New Haven: Yale University Press

Sprigge, T. L. S. (1985) *Theories of Existence* Harmondsworth: Penguin

Stacey, M. and M. Price (1981) *Women, Power and Politics* London: Tavistock

Stapleton, W. and L. Tietlebaum (1972) *In Defense of Youth* New York: Russell Sage

Stang Dahl, T. (1986) 'Taking Women as a Starting Point: Building Women's Law' *International Journal of the Sociology of Law* 14, p.239

—— (1987) *Women's Law: An Introduction to Feminist Jurisprudence* Oxford University Press

Stone, J. (1946) *The Province and Function of Law* Sydney: Associated General Publications

—— (1964) *Legal Systems and Lawyers' Reasonings* Sydney: Maitland Publications

Stubbs, M. (1986) 'Feminism and Legal Positivism' *Australian Journal of Law and Society* 3, p.63

Sugarman, D. (1986) 'Legal Theory, the Common Law Mind and the Making of the Textbook Tradition' in W. Twining (ed.) *Legal Theory and Common Law* Oxford: Basil Blackwell

Sugarman, D. and G. R. Rubin (1984) 'Towards a New History of Law and Material Society in England, 1750–1914' in G. R. Rubin and D. Sugarman (eds) *Law, Economy and Society, 1750–1914: Essays in the History of English Law* Oxford: Professional Books

Summers, A. (1975) *Damned Whores and God's Police* Pelican

Tapp, J. L. and L. Kohlberg (1971) 'Developing Senses of Law and Legal Justice' *Journal of Social Issues* 27, 2, p.65

Tapp, J. L. and F. L. Levine (1974) 'Legal Socialization: Strategies for an Ethical Legality' *Stanford Law Review* 27, p.1

Taub, N. and E. M. Schneider (1982) 'Perspectives on Women's Subordination and the Role of Law' in D. Kairys (ed.) *The Politics of Law: A Progressive Critique* New York: Pantheon

Taylor, I. (1981) *Law and Order: Arguments for Socialism* London: Macmillan

Thompson, J. (1986) 'Women and Political Rationality' in C. Pateman and E. Gross (eds) *Feminist Challenges: Social and Political Theory* Sydney: Allen & Unwin

Thornton, M. (1986) 'Feminist Jurisprudence: Illusion or Reality?' *Australian Journal of Law and Society* 3, p.5

Tomasic, R. (1978a) *Lawyers and their Work in New South Wales: Preliminary Report* Sydney: Law Foundation of New South Wales

—— (1978b) *Lawyers and the Community* Sydney: Law Foundation of New South Wales and Allen & Unwin

—— (1983) 'Social Organisation Amongst Australian Lawyers' *Australian and New Zealand Journal of Sociology* 19, p.447

Tonnies, F. (1955) *Community and Association* London: Broadway House

Unger, R. M. (1976) *Law in Modern Society* New York: Free Press

Visher, C. A. (1983) 'Gender, Police Arrest Decisions, and Notions of Chivalry' *Criminology* 21, 1, p.5

Wacks, R. (1987) *Jurisprudence* London: Financial Training

Weber, M (1954) *Max Weber on Law in Economy and Society* Cambridge, Mass.: Harvard University Press

—— (1968) *Economy and Society: An Outline of Interpretive Sociology* New York: Bedminster Press

—— (1971) 'The Ideal Type' in K. Thompson and J. Tunstall (eds) *Sociological Perspectives* Harmondsworth: Penguin

Weisberg, D. K. (1982) *Women and the Law: A Social Historical Perspective* 2 vols, Cambridge, Mass.: Schenkman

Weizman, L. J. (1981) *The Marriage Contract: Spouses, Lovers and the Law* New York: Free Press

Whitbeck, C. (1983) 'A Different Reality: A Feminist Ontology' in C. C. Gould (ed.) *Beyond Domination: New Perspectives on Women and Philosophy* New Jersey: Rowman & Allanheld

Wilson, E. (1977) *Women and the Welfare State* London: Tavistock

Wolff, R. P. (1968) *The Poverty of Liberalism* Boston: Beacon Press

—— (1976) 'There's Nobody Here But Us Persons' in C. C. Gould and M. W. Wartofsky (eds) *Women and Philosophy: Toward a Theory of Liberation* New York: Perigree

Wundersitz, J., N. Naffine and F. Gale (1988) 'Chivalry, Justice or Paternalism? The Female Offender in the Juvenile Justice System' *Australian and New Zealand Journal of Sociology* 24, 3, p.359

Index